I0153139

Burning The Candle
At Both Ends

Reader Reviews

Burning the Candle at Both Ends touched me all over. I could relate to this story in so many different ways. I know that so many people will be motivated by this story. Bryce I wish you much success.
Jenny White (house wife)
L.A., California.

Burning the Candle at Both Ends is very educational concerning the game of the streets and life. I know this kind of lifestyle is quite common in the underworld. I loved this read from beginning to end. Yo Bryce, keep up the good work. I can't wait to read your next project.
Melvin Duval (truck driver)
Washington D.C.

Burning the Candle at Both Ends made me realize that life and freedom is not all fun and games out here on these bricks. If you do decide to get down making some fast money, you should very well know the consequences. We love you Bro.
Your Boy, Sir Roxy
Harlem N.Y. {The Concrete Jungle}

Burning the Candle at Both Ends is a cold piece of work and you remind me so much of Ice Berg Slim and the late Donald Goines. It's unbelievable. I wish you much success International Buck. I can most definitely see your work transformed to the big screen and in movie theaters worldwide. Please, whatever you do, don't stop writing. Keep up the good work.
Big Rodney, The Crusher
Oklahoma City, Okla.

Burning the Candle at Both Ends made me laugh and angry at the same time. The book grabs you and keeps your interest from beginning to end. It is truly a page turner; just like your freshman project "OFF THE FRONT LINE." Burning the Candle at both ends will most definitely be in the top 10 of anyone's book collection. I really enjoyed this read. I can envision your work in a play or some kind of motion picture. Big ups to you Bryce, and keep up the good work.
Curtis Mayes, Criminal Lawyer
Louisville, Kentucky.

Print 2014

Bookstore Distribution

Contact: Bryce Turner
Big Chief Publishing
www. BryceTurner.Biz
ISBN: 0 – 9761052 – 1 – 7

Printed in the United States of America

Acknowledgments

I would like to give special thanks to JEHOVAH God first, and his only Begotten Son Jesus Christ. Thank you JEHOVAH for giving me the ability to write and stay focused on my projects, making a way, and opening up doors for my work to spread throughout the United States. It reaches so many people of all different nationalities. AMEN

I would also like to thank my backbone, play maker, and brains for working so hard to make my dreams come true. My love, Shanta Turner. I must let it be known that I truly understand what it means to have a good woman on your team. Behind every good man is a strong, smart, and beautiful woman. They may also be on the side of you. Oftentimes, they are in front of you. Just ask President Obama about Michelle if you don't believe me.

In loving memory of my boy Walter (Heat Cliff) Garland, who was like a Big brother to me. Heat Cliff helped inspire me to write in the first place. Love you Big bro. In loving memory of my first cousin Marcus (SS Boy) Turner. He was one of the coldest and most down hustlers to fall out of Memphis, Tn. We got plenty of money together. Rest in peace lil cousin and we love and miss you dearly. Pops and everyone from coast to coast is still laughing at us to this very day about all the crazy shit we use to do together (lol). It's also a blessing that I'm still here. Thank you JAH.

I would also like to thank my mother and father for hooking up and getting married. Bernice and Obbie Turner allowed Bryan, Brent, and I a shot at life. They taught us some very valuable lessons in life. Thank you Mom for staying strong, loving, and being an independent woman who didn't give up on us. You pushed and kicked our asses until we were something in life. Thank you very much Momma. We love you.

I also would like to thank Mrs. Wilma (momma) Scott who was vice president at First Security Bank in O.K.C. She always had much faith in me and had my back at all times. Mamma Scott supported my goals and dreams when I touched down from prison out of Kentucky. Rest in peace to you Momma Scott. You'll never be forgotten. The community, along with the Turner family, and we love and miss you very much.

Thank you Jehovah for blessing me with (6) six beautiful kids: Deshanna, & Cameron Goldsby, Brandus and Jajuan Clayton, Erica Clark, and my baby girl Ashley Miller. Also thank you for my (11) eleven beautiful grandchildren. God is good. The lifestyle that I lived, I never thought that I would live to see grand kids. Again thank you JAH.
I would also like to give all of my real people on lock down a special shout out.

Pac said, "Keep your heads up & stay close to JAH."

To my big Bro. Curtail and all my real ones in Kentucky, you know who you are. Also to my boy Messy (Boy Wonder) and my real ones in El-Reno and the rest of the federal system. To all of my people in Oklahoma City county jail, and D.O.C. We love you, and keep writing and requesting my books. Help me with my quest to have an Oklahoma native to land "Off the Front Line" and "Burning the Candle at both Ends" in every prison system in the United States. Let's start off with the state of Oklahoma. Please take all of your required courses with no write ups in order to come home. They don't let you out now. You have to graduate out of prison, you dig? No write ups if you can help it.

Take it from your boy B.T. I had to do ten calendars in different states. I am living proof that it can be done. The sun always shines after the storm. I wrote (3) three books while incarcerated and so can you if that's your dream. Anything and everything is possible in the U.S., you dig? So again keep your heads up and think positive. They only can lock up your physical body. They can't lock away your character or mind. So do the time and refuse to let the time do you. Most of those people who work for such places love misery. Never give those kind of people joy by letting them see you sweat. Your boy till the wheels fall off, International Buck.

Also I would like to thank my sponsors: B.T. 4 Restoration, Big Timer's Detail shop, Global Interiors, and Big Chief Publishing book store & more. Those are some of the fine people who helped me out. Hope that you love my sophomore project, "Burning the Candle at Both Ends."
Peace and hope you enjoy, B.T.

Chapter 1

The big O.G. (Oklahoma Gangster) was one of the coldest brothers I have ever met and for some reason he took a liking to me. Everyone called him "Big Timer." He dressed like a million bucks and drove some of the coldest vehicles in the city. He also wore top flight jewelry, & had a total of about 25 to 30 karats. Big Timer had a big 4 oz. medallion covered with quarter karat solitaires and half karats. This guy even had whole karats as well as solitaires of some of the finest stones money could buy. That medallion had to have a total karat weight of almost 15 karats.

Big Timer always said, "It cost over thirty thousand dollars on a helleva discount."

Timer also had the Presidential gold Rolex with the diamond bezel and band. I priced a Presidential at $18,500, not including the ice band and bezel. Big Timer had it going on, not to mention his giant rings dripped in ice. One of his pinky rings even had over five karats.

This guy was top flight, no wonder they called him Big Timer. He was exactly what everyone wanted to be. Women would practically throw themselves at him. They knew he was a hustler, pimp, D-boy, O.G., gambler, and killer. This man was different from all the rest of the ballers.

Big Timer was in a class all by himself. He had style and was smart as hell. His game and conversation were well rounded, while owning a mansion in Dallas Texas. Timer also had a phat condo in Memphis and a beach house on South Padre Island. He was constantly on the highway "getting paid" as he would call it. Everyone loved this gangster. He reminded me of a black Robin Hood except he didn't give his money to squares. The only way you could get anything is if you and Timer were doing business together or you had to be very poor.

Timer mainly hung with pimps, Crips, and Bloods. He was the only one that I ever saw driving a red Porsche through Crip territory pounding his Alpine and wearing all of his jewelry. Women would be calling his name and running over to him like he was a celebrity or something. As a matter of fact, he was probably selling dope or collecting money.

Gang members and gangsters constantly paged him and would practically beg to be put down on any kind of hustle. These young gangsters would kill for him in a heartbeat just to get his nod of approval. Now that's what you call having respect, money, and power to the highest degree.

Every time he showed up in Oklahoma City, he would go to J.T. Cut n Stack. Sometimes he would have some of the meanest killers with him who treated him like a king. Their faces didn't look treacherous, just their eyes. They all tried to follow his style and that was with a big smile on their faces. You could look at these guys and figure they would kill everybody there with the snap of Big Timer's finger.

Big Timer had a million dollar smile with a killer's eyes also. I can imagine him putting in work on some fools if they rubbed him the wrong way. He wouldn't even have to be present. His boys would be honored to put in work for him. That way he wouldn't mess up his manicure or his hair.

Big Timer was international for real. He would have gangsters and ballers with him from various states like Houston, L.A., Detroit, Memphis, ATL etc... All those guys were big major players in the game looking like gangsterized business men. They rolled around town in 600 Benzes and Burberry. They also pushed old schools with Dayton's and 20 inch rims and tires worth $7,000.00.

I could also understand how the rich got richer and the poor got poorer. People always give rich people free shit: like haircuts, dope, weed, liquor and food. Women gave pussy and their bodies to them just for a chance to ride. Women would bounce from the truck stop to the rest areas selling pussy.

Big Timer was a very likeable person. Just because he was well off, he didn't forget where he came from. He would talk to the poorest of the poor and give them encouragement, advice, and even a few dollars if they needed it. He constantly fired up blunts of Indo with everyone. Then he would ride off into the sunset on his 20 inch rims. All the homies would be watching and admiring Big Timer's vehicle and giving him props. One thing about Big Timer, he never looked down on anyone just because he had it going on.

Big Timer and I became extremely close.

He would tell me, "No one is aware of how much money passes through Oklahoma City from the dope game. I make hundreds of thousands just being a coyote, which was someone who transported dope from state to state. I have major hook ups from the SA's, (Mexicans). The SA's trusts me with millions of dollars."

The average person would have cut out with the dope and never returned home. Take me for instance. It would be tremendously hard to pass up a life time of dope and dope equals money. Imagine a person trusting you to deliver a half million dollars' worth of kilo's and sticky green to another state. Tell me it wouldn't cross your mind to keep everything and move your family and yourself out of town, on the down low?

It was also a rumor around the city claiming that Big Timer was traveling from state to state robbing jewelry stores. I believed it.

He would ask, "Do you like my jewelry? It's not shit to get, just put it down. Your game that is!"

All of his little young gangsters was rolling tight, looking good, and constantly drinking Remy Martin. They also smoked Indo blunts and that Water (PCP). I guess that's why everyone would be holding his nuts, trying to get in where they fit in. They were buying keys, pounds, or trying to get put down on a helleva lick.

Big Timer was smart and had the heart of a lion with big nuts.

He always said, "Have heart. Have money."

One thing about it, if he took one of his crew members (Crips or Bloods) with him out of town, whenever they got back all of them would have thousands. The whole crew would be buying everything: new clothes, Burberry, Drop tops, triple gold Dayton's and big karats in their ears. Their smiles would be from ear to ear. Big Timer would be sitting there like it wasn't shit and he would either leave with another crew or ride out alone.

I believe he supplied the whole East and North sides with work (weed). He fronted a couple of homies of mine 30 or 40 pounds of sticky green and two or three kilos of that butter straight drop.

Big Timer was major and the Feds wanted him, but couldn't touch him with a ten foot pole. He had workers and never touched anything. Again I really believed that he was also making jewelry store licks. I doubt if he went in because he had soldiers who would do anything on his call.

I asked, "Do you trust your workers?"

Timer answered, "Yes, why not? Believe me they know the rules of the game (death) and if I can't reach them I'll reach the next closest thing to them. Their Mom, dad, brother, sister, baby, dog, or cat. Plus the other homies would love to peel his or her cap. That's why we all sit and kick it at each other mother's house. That's letting me know you have nothing to hide and you will not snitch or fuck up. It's a life time contract baby!"

By the look in Big Timer's eyes I could tell he wasn't bullshitting. As a matter of fact, he was getting heated just thinking about it.

Once he put you down, he explained the rules thoroughly.

He always said, "You youngsters got the game all fucked up. You kill your best friends and steal from each other. Tell everything you know on him or someone else. No respect for others and so on. I keep it old school rules. I live by loyalty, respect, no snitching, and keeping it in the family."

That was true. His crew bought work from him constantly, especially after they would come back from a long trip on the highway. Big Timer's team ranged in ages from 17 to 55 and they all listened to him. I'm sure some of them wanted to cross him out, but they couldn't discuss it with one another. Because someone would let Big Timer know who the culprit was and that would mean curtains for that person. The game is a mother fucker.

Big Timer introduced me to one of his older Gs from Chi-Town (Chicago). The guy was a genius who could do almost anything.

Timer said, "That older guy taught me a lot of game and he's down like four flat tires. I would do anything for him and I mean anything."

If I didn't know any better, I would bet that this guy was brain washed just like all the others.

The old guy's name was Gator. I didn't have to ask where that name came from. When I first met him, I noticed his crocodile shoes he was sporting. It really made me wonder what Timer knew that attracted everyone to him. What would make an old man come out of retirement to get with a person and take a penitentiary chance?

Timer even put the old man through the test. When Gator came to town, a couple of hits went down. I assumed he did it. After the murders, the next day, Gator was gone back to Chi-Town, & Timer was also gone.

When he came back to OKC, I asked Timer, "Did you hear about the double homicide?"

He said, "Yeah, I just heard about it. That was fucked up wasn't it?"

Then I started noticing Gator with Timer quite often in OKC. I guess Gator was in now and had earned Timer's trust. They were doing business together and having much money. It was something about Gator that I didn't like though. He was too nosey and had shifty eyes. If it was me, I wouldn't be able to trust Gator. I guess because he watched and listened to everyone's conversation.

Gator would often ask, "What did he say?"

He would do that even when that person wasn't even talking to him. I hate a nosey person like that. I know Timer didn't like shit like that either. He was trying to learn the game over night. If my boy made one step, Gator made two. He was trying his best to keep up with Timer.

My boy told me that he, Gator, and one of the crew were going out of town for a couple of days. They would return in a week or so.

Timer said, "I'll bring you something back just for being real and for keeping your ear to the streets for me."

I was hoping that he would bring me one of those phat diamond big face Rolex's.

I asked, "What are you going to bring me back Timer?"

"Don't sweat that. Just chill and stay down lil Bro. Do what you do and let me do what I do."

Timer, Gator, and his crew left town that week.

They all had a look in their eyes like, "Let's hurry up and go & get this shit over with!"

Whatever it was they were up too, I already knew what time it was. They were probably going to lay it down (set it off), in other words.

They left town in Timer's Travel Time Conversion kit Suburban. It had butter soft leather, wood grain, TVs, VCRs and Sony Play Stations. Also sitting on some 20 inch chrome Trancula rims and tires. It was squatting down in the front, low and jacked up in the back a little bit, and pounding on Tela (Watch Your Mail).

The shit looked like the movies or something. They all wore Fubu & Karl Kani from head to toe; with diamonds glistening from everyone in the 'Burban. Big Timer pulled up with his crew and hit the pimp horn on me (beep beep).And they punched out toward I-35. All of them threw up the peace sign to me.

In a way, I wanted to go and get down with whatever it was they were doing, but in another way, I was a little nervous.

Timer always said, "Have heart. Have money."

I guess I didn't have the heart to jump in the action or even approach him with it. The meaning of the word anticipation is a mother fucker. I was probably more nervous than they were. And I was at home safe as a baby, just waiting and hoping. Hoping & anticipating that everything turned out okay for them. Wishing that they would come back home without getting caught up. That put me on the edge like I was there.

As I slept at night, my woman would shake me to see if everything was alright. I was tossing and turning so much. The game is a mother fucker. If you're not 110% down, don't even get involved point blank.

About two weeks after Timer left, I was at the car wash cleaning up my shit. I heard an extremely loud car stereo system coming down NE 23rd Street pounding on Spice One. From the sound of the system, it could be no one but Big Timer. I looked up and it was Big Timer and the crew. I flagged them down and they pulled into the car wash right behind me. All of them were smiling from ear to ear. The whole crew jumped out dancing, doing the C-walk, and talking cash shit.

Timer put that Tela back in (I'm So Tired of Balling).

And said, "Come here lil Bro."

Timer hit the secret compartment in the 'Suburban, & showed me brand new big faces about $50,000.00 worth. His boys had about 20 to 30 thousand dollars each.

Gator was popping it, saying, "Timer is the coldest young brother he has ever met in his whole life!"

Chapter 2

At that point, I really wanted to kick myself straight in the ass for not going or even asking to go. The only thing I could concentrate on was that I just missed out on thirty thousand easy dollars with the most downest O.G in the Southwest.

Timer asked me, "What's happening, you're sick aren't you? Don't sweat this little shit, because the game isn't for everybody."

Then he reached a little further in his secret compartment and pulled out a silver oyster Rolex with a blue face. It had pave diamonds with the diamond bezel. I almost started drooling when I saw that Lex-O.

Timer said, "Here little bro. This is for you for being down."

I couldn't understand what he was saying at first about me being down.

Timer explained, "That it's more ways to be down without getting down. Even though I feel you will do anything for me."

He was right. At that point, I would do a mother fucker right now for him. I would do whatever just to show him that I was down all the way around. Timer was smart. He already knew that about me before he gave me that Rolex.

He told me, "I have to go and handle some more business and drop my crew off. I will get with you later before I leave town again. Don't ever get rid of that watch. Whatever you do, don't pawn it. Take it to a friend of mine and have the serial numbers grinded off. Just in case you ever get jammed up with it, tell the folks (police) you found it or bought it at the car wash from some smokers or something. If you're smooth with your game, you won't have any trouble homie."

Later that same day, I met up with Timer again at J.T. Cut-n-Stack barber shop. Timer was getting that DC fade touched up and I was flossing my brand new Lex-O.

Everyone was asking, "How much did it cost? Where did you get it?"

I told them, "The game paid me."

Timer just sat in the chair cool as ever, smiling while listening to my conversation. Half of the busters and player haters were asking me about my Lex-O.They didn't know the difference between a real one and a fake one. They were just nosey. I learned to always keep my business to myself. It didn't cost a mother fucker a dime to stay out of mine!

Timer continued getting faded up by the best barber in OKC. This barber wins all the hair shows from state to state in the Southwest. Timer pulled me to the side and we walked outside toward his vehicle.

Timer whispered, "Now remember what I said. Don't flex so much because these haters just don't understand this kind of shit. Hold everything down. I will get at you whenever I get back to OKC. Before I leave town, I need to holler at one of my down pimp partners who just got out the penitentiary. This brother is down. He pimps from coast to coast and he still got a major stack (money)."

I went home that night and my old lady gave me the third degree about my iced-out, diamond covered Lex-O. There was no doubt that she liked it.

I told her, "I brought it from a fiend on the East Side."

She asked, "Do you think you could get one for me?"

I laughed, "If I ever see those smokers again, I'll check on one for you."

I can't ask Big Timer for a lady's Lex-O for my bitch!

You must be aware when wearing an expensive piece of jewelry. You have to watch your back at all times. If you're in a bad area or company, be real discreet. Pull your Lex-O off and put it in your pocket. One thing for sure is these brothers and bitches in OKC were no joke. They will rob or set you up in a New York minute. I didn't wear it every day because I noticed white people looking at my watch. Since I'm dark skinned, you know they were thinking negative about a young player anyway.

"How can he afford that $13,000.00 watch? I can't even afford one! He's selling dope or he stole it!"

You know how Caucasians are. They are some real jealous and nosey individuals that will call the police on you just for suspicion. Don't get me wrong. It's a lot of blacks and other races will do the same shit.

Timer's pimp partner was named Pimping X and he was a true pimp. Everyone in the city was talking about this big pimp. I heard he was also a Crip. That fucked me up. I was taught that pimping and Cripping didn't mix.

Like Biggie said, "It's like two dicks and no bitch. Find yourself in serious shit."

That was real. How can you be out on the track pimping hoes, gang banging, and dodging bullets? From the talk around town, Pimping-X was a true pimp and a true Crip. One day at J.T.'s on the East Side, Pimping-X walked in to get his perm washed and conditioned.

This guy looked just like Wesley Snipes who starred in Passenger 57. The ladies were just whispering and smiling at Pimping. He had all kinds of action, especially since he was driving a brand new big body Benz with chrome Octavo rims and vogue tires. His brand new hoe catcher (car) was Carolina blue with the paper tag still in the back window. Pimping-X was Versace down and talking cash shit (pimping shit) while getting his perm whipped up. Pimping-X was fresh out of the state penitentiary for some gang related shit. And was already three hoe's deep, steady accepting applications for more hookers and wanna be hoes.

That goes to show, once you have the game, you'll always have it. That's one thing no one can take from you (how to accumulate capital) how to get money. Big Timer, Pimping-X and several other real players proved that. They would come up as soon as they touched down, hit the bricks, or got out of prison, plus rolling in brand new cars. With brand new clothes, jewelry, cribs, and phat bank rolls. They stayed talking shit. These players were picking up where they left off.

I hit Big Timer on his 1-800 pager after I saw Pimping-X.

I told him, "I ran into your homie who is fresh out."

Timer asked, "What do you think about him?"

"He's a real one."

Timer said, "He's cool as a mother fucker too. Pimping-X laid it out for me in the penitentiary. We drank yak, (Hennessey) smoked sticky green, and had plenty of food. We ate steak sandwiches, fat burgers, fried chicken, drank soda, and the whole nine. Pimping-X walked around the penitentiary with silk pajamas and house shoes on. He had bitches coming to visit him every weekend. That's how real players do it. You ball no matter where you are. It doesn't matter whether you are in or out the penitentiary."

Mostly all the ballers and rich brothers I know have been to the penitentiary. Some of them have been more than once.

Timer said, "Yeah he is real cool. He can get whatever from me because I know he'll give me his last and that's real. Dig that!"

They were supposed to hook up this weekend in Dallas at Deon Sander's club. Pimping-X called Timer yesterday to pop pimping with him. They made arrangements to chop it up at Primetime 21 (Deon Sander's club) this weekend.

Timer said, "I'll call you next week because it's going to be some big shit popping off once me and Pimping-X hook up. He is an OG just like me with plenty of soldiers that will move on his call just like the Big Dog (me). We have a lot in common. Let alone, we have pimping in common."

The weekend came. Pimping-X showed up in Dallas at the mansion with another pimp named Young City. Young City drove an early 90 model Rolls Royce. It was black and clean as a mother fucker. Young City was from OKC, & also an international pimp. He was home maybe three months out of a year. Mostly in Hawaii pimping up a storm &, six hoes deep. Young City had Chinese, Hawaiian, black, and white girls. Young Pimping doesn't turn down anything but his collar and sometimes don't turn that down.

Needless to say, he and Pimping-X were Versace down again. Versace suits, brims, canes, and ready to chop it up at Deon Sander's club. Timer stepped into his walk-in closet and picked out a Versace suit and brim with the crocodile shoes. Then he put on about 38 karats worth of grade A diamonds. There were 15 karats around his neck, 15 karats on his fingers, 8 karats around his wrist along with the Rolex watch and bracelet.

Big Timer came down that curly staircase in the mansion. Those pimps jumped off the leather couch in the den & both of them admired his ice (diamonds) and giant pieces.

They told him, "You're looking like Puff Daddy."

Timer had the Versace shades on. X & pimping country couldn't believe all that jewelry Timer had on which was almost $200,000.00 worth. They gave a hustler his props.

Afterward they had another drink and smoked another Indo blunt. As they prepared to leave the mansion, Timer still wasn't finished flexing. He had one more item for that ass. That snow white mink to the floor.

His pimp partners also had their minks in the Rolls. All of them were clean as a mother fucker. We knew that these hoes and women were in trouble tonight. We were barring none. All three of us pimped to the Rolls parked in front of the mansion. This was some real shit.

As they pulled off, Young Pimping put in the new Keith Washington. Timer pulled out his nose kit for a one on one to set the evening off. It was safe and perfect to say that he had the best yola (cocaine ether base) in the Southwest.

Pimping-X said, "Timer you haven't been bullshitting since you got out on these bricks. You've been about your scrilla (money, paper)."

Timer told Pimping-X, "That's right."

Pimping-X said, "You have the phattest crib I've ever been in. You got the swimming pool, Jacuzzi, minks, diamonds, Benzes, 'Burban, and a down crew. You are truly the most down all around hustler from OKC. You represent how we do it in OKC, from state to state.

Timer said, "That's right."

Before they fell up in Deon's club, they took a stroll to the hoe stroll in Dallas, off of Harry Hines Boulevard. Hookers don't walk up and down the track anymore. They drove buckets to pick up their dates. So if you are a trick, just keep driving up and down (back and forth) on the hoe stroll (track). It won't be just one hooker either. There will be several hookers pulling up on the side of you at the red light propositioning you.

The girls pulled up on them in the Rolls Royce and burned rubber away from them. Pimps would always let those tinted windows down, to show that they were far from tricks. These were real pimps and they were prospecting for dedicated, hard working hoes.

A true dedicated hooker knows if she smiles or conversates with a true pimp, she will have to break herself right there on the spot. She will either comply or suffer the consequences. When a true pimp mentions break yourself. That means a hoe will breaks herself of every dollar. She won't hold back not one dime. That's what they call choosing fees and breaking a bitch.

Young Pimping played the new Case, which was right on time & mellow. That really fit the mood. Big Timer was feeling good after tooting the coke and drinking Don P. By now he was ripped, feeling good, and spitting at every hoe that pulled up. Timer was trying to get the hoes out of bounds or re-choose on some new pimping. All three of them rode up and down the track for about thirty or forty minutes. It wasn't that much action happening yet on the track because it was still early. It wasn't even eleven o'clock yet.

The Rolls jumped on toll way North hwy. until they got to Deon's club (Prime Time 21). By the time they arrived at the club, it was jammed packed. Everyone was fly too. Players from all over Texas and Oklahoma was there. There was valet parking. They even saw Deon's black Lamborghini. There were ballers in Benzes, limos, Bentleys, and 'Burbans.

Deon held a small party that night with special guest appearances by Howard Hewitt and Faith Evans. As they pulled up to the valet parking area, a man came to open the doors of the Rolls Royce. The OKC. Pimp's pimped on in the club. Once they walked in, it seemed like all of the music stopped. All attention was focused on them. All the ladies and even brothers watched them walk up to the VIP section.

It seemed like the music came back on and everyone proceeded with their evening. They looked like celebrities who were used to that kind of attention. Those three were the cleanest brothers in the house that night. They started ordering bottles of Don P., popping pimping, and parlaying.

The bitches were walking by, waving, whispering, smiling, and shit. The girls were giving them all kinds of rhythm. My boys don't fuck with square girls. They prefer hookers; but me, I'm a hustler. I'll accept a pig with a wig as long as her paper is longer than mine. She has to love my dirty drawers and that's real.

I guess they were spending a nice piece of change on all the Don P., and Cuban cigars. The man himself had to come see who these players were, that was spending all this money. Deon Sanders came out to meet & greet them.

Deon asked, "Where are ya'll players from?"

They told him, "OKC."

Man, "You players sure are looking good."

As they introduced themselves and shook hands.

Deon said, "Is this how they do it in OKC?"

Timer said, "That's right."

Deon laughed and nodded his head saying, "Dig that!"

He immediately called one of his fine waitresses.

And told her, "Bring them two more bottles of Don P., on the house! Compliments of Prime Time 21! Cheers to these to Oklahoma City cats!"

Everyone was really looking at them because they probably thought that they knew Deon personally or something.

Also in the house that evening was Jason Kidd, Sam Perkins, and Mike Irvin. Celebrities are always at Prime Time 21. All those millionaire brothers were cool as hell. They probably thought we were millionaires as well. I guess that's why Mom always taught me to dress like a million bucks even if you don't have any money. You don't have glass pockets. How will they know if you are broke unless you tell them?

They had a ball at club Prime Time 21. After they left club Prime Time 21, the Rolls went directly back to Harry Hines, the hoe stroll. The hookers were out now. They were in full swing and making plenty of money. That meant, the hoes were turning plenty of tricks. Pimps everywhere. They even saw their pimp partners from OKC, with their hoes.

Pimping Long Perm, Eyes, Pimping Cobra, Young Bryan (rest in peace), Big Pimppin and some pimps out of Memphis, Kansas, and Houston. It was on now, with everyone meeting up at the hotel. Players & pimps was popping pimping and getting high for hours while everyone's hoe was getting that paper(money).

Timer told Young City and Pimping-X, "Let's hit the track again. I need to knock one or two new turn outs to get in my stable."

We jumped back in the Rolls and went to the track. Then we set up camp at the adult book store. Broke a bitch and sent them out the door with instructions. Timer got a few phone numbers and passed out a gang of pimp cards, (business cards with your name, number, and occupation on it).

That's one thing about pimping. You stay down and you're bound to come up with a hoe or two maybe three. Keep spitting at the hoes. Don't fall apart if you don't knock a bitch that night. Keep dressing and progressing.

They parlayed all night. Timer was twisted and full of that good nose candy (coke). Now it was time to retire for the evening. The sun was slowly coming up. We jumped on the highway headed toward the mansion. As soon as we got there, Timer showed us to our quarters (rooms).

Timer passed out in front of the big screen. Pimping X & Country woke up the next morning and had a hearty breakfast. They talked about what had happened last night and how many hoes they knocked.

Timer usually knocks hoes 24/7. Maybe he was too pimping for them last night. It gets like that every once in a while (smile). Timer was full of Indo, cocaine, and Don P. That mixture will make a pimp talk shit to those punk bitches. Especially if they aren't saying what he wanted to hear.

Immediately, Timer's pimp partners started inquiring about that ice (diamonds).

They said, "Timer, you were clean as a mother fucker last night. Those hoes couldn't understand you. Let alone see you because you were glittering too much. You probably scared those popcorn hoes off. They knew if they choose up with a pimp with all the ice on, he was going to work her until her feet look like deer hooves."

Timer said, "That's right, dig that."

Pimping-X and Young City both asked, "Timer, when are you gonna hook us up with some of that ice and Lex-O's?"

Timer played them off at first, but they just kept on inquiring about the jewelry. Now they had jewelry, but not any monster shit like what Big Timer had. & that's what they wanted. Pimping-X was more amazed about how he got the shit than anything.

X said, "Timer, you and your crew are about your paper. I need to put my young gangsters down on some gangster shit like that."

Timer smiled and didn't reply on anything because the golden rule is: the game is to be sold and not told. Sometimes it's not even sold because this shit isn't for everybody. Some people get so big headed that you can't even talk to them anymore. Sometimes they forget where they come from & let the money go to their heads. This game is only for a chosen few. Needless to say, both of them had to show Timer how serious they were about purchasing some jewelry.

Pimping country & X said, "Timer, we'll tell you what. We want to spend $20,000.00 with you. That's 10 stacks each."

Timer said, "Well I don't really work like that. I'm not splitting up my sack (jewelry). I sell the whole sack at one time so I can take care of my people. I try to keep everyone happy. I know a little lick that you might be able to have, but it will cost you about $80,000.00. That's a cool deal because I could get $110,000.00 for it easy."

They said, "We don't want that much.

Chapter 3

Timer said, "Well sell what you don't want to the rest of your pimp partners."

Timer knew they needed a minute or two to think on it. He offered them some Remy Martin and twisted up an Indo blunt while they conversed. Timer came back to the room with the drinks and blunts.

Pimping-X said, "Timer here is the deal. I want a Presidential Rolex with the iced-out bezel. I want them big chunks of ice for some monster rings. Young City wants the same. How long will it take to get it?"

"Yesterday," Timer answered while laughing.

Both of them said, "Give us a day or two to put together $80,000.00. We have $20,000.00 up front just for some highway money & trick off money at the casinos for you & your crew."

Timer asked, "Is that right?"

Yes, "But when are you coming back to OKC?"

Timer answered, "In a couple of days, or so. I hope that's cool with you."

"It's on Timer. You can follow us now to get this little $20,000.00."

Timer laughed, but right then he knew that they were serious as cancer. He still had a little unfinished business in Houston that he needed to attend to first.

"I will be there in two or three days. Plus I will page you when I am on my way," Timer told them.

They replied, "Dig that."

There were smiling from ear to ear once again.

Timer never called me back. He just showed up in OKC like he always did.

Timer said, "Little homie, we really popped it last weekend. I told you we were going to hookup and it would be on. How is that Oyster Lex-O of yours?"

"It's cool, but I don't wear it every day."

Timer said, "You're not supposed to wear it every day."

"How long are you going to be in town?" I asked him.

Timer replied, "I will be out of here in the morning. I'm headed to the East Coast."

I was thinking to myself, "It must be fun just to travel to any state you want and get paid for it."

Timer said, "We are going to pull out in the morning. We'll be back in a week or so."

I sure wanted to be down with him. I always hated it when I missed out on those thousands. I didn't see my boy Timer before he left OKC this time. I just knew that he was already gone with his crew. I saw Pimping-X and Young Pimping in the city with a car load of hoes and checking their paper (money).

I didn't see Timer for almost three weeks. Needless to say, he was phat (plenty of money) when I did see him again. His boys were phat too. He also had those pimps' sack. That made me wonder just how many licks did he make?

"It was a double play made. We hit two stores that were side by side. Hit them both at the same time. We took home about a quarter million between the five of us. My crew will get 40 thousand each and I will get about 90 thousand. Now that's some real money for some ghetto brothers."

I had to ask, "So how come you get the biggest cut of the money?"

Timer said, "Because it was my lick! I sponsor the whole trip! I pay for the hotel rooms and the food! We stop at casinos and gamble off thousands and shop. Plus I have the blue prints and I have to move & sell everything with no problems involved! My crew understands that. Besides, I only promised them $25,000.00 a piece! They ended up with $40,000.00 a piece! Now would you complain after you agreed to do the job for twenty five thousand? Another thing, you were dead broke before you jumped in the 'Burban!"

I think Timer got a little upset with me for asking him that question.

He went on to say, "Since you're asking so many questions. Why don't you answer one for me? What if I told you that they all bought birds from me as well for $15,000.00 a piece? I ended up with another $60,000.00. Now do you think I'm wrong for that?"

I said, "No, that's a good deal. $15,000.00 for a bird (a kilo of cocaine) is love."

Timer said, "$40,000.00 is a good deal when I could have given them $25,000.00. I'm not like that and that's why my people love and trust me with millions. It's not like I'm stealing. They already know I get more on most occasions. I'm the OG. The game costs, especially if I give it to you. Well I gotta roll now. Time is money and money is time. It's about time for you to pay dues on all this game I'm giving you."

One thing I know about Timer, he's not joking about anything he says. He was always laughing and grinning anyway. Once again he left me with that same thought stuck in my mind. How come I didn't go? I could have had a bird and $25,000.00. Shit!

I was slowly lighting a fire under my own ass. That fire made me want to get down even more. I would often have dreams about bashing and grabbing Rolex's and ladies diamond rings & shit. I had a dream that I stole a truck (popped the steering column) and drove it to the front door of the store. I walked in, smashed a case, walked out, got in the truck, and drove off in my vehicle that was parked a couple blocks down. That's probably how Timer does it, but I know that he doesn't drive the Suburban to the front door.

However they do it, it's working and paying off like a Las Vegas slot machine. Timer went home with $150,000.00. Just a few weeks ago, he made $50,000.00. That's $200,000.00 in a month. That's not counting his other drug deals and hookers in his stable. This man here was larger than I thought. He's had a million plus run through his fingers in six months to a year.

I saw those pimps a few weeks after Timer left town and these guys had on some giant shit. Their rings were bigger than Timer's. Pimping-X had one ring with over 10 karats and a gold Presidential Rolex. His other 3 rings weighed at least 2 ounces each with 7 or 8 karats. Pimping X was popping big shit and flexing. This time I saw him with about 3 other little Crips. They looked treacherous and hungry (for money). Pimping-X also had a couple of crack houses. With the little gangsters running the dope houses.

I was broker than ever. This little 8 to 5 job I had at the barber shop just wasn't cutting the mustard. I had to get my grind on. So I called Timer.

"Could you front me a few pounds of that sticky green?" I asked.

"You called me in the nick of time lil bro. I got something major for you".

"Like what Timer?"

"How long would it take for you to move 100 pounds of sticky green?"

Wow I couldn't believe that he was going to front me all of that. I only wanted about 5 or 10 pounds.

I quickly answered, "No more than 60 days. & I'll be finished with it. How much do you want for each one Timer?"

"Just because it's you, I'm going to give you a cool deal at $600.00 a piece. So that's $60,000.00 for the package. Can you handle that?"

"Hell yes! When can we meet?"

"I'll be there next week and I'll page you when I get there."

I was thinking about how much I would make, selling each pound for $900.00. I could make $300.00 profit off each one. I'd have 100 pounds. I should come out with 100x300=$30,000.00. That's a nice little lick and boy could I use it!

The next day, Timer was at the barber shop. I was sweeping, hanging out, and rapping to the honeys.

Timer walked in and said, "Let me holler (talk) at you outside for a minute."

As I went outside with him.

"You drive that old pickup truck over there with the lawnmowers in the back and get your shit. I'll be back here in one hour. So that homie can pick up his truck. He's on his way back to Dallas," Timer said.

Timer pulled out in that white on white big body 600 Benz sitting on 20 inch rims and low profile tires. I drove homies' truck with the weed in the bed of it, to the country on the out skirts of OKC. Then I put it up in my good hiding place. It was on now. When I arrived back to the Barber Shop Timer gave me dap (hand shake).

"Don't fuck the money up little bro!"

"I got this big bro. I'll be paging you every week or two with a stack of money until I get you paid off."

"Yes sir," Timer replied as he punched out in the big body Benz.

I thought Timer had left town, but I saw him and Pimping-X flexing in the big body Benz. They were checking hoes and running back and forth to the track (hoe stroll) in OKC, on S Robinson, and to Black Welder Road. They were back and forth to Guthrie truck stop, pimping up a storm, and checking hoe money from the womb. This guy never gets tired of making money. How much is enough for this guy? Well I couldn't sweat Timer and watch him get his grind on. I had to handle my own business and move these pounds of that ganja.

I liked selling weed much better than selling rocks because almost everyone smoked weed. The police don't sweat the weed man that much. The five-o would rather bust the crack man. Besides, I can move weed just as fast as a person moving rocks. I was going to keep pumping, stacking, (saving money) and putting almost all my profit back into the business. That wouldn't be hard to do with the hook up (connection) I have. A month had passed and I only had about 25 or 30 pounds left. Now I had a few brothers that owed me money, & boy was I looking good. Plus Timer was already paid off, & Timer loved it.

"Little bro you can sell the shit out of some weed can't you?"

I replied, "Yes sir. Plus I'll have a down payment of my own money." I've been stacking. Big Bro. I'll call you in a week after I finish with the rest of the weed. I got to collect a few loose ends out here. It's on big baby. Ha ha."

Timer said, "You know I'm going to take care of you little bro. I need to ask you a serious question. You think I ought to put Pimping-X and his crew down on the game?"

I said, "I don't know Timer. He looks cool; but you know him better than I do."

Timer said, "I know that. Its just this game isn't for everyone. It's like having a money tree in your own backyard. Would you pick all the money off the tree at once or just pick how much you need at that time? The money isn't going anywhere. It's your money tree and it's on your property. So what would you do?"

I answered, "Of course just get what I need Big Timer."

Timer said, "You're a smart man and that's why I fuck with you. That's exactly how I treat my money tree. I can go get money anytime I want. Seven days a week. There is no need to get on a robbing spree to make several million dollars in a month. You can get 50 or a 100 thousand anytime. That's why I have lasted over 15 years in the ice game and have not been caught. But how will Pimping-X treat the game? Like I told you before, Pimping-X took care of me in the penitentiary. He threw me $20,000.00 up front for highway money. I honestly believe if the shoe was on the other foot he would give me the game and put me down."

I said, "Well, you just answered your own question. Go with it."

Timer smiled and said, "Feel that. Besides, me and Pimping-X can put our teams together and hit a monster lick. We can sit back and watch them work. We are Gs. So it might work. Thanks little bro. Remember everybody always need somebody. I could see in your eyes that you couldn't figure out why I talked to you about this. Even a millionaire needs somebody. Maybe not for capital (money), but that's how I look at you little bro. You really helped me out and you don't even know it (smile).Well little bro, I'm headed to Nashville to drop these hookers off at Meko's (hoe house). Call me once you get your ends together."

"I'll be ready by this weekend," I told him.

"I will be back by then," he said.

Friday came and I was sitting on about 25 thousand dollars. And was going to put 20 thousand back into the game.

I paged Timer.

"I'm ready. Let's kick it again. This time I have some gas money. I have about twenty dollars," I told him.

That's how we talk over the phones. It doesn't matter if it's a pay phone or whatever.

Timer said, "Is that right?"

"Yes, I replied."

"Well I'll be there in a couple of days, lil bro."

Timer was there the next day just like last time. He never gives you the exact day or hour when he is coming. I guess all real ballers do the same. I would too. I wouldn't want anyone to know when I was coming or going either. Someone might set me up or tell the five-o what kind of car I was driving. Just like Timer, you never know when he's coming or what he's driving.

Big Timer fell up in the barber shop for a DC fade from JT. All these brothers loved Timer, but what I think people like most is his style. After Timer got faded up, I walked outside with him. Two white girls pulled up and they were fine as a mother fucker.

I said, "Who are those hoes?"

Timer answered, "They are with me. These are two of my new turn outs. These hoes are ready to hit the track and work their jelly. Come over to the Fifth Season's Inn on NW 63rd. I'll be in room 213."

I said, "Word."

Big Timer jumped in the Suburban and told the white hoes to follow him. They didn't know their way around because they were from Houston TX. The white girls were driving a brand new Chevy Tahoe and looking very, very good, if I must say so myself. When we arrived at the room, they really surprised me because they weren't ordinary white girls. These bitches had asses fatter than black girls. They were freaky as hell too.

Timer told the girls, "Let me fill your gas tank up and pick up some drinks. When I get back, we are going to sit down and talk. Have a good time okay."

"Okay baby," they laughed and giggled.

He said, "I'll be back shortly. Just chill out."

Timer secretly asked me, "Where do you want the weed?"

I said, "Follow me to my homies' house in the country."

Me, & Timer drove to my homie's house in the white girl's Tahoe. Then pulled in the garage and closed the door. Big Timer climbed in the Tahoe's back door to pull out the spare tire.

"Here you go. Now get this shit out of the tire and bring it back to the hotel room," he said.

I said, "Those are some down ass white girls to drive from Texas with a hundred pounds of weed."

Chapter 4

Timer replied, "Yeah, kind of. They probably would have tripped if they had known that weed was in their truck."

"So you mean to tell me that they didn't know about the bud in their truck?"

Timer said, "That's right. I never let a bitch or a nigga know anything! Never let your right hand know what your left hand is doing. That's the golden rule. You have to keep your nose clean. Meet me back at the room and stay down little bro. I like the way you stack your chips instead of tricking it off. I'll help you get the 100 thousand. After you finish this, you should have fifty thousand dollars. I'll sell you 100 pounds for 50. Is that cool?"

I said, "Hell yeah, that's cool! Then I'll be real close to a 100 stack (money)."

Timer said, "Alright. I'm out of here. I'll go and pick up some Remy Martin. You want some?"

"Yes I do. I'll have a drink with you and those fine white girls."

Timer ask, "So you like them huh?"

"Hell yes! I bet they will make money on the track."

Timer said, "Feel that."

Timer left and I went up to a friend's service station on 23rd street. I had him to break down that tire and rim. Then paid him 200 dollars for the job. Then quickly went out to my stash spot to put my weed up. Now I owed Timer $40,000.00. I planned on paying him off in less than a month.

I also stopped at Bryon's liquor warehouse and picked up a 5th of Remy Martin & headed on over to the Fifth Season's Hotel.

When I got there, it was on. Timer had those hoes sucking each other's pussy and freaking each other. He was sitting at the table fully dressed with about a quarter ounce (7 grams) of that good ass coke, (cocaine) a fat sack of Indo weed, and a 5th of Remy Martin on the table.

I sat down with Timer at the table to watch the girls freak. While twisting up a fat Indo blunt mixed with some of that pine cone sticky green. Timer poured me up a drink. I even got loose with the powder and started snorting up a storm. Next thing I know, I was fucked up.

Timer was over there putting coke on their little man in a boat (on their clits). Those bitches were hot! It made me get hard as a mother fucker just watching them, but Timer never took one stitch of clothes off. All he did was laugh and had a good time.

He asked, "Do you want to freak with them?"

"Well," I hesitated.

"Go ahead, Timer implied."

The girls said, "What's up Timer? We came here for you."

Timer said, "Are you? Well, if you two are for me, I want you to freak with my little brother. I want you to imagine it's me. How do you call yourselves choosing me if you can't do what I'm asking you to do? How can you turn a trick if you are worried about who it is? Besides, I'm putting you two down. You're not putting me down on the game. Now handle your business ladies."

I proceeded to get undressed and climb into bed with the hoes. It was on. Both of them were licking me from head to toe. Then they started licking my nuts and sucking my dick. That had me going crazy.

Timer was over there at the table snorting cocaine, drinking Remy, laughing at my facial expressions, and shaking his head. While talking on his cell phone making big deals I'm sure.

Since I snorted all that good coke, it took me a long time to climax. Those freaky hoes wanted me to cum all in their faces. One bitch even started licking my ass hole. As crazy as it may sound, that ass licking shit had me groaning like a moose. I had butterflies in my stomach like I was riding on the Texas Giant roller coaster at Six Flaggs. They were licking, jacking, and sucking on my dick until I came. The girls were almost fighting over my cum. Sort of like it was honey or something. They took turns swallowing my cum until there was no more. While still jacking me off and sucking trying to get more cum out of me.

I had to push those hoes off of me. I couldn't take it any longer. My dick was tender as a mother fucker, especially after a good orgasm. Those hoes would have given me a heart attack. I see why women can sell sex. They never get tired of it. After they sucked me dry, they kept freaking amongst themselves.

Timer was laughing so hard he almost fell out his chair. He was mocking me. Even those snow bunnies (white girls) were laughing at me.

They asked Timer, "How did we do? Did we pass your test?"

Timer said, "Half of it. Now it is time for you to pass the other half. Girls get dressed. Put on your ladies of the night outfits and let's go to the track. Let's make some money. That will let me know if you two are real hookers or just some free fucking, trailer park white hoes."

They quickly replied, "We aren't any trailer park white trash! You have to pay the cost to be the boss with us! That's right."

Timer and I sat at the table getting fucked up while they were getting cleaned up, dressed, and putting on their makeup.

Timer asked me, "Do you want to kick it with me tonight for a little while?"

"Yeah, I'll chop it up with you Big Bro. I'm not doing anything until this pager goes off."

Timer said, "I'm going to put you down on this pimp game. All these broke bitches out here free fucking & shit. They can get paid for it and cum at the same time. All you have to do is dress them, keep their hair, nails and toes done, keep some bond money, and it's on. Take notes tonight and check out this pimping. I've been spitting at these square hoes for only a week or so, and they are already, ready. They followed me all the way from Houston TX, to sell some pussy here in OKC. They didn't want to sell any pussy locally. Their family, friends, or someone might see them. You know me. I'm international with my pimping. I'll work the bitches in Tokyo if I have to (lol). It doesn't matter to me, just get my money."

The girls were finally ready. Timer had already slid the girl's spare tire back in their Tahoe without them ever knowing anything. We climbed into Big Timer's new Suburban with the leather and wood grain everywhere. It was sitting on the Enkei 20 inch rims with the rubber band tires (low profile tires). We were in the front captain seats and the ladies were in the back captain seats. The girls loved Timer's 'Suburban. I guess Oklahoma and Texas girls loved trucks.

We pulled off the parking lot and Timer turned on the CD player. The first song was that new Silk (There's a meeting in my bedroom). His system was crystal clear with that deep, rich bass. There were tweeters in each corner of the truck. Big Bro. had the surround sound system, Timer had it all.

You couldn't go wrong being dressed and smelling good. With good music and movies on, a bitch had to break herself if she enjoyed that lavish lifestyle. Besides, I was curious to know how their first night out on the track was going to turn out. We headed to the South side of OKC off of SE 29th and Robinson Ave. Timer was putting his pimping down every inch of the way to the track. He gave the hoes pimping and sent them out the door with instructions.

These hoes had never walked up and down the track before. From what it looked like, they enjoyed the adventure and challenge of strutting their stuff. Once they turned their first trick, they were sprung. Hoes get a major rush from getting paid for just a piece of ass. That's the tricky part of the game. The way I seen those tricks on the track, no woman should ever go broke. They were sitting on a gold mine.

I really started feeling that pimp shit after we popped it with some other pimps from OKC and California. We even saw Pimping-X. Timer formerly introduced us. I sat there and took notes for a minute. I listened to them talk about pimping and checking hoe money. That is, until my pager blew up with a $5000.00 bite.

I immediately asked Timer, "Could you take me to my vehicle? Now it's time for me to check my grip (money) and I hadn't even weighed my shit or separated it into pounds yet."

I had been out with Timer trying to pick up on some pimping. But for now, I needed to stick with what I know. I guess Timer mentioned to the pimps that I had the sticky green. Ten of them wanted an ounce for a hundred bucks each. So now I had six thousand to pick up right quick. That's a nice lick for one day's work; $6000.00.

Timer and I jumped in the 'Burban and mashed out. Timer wanted to hurry because these were some new turn outs. A lot of pimps were out tonight accepting applications. One thing about it, you can't do anything if your bitch re-chooses on you. That's why you work a bitch like there is no tomorrow because you never know when you might get peeled for her. So if you pimp a 'Lac or a new Benz out of a bitch and she leave, who is the winner?

Bitches, hoes, and women period are subject to re-choose on a player at any given moment. Never say what your bitch will or will not do. You might get heartbroken and that's real. You square mother fuckers out there can't take it. That's when you want to fight and shoot another player just because your bitch re-chose.

Fellas check yourselves out there. Don't check pimping. Check your bitch and don't be afraid to let the bitch go. Just because you bought the bitch some leather and fucked her don't make the pussy yours forever. That's not your pussy fellas. That bitch own that pussy and she will give it to whoever she wants.

I guess that's why Timer was rushing to drop me off.

Timer said, "These are my new turn outs and they aren't ready to be put on automatic yet. They do know the rules about speaking, waving, or smiling at another pimp. The bitches know that they would be out of bounds for that type of behavior. If I can get a good month out of these square hoes, that would be terrific. Hopefully, these hoes can make at least 4 or 5 hundred a piece. I'll work them 7 days a week. My pimping is open 24/7. It never shuts down."

We finally made it back to my old bucket.

"I'll page you in about 30 to 40 minutes when I'm ready for those pimps," Timer.

I jumped in my old school bucket. It was a 1985 drop top Monte Carlo SS with all gold 100 spoke Daytons and Vogue tires with the candy flip flop paint. I mashed out peeling rubber and fish tailing. I was showing out and feeling good. My Alpine was jamming on that old Al B. Sure (Naturally Mine). My shit was no punk and it was a hoe catcher as well.

I pulled different types of women. They were either a hood-rat or a gang related bitch. I was ready to pull hookers and hoes now. Fuck those square hoes. I punched it all the way to my hiding spot in the country. I was thinking about pimping me a bitch all while I was jamming and listening to AL B. Sure and R. Kelly's 12 play.

I rushed and sacked up 7 pounds for the 5 thousand and weighed up 10 ounces. That was a half pound and 2 ounces. Me, & the Monte Carlo SS was headed to the East Side to meet my partner who wanted the 7 pounds. I met up with him and collected that little 5 grand. I then paged Timer.

And told him, "I'm on my way to the track. Make sure those pimps don't leave. I'll be there in 10 minutes. Feel that."

I pulled up on the track still bumping that old R. Kelly (Summer Bunnies).That Alpine with the 6 twelve inch Alpine woofers along with the mids and tweeters really sounded good; If I must say so myself. It was being powered by two Alpine amps and Alpine cross overs. I was really surprised because bitches were just looking and jamming to the grooves. I pulled up on the lot where the pimps were and they all started doing the pimp step. Pimps were shaking their heads and admiring my old school drop top.

I served the fellas ounces and chopped it up with them for about 10 minutes before my pager blew up again. This time it was a $1,500.00 bite for 2 pounds. I was giving good deals that night, just wanting to move this shit. If I made a 100 or 200 dollars off a pound, fuck it. I had plenty of pine cones.

A hustler had to cut the pimps short and get on my grind. I had to get my skrilla, & those pimps loved my bud.

"Can we get your pager number S.S. Boy? We'll be calling you every day while we're in town for this sticky green," they said.

"Feel that. I'll come serve you, just call," I told them.

Timer was standing in the cut as usual, just smiling and giving me the peace sign. I jumped in the Super sport and bumped the R. Kelly again (Sex me remix). I drove off the track hitting the pimp horn at the hookers. I was trying to knock me one. I didn't see Timer's new turn outs, which was good, because they were probably selling plenty of pussy.

All I could think about was making this money; which will be $7,500.00 in one night. I was doing a hundred down the highway with my mind on my money and my money on my mind. As I rushed to the country to pick up 2 more pounds.

My pager blew up again from my cousin. It was a 5 pound bite for $700.00 a piece, which equaled $3,500.00. These hustlers really loved that sticky green. I weighed 7 pounds and dropped them off. Everything was going rather cool. This slow night had turned into a great night. I clocked over $11,000.00 in a couple of hours.

I had moved over 14 ½ pounds and still had 85 ½ pounds left to work with. I got drunk as a mother fucker that night. With a mean dick sucking and made $11,000.00. I had a good night for a small timer. Immediately paging Timer again.

"Come pick up this little change," I told him.

Timer said, "That's right. Feel that. If I don't get with you tonight, I'll be by your house in the morning. I'll call you when I'm on my way. I'm working these white hoes right now. I've already clocked $1,200.00 from them and they're still turning tricks. It's a pretty good night little bro. My pimp partners are inquiring if there are more of these dedicated white hoes in Houston, TX! You know me. I'm going to let the blind stay blind and let the sleep stay sleep. If these hookers know more hookers they will recruit them for me, feel me?"

"That's right. I'm trying to knock me one now Big Timer. I want a hoe. Fuck these broke square bitches waiting on me to take penitentiary chances so we can live good. These square ass hoes need to take some chances if they want me. Now feel that."

Timer laughed and said, "I can dig it."

Chapter 5

The next morning, about 10:00 a.m., Timer was ringing my door bell. I had a hangover that wouldn't quit. It must have taken me five or ten minutes to answer the door. I let Timer in. He had his new turn outs at the room resting up and getting ready to hit the highway.

Timer said," I pimped almost $1,500.00 out of them both last night. They are turned out on this pimping and tricking. These snow bunnies are ready to go coast to coast and sell plenty of pussy all across the United States. I told them we need about 2 or 3 more hookers first. Then we will take a 3 or 4 month trip across country. International baby."

"It ain't no problem. We have 3 more friends who would love to travel, make money, and go shopping with us Timer."

"Go and get them. Ya'll introduce us and let the pimping begin."

I couldn't really pop pimping because of my rough night.

I told him, "Hold on and twist up a joint."

Timer likes blunts but, he would prefer a phat joint rolled with those Zig Zag papers.

I went in the bedroom and grabbed that $11,000.00 I made last night and handed it to Timer. I had given him $20,000.00 plus $11,000.00, which equaled $31,000.00. Now only owing him $29,000.00 and still had 85 ½ pounds left.

Timer appreciated how I treated the game, & paid him off before I started spending money.

Timer said, "It's on with you. That sticky green sells like hot cakes. Well little brother, I'm out. I've got pimping to do. You know what little bro?"

"What big Bro?"

"I think I'm going to bust out in me a new Silver Spur Rolls Royce. Maybe not brand new, but at least a 96, 97, or 98. I'm going to charge it to all these hoes. Pimping is five hookers deep now. If these hoes knock me two or three more, I'll be 7 or 8 hoes deep. Keep up the good work little bro. Call me. Let's get down while the getting is good. I'm headed back to Texas after I talk to Pimping-X about our two teams hooking up on something major. Pimping X wants that Hummer just as bad as I want that Rolls. Every mansion has a Roll Royce or two in the garage or in the driveway."

I said, "That's right. Timer, I think I'm just going to pay my little house off. I only owe about $30,000.00 more on it. Then I might bust out in a new hoe catcher."

Timer said, "Keep a steady pace like this. Keep your job. & it should be no problem for you to get that accomplished.

Timer left OKC and was gone about three days before I came up with another $10,000.00. I paged him as he was on his way to Denver, Colorado with those same two snow bunnies. Timer had been pimping up a storm. He was also on super charge (feeling good) about his pimping and accepting all applications from hookers in Denver.

He said, "My hoes have been pulling in close to a thousand each and every night. I have already pimped almost $10,000.00 total out of them. They both want to buy Daddy that new Rolls. We are working overtime to get that accomplished too. I told them that I need thirty thousand for the down payment. Hold on to that $10,000.00 you got for me. Try and make it grow. I'll get with you in a week or so. Pimping-X and I came up with a master plan. I'll have to see if his team can follow instructions. They need to handle business first before we execute this major lick. I'll call you. Keep that hundred thousand on your mind. Be about your paper, like me, little brother. Nothing comes to a sleeper but a dream. I have dreamed long enough. It's time for my dreams to come true about that Double R (Roll Royce). It just won't fall in your lap. You have to go and get it by any means necessary. How bad do you want it (money)? One man's loss is another man's gain. What one man won't do, another man will. He'll get away with it, if he play his cards right. So handle up. I'll get at you in a few days. Peace."

Hanging up in my face again. He always left a serious thought and something real on my mind. I continued stacking my chips and this weed was selling quicker than crack. My pager was constantly blowing up with pound bites. OKC weed houses stand tall with plenty of business. Brothers from Arkansas and Kansas stay coming up to the city for the bomb weed.

Timer finally came back to OKC. He would then be on his way back to Dallas with a phat bank roll which he pimped straight out of those two white hoes pussy.

"I'm going to pull a Rolls Royce out of their womb and keep it pimping, Timer replied."

I made that little ten thousand grow to seventeen thousand. I only owed Big Bro. twelve thousand more dollars and I still had sixty pounds. I was looking alright, but not as good as I should have been looking on my money. The only reason why I wasn't fully satisfied was because I sold them for seven hundred each, when I should have sold them for nine hundred. Fuck it, at least I'm moving this shit fast and earning Timer's approval. I'll get my money in later. I just need fifty thousand so I can pay cash for the hundred pounds.

Timer told me, "You are really getting down and I will start working on the 100 pounds of sticky green for you. I'm going to check my traps and see how many pounds I got left. I'm about ready to re-up (buy) myself. My workers in Dallas move the hell out of pounds and birds (weed and kilos of cocaine)."

Timer left with the seventeen thousand dollars and however much he broke his hoes for. It was probably 20 or 30 thousand knowing him. I had the rest of Timer's money, which was $12,000.00 in about two weeks after he left. I paged him on the 1-800 number and he called right back as usual.

"I'm ready to ride and I have some gas money, Big Bro."

He said, "Cool, I'll be there in a few days. I'm trying to wait on my check so I can fill up my gas tank to make it down there. Then we can chop it up and kick it for the weekend. Why don't you send me those few dollars and I'll pay you back on pay day?"

I said, "Cool, I'll do it."

I went to four different banks and purchased a cashier's check for $3,000.00 at each bank. I used Timer's fake name that he had an ID for. Then I took those four $3,000.00 checks which totaled up to $12,000.00 and put them in a large card board federal express envelope. Then had it delivered over night to Timer.

When I paged him back.

I told him, "It's on. You'll have a few dollars tomorrow."

Timer replied, "Feel that. I'll call you later."

Now I was feeling good because I had Timer paid in full. I still had almost 45 pounds, which made me short of the 50 thousand dollars. Fuck it. This was all mine and I'm selling each pound for $900.00. That way if I'm short, I won't be that short. I will only owe a little bit. All of my clientele was spoiled from the $700.00 deals though. It took me a lot longer than I expected to move those 40 pounds. My luck couldn't have been better because Timer was still waiting on the sticky eye closer anyway.

He said, "I could have gotten some of that old Mexican brown or dirt weed on a good deal, but I passed that up. My other people should be back soon. Just keep clocking your money and it will be on before you run out. I'm almost out too, so something got to give quickly. I put those two white hoes on automatic in Nashville at Meeko's whorehouse and they are doing just fine. My other hoes are getting down too. Have you knocked a hooker yet or flipped a square bitch S.S. Boy?"

I told him, "No, not yet, but I'm working on it. I'll have one sooner or later. Bet that."

So I continued pumping my pounds and getting $850.00 to $900.00 each. It took me almost a month. Timer was just waiting for my call. I finally was finished with those 45 pounds. & had approximately $39,500.00, which was all mine.

"Timer, I'm ready with about $35,000.00 for you."

I was going to keep $4,500.00 just for bills, necessities, and bond money if needed. A young hustler was feeling pretty good because I was still about $40,000.00 strong. Yeah, I had come from broke to now sitting on forty thousand free dollars. Now I'm about to buy 100 pounds of sticky green eye closer and it will damn near be all mine. I'll only owe Big Timer a little $15,000.00. That's a lot better than owing him $60,000.00.

I had the whole East Side sewed up and everyone was waiting on me to re-up. People were also trying to figure out my connection and where is it coming from. I hate nosy mother fuckers.

I told them, "Don't sweat mine. Just be happy that it's on at a good price."

Why do people always ask questions like, "How much do you have? Who did you buy it from? Where is it from? How much did you pay per pound?"

I told them, "Never ask me any questions again about my business. By the way, let me pat you down just to make sure you're not wired."

I immediately left those busters and headed to the Barber shop. Once I got up there, I heard the homies talking about this brother getting in a brand new white on white Rolls Royce. It had gold Lexani 20 inch rims, a gold grill, and a touch of gold all the way around it. They were going on and on about this brother. It was a young black brother in the Double R. I immediately thought about my boy, Timer. He was the first one came to mind.

I put this on everything. Just as we were talking, this white on white Double R (Rolls Royce) pulled up with the gold grill and rims. A fine ass Mexican bitch was driving. She jumped out and walked around to the back door on the passenger side. This beautiful woman had a little see through sundress on that was very low cut. The high heel shoes that she wore exposed her pretty toes with long black, curly hair. She reminded you of Selena (the late beautiful Hispanic entertainer). She opened up the rear passenger door and guess who jumped out?

He was Versace down from head to toe, with all of his diamonds on. Or shall I say a lot of diamonds. He had on about 35 karats. Everyone in the Barber shop was motionless and speechless.

I replied, "It's my boy, Timer. He told me that he was going to get him a Rolls Royce."

I couldn't believe how clean this car was. He really looked like a millionaire now. Niggas was shocked. They were commenting on the girl and the car. This fine ass Mexican girl even opened the door up for him. She treated him like he was Don Juan, (the big pimp out of Chi-Town) or as if he was Puff Daddy or someone.

I had never seen my big homie flex like this before, not too many brothers from OKC had come through with a Rolls Royce. Timer came in, spoke to everyone, and sat in the barber's chair for his DC fade. Everyone was paying props and giving him dap. Everyone walked outside to get a closer look at this six figure car with the ten thousand dollar rims and tires on it. I know I did.

The closer I came to it, the cleaner it became. That big gold grill with the gold emblem on top was just too much. That meant money. He had that big white leather on the inside with the high back leather seats. It looked like the front seat could touch the headliner of the car. His shit was Alpine down with brand new 2000 equipment.

Timer told us, "I'm not pounding. It just sounds good and clear with three 10 inch Alpine woofers."

Timer looked all the way different. He looked like he just graduated to another level; which he did. JT finally finished fading Timer up. That pretty ass Mexican bitch just sat there patiently while he was getting his hair cut. She was one of Timer's hookers who had been in Nashville at the whore house for a couple of months. She came home to Texas for a week or so.

Timer said, "She came to visit her family and child."

This bitch was just too damn fine to be selling pussy. She could have been anything besides a hoe. She could've been a model or an anchor woman or making commercials or something of that nature. This Selena was so fine I probably would have bought a shot of that pussy if I could have kept it in the closet.

Those clowns in the barber shop were feening for that girl and not necessarily to have sex with her. They wanted to take her out on the town and show her off. Her voice was so soft spoken and sexy. Her body was either a ten or better.

Timer knew she was a bad bitch. We all knew that. We all were tweaking, (wanting her). I'm sure he would have let her make some money if one of us had approached him or her with a proposition. Timer would not turn down shit but his Versace collar. As Timer walked out of the barber shop with his bitch, I walked out behind him. I was trying to see what's up with my shipment.

Timer said, "I will call you later on tonight after I handle some other business. Chill out. It's on."

That fine bitch opened his passenger side back door. Baby closed the door once he got in. I just stood there smiling and admiring this hustler. I called him a hustler, because he was much more than a pimp or a dope boy. He was a jack of all trades. He did it all: sold dope, weed, robbed, pimped, gambled and most importantly hustled.

His girl got in and started up that pretty pimping ass Double R. I couldn't even hear it running. Timer let his window down and winked his eye at me. He was jamming on that old Jodeci (Dairy of a mad Band). Timer slowly let the window back up with a fat ass Cuban cigar in his mouth. The girl pulled that car off real slow.

Everyone was staring in amazement.

Chapter 6

They were giving each other dap and saying, "Timer is doing too much! Way too much! He is the top dog! He is the coldest mother fucker from OKC, and his game is well rounded!"

Later on that evening, Timer paged me and asked, "Can you meet me at Pearl's Oyster bar off of 63rd and Western? Come have a drink with me."

Pearl's is where all the upper class people hang. You can find whites, blacks, business men, doctors, lawyers, and ballers. I had to get clean & put on one of my exotic skin suits. A crocodile jacket, pants, shoes, and hat, with my little drips (jewelry); the blue face Oyster Rolex, my phat rope, and diamond medallion.

My bitch was all over me sweating the shit out of me.

She asked, "Where are you going?"

I had to check that square bitch and put her in check real quick.

Bitch, "Don't sweat me. I don't ask where you're going when you go out with your friends. So I would appreciate it if you treated me the same. Now excuse me please, so I can handle my business."

Boy was she heated (angry)!

As I walked out the door, she shouted, "You think you're all of that don't you?"

I replied, "No I don't."

"You think you're the shit since you and Timer have been hanging together. All of a sudden you've been having money."

"Bitch, you must think I'm the shit. I'm the same old me; except being introduced to some new & improved game. That new game is pimping. Finding me some hoes and getting that hoe money every night."

She said, "Timer has turned you out! You're not a pimp."

"Bitch you always paid me with that small ass paycheck you earn!"

She was really heated now! She knew it was true and couldn't say shit about it.

"If you're going to mess with some nasty prostitutes, I'm out of here!"

I asked, "How are they nasty? You do the same shit! Fucking and sucking dicks! Except you don't get a dime! Now if I was a bitch, I would rather get paid for my services. That beats getting a hard dick running in and out of my pussy for free! Now you analyze that!"

"But I only get down with my boy friends like that," she said.

"Well how many boyfriends have you had?"

Her eyes were fire ball red. If she was a man, I believe she would have stole on me (hit me). I pimped on out the door and jumped in the SS. I punched out and this time I left someone else with something on their mind (smile), wondering how she liked those apples (lol).

I really need to flip that bitch and get her on out there now. The first chance I get, I will, you feel me? I fell up in the parking lot of Pearl's Oyster Bar and saw Timer's Double R parked at the front door. The valet attendants were admiring his car. I even had to take a second look at it again while walking in the front door of the restaurant.

Timer was sitting at a special reserved table just for us. His Mexican bitch was there and I also saw a few local ballers. They were just staring at us and coming over to the table giving props.

Timer said, "Little bro, you have come a long way in a short time. The average person can't do that."

I said, "That's right. I'm just trying to pick up on my pimping. I'm tired of being broke and working from paycheck to paycheck. I can barely make it."

That's the way we talk in front of anybody. We are firm believers of not letting a woman or anyone else know anything about dope, robberies, gambling, or getting money period. The only thing we will let a woman know about us is some pimping and accepting hoe money. That's where a lot of people fuck up in the game. They let their women listen to their conversations and pillow talk & shit. Then a bitch can set you up or some other fucked up shit. Real players and hustlers keep their women out of their business.

We started drinking those Long Island Ice Teas.

I asked, "Timer when can I push the Rolls?"

Timer answered, "Once you knock a hoe. I'll let you drop her off at the track. The Double R only drops off and picks up hoes with fat bank rolls. Isn't that right baby?"

That fine Mexican girl just smiled with the prettiest smile.

And said, "Yes Daddy."

That hoe made my dick hard just listening to her speak. She had a pair of the prettiest lips I had ever seen.

Timer told me, "Gator will be flying in tomorrow. We are probably going to push the Rolls cross country to Jersey. I need to check on my hoes and scope (look) out a lick. We need a major lick. I need a diamond necklace made with whole or half karats with nothing but ice. Before I make any moves, I will be getting with you."

Okay Timer, "I'm ready & can't wait."

I was feeling real good after a few drinks.

My tipsy ass had to ask, "Can I ride with you? Can I get a necklace too Big Bro?"

I couldn't believe that even came forward from my mouth.

Timer said, "What? You know I always have room for my little homie if he really wants to ride."

Timer, "I had a dream that I got down and it felt good pimping in another state."

He knew what I was talking about because all through the conversation we were talking in codes.

It felt good knowing that it's on. I would be in power with a hundred pounds plus, I might get to get down on a lick with Timer. I must admit that I was a little bit skeptical about putting a lick down and getting some superfast money. Fuck the word skeptical! I was nervous! That Long Island Ice Tea made me say that shit anyway [lol].

Timer told me, "Pimping X will probably roll with me and Gator tomorrow or whenever I decide to leave. Little bro, just keep getting your scratch with the sticky green and don't sweat the other shit."

I said, "Word. I just want that hundred thousand now. I want to sit back and take a cruise to the Islands or something, you feel me?"

Timer said, "I feel you baby boy."

Timer and I were ripped and so was his bitch. She was running back and forth to the restroom and to the wet bar while we talked. I think she had already lined up a few dates.

Timer said, "Just go home and wait for me to call you and it's on. I've got you covered."

Okay, "Cool, I'll scream at you tomorrow Big Bro. I'm fucked up; but first I'm going to see what's happening on the track."

Timer said, "That's right. Stay down and besides, tonight might be your night."

I asked, "Timer where are your white hoes?"

"In Arizona on automatic, (auto means sending them out alone with instructions) getting a pimp his money, and at the whore house loving this pimpin."

I replied, "Feel that, I need me some hoes so I can put them on automatic. I'm going to see how much this square bitch at home loves me. Fuck that little $8.00 an hour job. The government puts taxes on it anyway. I want her to pay taxes to my pimping. Fuck Uncle Sam right now (lol)!"

I flexed in the drop top SS to the track and it was plenty of action out there. Pimps and hoes was everywhere. Tricks were riding and holding up traffic talking to hookers.

I went home and here stood this square broad in my face who thinks she has game.

She asked me, "What did you mean before you walked out the door earlier?"

I replied, "What part of it you didn't understand? I need a hooker. I need a woman who will go out and get money. Baby, by the way I seen those tricks buying pussy from all those girls, we will be living large in no time. Especially how pretty and thick you are with those big pretty, golden brown titties. Maybe it's time for us to try something new Baby. I know that our little jobs ain't hitting on shit. The way I see it, you probably could make almost a thousand dollars a night."

She asked, "You don't love me do you?"

I replied, "Of course I do Baby."

"Well how could you let me go and sell my body?"

"Baby, I sell my body for you taking penitentiary chances whenever we need extra money don't I?"

"Well that's different."

"How is that different? We both take penitentiary chances. We both make money. So how is my hustle different from yours?"

She said, "How can you sleep with me knowing I've sold my body? Besides, you know that you would trip out if I sold this good pussy to someone."

"No baby. The only way I would trip out was if you gave it away for free. You know what else? I would respect you even more if you sold that good pussy instead of giving it away. Baby, most tricks just want to take you out to dinner and suck your pussy or something. You know you love that and besides, you'll get paid for it. Now think about that."

S.S. Boy, "I can't believe you came to me like this. You say you love me more than anything and you want me to sell my body for you?"

"Yes Baby. That is true. I do love you more than anything. Yes, I would like to see if you would sell your body for me. Then I'll believe you when you tell me that you will do anything for me."

"You think you have game nigga?"

I said, "No."

"Well I ought to sell some of this good pussy. Just to watch you get angry and beg me not to do it again (smile)."

I said, "Baby, I'll try not to get angry."

She said, "I could get hooked up on a date with my friend. He is an old sugar daddy and he was inquiring about me through my friend. Plus he has money, & retired from GM."

"Well, what's up with him Baby? We need some help around this camp."

I thought to myself, "I can't believe this broad is going for it. Maybe she wasn't as square as I thought she was. It was always in her. Who knows? Maybe she's already sold some pussy. All this time, I had a hooker and didn't even know it. She was playing me."

I quickly went to the kitchen and pulled out two champagne glasses from the cabinet. I poured us up some drinks and rolled a phat blunt. Me & baby smoked and had about three glasses a piece before we ended up in the bedroom. I sat back to watch her do what she did best: sucking and fucking. I was talking to her while she was sucking on this night stick (dick).

I asked her, "How much do you love me? Will you do anything to keep this big black Indian dick?"

Her mouth was full while she moaned, and nodded her head up and down in the yes motion.

The bitch popped my dick out of her mouth like a charms blow pop sucker (lol) & ask, "Can you cum in my mouth please?"

The more I looked at my girl; the more I could see clearly now that she was a true freak. She loved to get freaky.

I had to step my game up now and get this fine thick mother fucker out there somehow. Fuck a sugar daddy! I need fresh hoe money every night or as often as possible. Baby gave me something to think about now. I needed to flip her completely. Get her mind and thoughts completely on me and my pimping. I must admit we had a really nice time that night. It seemed like we turned over a new leaf in our relationship. It was now more like a pimp and hoe relationship.

The next morning about 7:30 or 8:00 am, Timer popped up at my house and rang the shit out of my door bell.

Chapter 7

I opened the door to him saying, "Meet me at the car wash on Air Depot Blvd. and 23rd street. It's almost in Midwest City. Be there in about ten minutes & give me the grip (the $35,000 dollars)."

I knew it was on now. Timer came in and I stacked all the money neatly in a papersack.

Timer said, "Come on. Hurry up and be there in ten minutes homie."

I rushed into the bathroom to put my clothes on as quickly as possible, & didn't want to be late. I made it to the car wash and didn't see Timer or his Rolls Royce. I saw some other people there early that morning washing their cars and trucks, but no Timer. I fell in line to wait to wash my car next. This brother, whom I had never seen before in my life, came up to my car and knocked on my car window.

He asked, "Can I wash your car for you? Your car is hitting (nice)."

I looked up and there was Timer in an old bucket (car) in line next to me. He was nodding his head yes.

I told the guy, "Yes you can wash it. How much do you charge?"

He said, "Don't worry about it. As a matter of fact, why don't you go and get us some breakfast in my car? My car is in the stall directly in front of you."

I looked at Timer and he was giving me the go ahead signal. I climbed out of the SS Monte Carlo and jumped into this brother's bucket (old car). When I got in, I saw two big duffle bags. I already knew what was in them. The smell was very loud. It was the sticky green. It damn near smelled like Indo.

I had to hurry up and drop this shit off in the country at my hiding place. Boy was I happy. I now had 100 pounds of sticky green, and was getting ready to stack my grip and handle up. A young hustler wanted this hundred thousand dollar stack real bad. I dropped off my weed and unzipped one of the bags and broke off a phat block, about 2 ounces, so I could sample it to see how bomb (good) the weed really was. Quickly a hustler headed back to the car wash where Timer and his boys were.

Timer asked me, "What do you think?"

I answered, "It smells good, & I'm getting ready to roll a couple of blunts."

Timer said, "Cool, I'll be back by the time you have them rolled."

Timer and this other brother punched out leaving the other guy to finish up my car. He was putting the black magic on the tires.

I sat in homie's car and rolled blunts. Timer came rolling up in the Double R. He pulled in the stall as homie finished with my car. The guy immediately began washing the Rolls. Timer came to the car where I was and got in.

We fired up a blunt and this shit was the eye closer. I knew my clients would love this shit. Timer was just sitting there smiling, knowing that I was digging this sticky green.

"Timer, I've already paid you 35 thousand, & only owe you 15 thousand now."

Timer said, "No little brother. I'm just going to charge you 45 thousand for the 100 pounds. Now you only owe me $10,000. How is that?"

"That's cool Timer."

He said, "The only reason why I'm doing this is because you are staying down and hustling hard. You have come from skid row to the world of honey. Keep up the good work and stay sucker free. Always keep your mouth shut about your hook up. Now you should be even closer to that 100 thousand dollar stack that you want. Don't even sweat it; but also don't sit on your ass waiting on it to fall out of the sky."

I told Timer about what me, & my woman discussed, and what she said.

Timer said, "Is that right? Sounds like you might have you one. It's just how much you apply your pimping and how serious you are with her about it. Be sweet to her; promise her the world, or whatever makes her motor tick. Make sure to enforce to her how much you love her. Tell her that you won't ever look down on her for getting your money with her looks and body."

We sat there chopping it up while blowing those blunts and waiting on homie to finish cleaning Timer's car. I was sitting there taking notes from the realest hustler I had ever met.

Timer told me, "My Mexican bitch flew out early this morning. Pimping X, Gator, and I are getting ready to head to the East Coast. We need to come up with a plan to put Pimping X and his crew down. I will be back in a week or so. Be careful and don't get caught up accepting any wooden nickels."

Little homie finally finished cleaning the Rolls and it was spotless.

Timer dapped me and said, "I will get with you once I come back."

Okay &, "I should have that little ten thousand for you by the time you return Big Bro."

Timer said, "Okay cool."

Then he jumped in the Rolls heading to the East side.

I went back home and told my girl, "Get dressed and let's go get some breakfast at Jimmy's egg, Pioneer Pies, or someplace nice with good breakfast food."

I spit pimping at Baby all while we ate. That left her clueless on how much money I'm about to come across in the next month or so. I played the broke role with her all the way. I was trying to convince her that we needed to do something immediately.

I reminded her of how bad she wanted that short body Jaguar. Baby loved the one Juvenile had on the Bling-Bling video. She was really listening now. I must have struck a nerve when I mentioned the Jag. Baby was all ears now and I saw the twinkle in her eyes. She was definitely putting some serious thought into my conversation now.

I said, "Maybe we ought to take a trip to Dallas one weekend to see what we can come up with Baby."

Baby asked, "Can we get big money in Dallas?"

I quickly replied, "Hell yes. We can get paid royally."

"First S.S. Boy, I want to talk to my friend again about this sugar daddy to see what he's talking about."

"Baby I doubt if that old man will give up 10 or $20,000.00 a month. Will he?"

She said, "I don't know."

"Does he have big money with Gold and Platinum cards?"

She said, "Yes."

Well Baby, "He might just go and charge us a new Jag. So when are you going to check on this old fellow?"

"I will today. Can you first promise me that you won't get angry at me?"

"I promise Baby. Like I mentioned before, the only way I'll get mad is if you give away that good loving for free. Then I'll figure that you must have liked him. So don't ever let me find out anything like that. It will be over unless you can put over ten thousand dollars in my hand just for fucking up."

When we finished eating, Baby picked up her mobile phone to call her girl friend about the sugar daddy. She walked away from the table toward the restroom while still on the phone talking.

Baby came back and asked, "Would you drop me off over my friend's house?"

I answered, "Sure."

That sounded good to me. That gave me time to handle my business. I could pick up the digital scale, some large freezer bags, and start sacking up some pounds of the sticky. We jumped in the M.C. and I put my pimping down until we arrived at her girlfriend's crib.

"S.S. Boy you don't have to pick me up. My friend will bring me home."

So I went to the grocery store for the freezer bags and stopped at one of my homie's to pick up a digital scale. I then headed to the country to start my sacking process.

I started contacting my people and dropping off pounds to my homie's weed houses. I fronted out ten pounds to three of them at $850.00 each and they loved it.

"This weed is much better than the last time S.S. Boy. It will sell with the quickness."

My pager started blowing up with a couple of small bites for quarter pounds, which I sold for $225.00.

Afterward I went back home to finish watching the final four (March Madness basketball). There were two Oklahoma teams still in the tournament; Oklahoma State and Tulsa. I poured up some Remy Martin and rolled another blunt. While sitting on the couch and enjoying the rest of the evening in front of my big screen. All I could think about was my money.

My woman finally came home, tipsy.

Baby updated me stating, "I met the old man and he was pretty cool. He took me and my friend out for dinner and drinks. Wow, was this older gentleman really interested in me, my goals, and needs in life."

I said, "That's good. So what's up on the money?"

"He was just looking for a lovely young lady as myself. The John just wants to spend a little time with me, nor did he have a problem helping a single independent woman out."

"That's good Baby. So what do you think about how easy the game can be as long as you apply yourself properly?"

She said, "So far it's cool. He did ask me for a hug and kiss on the cheek when he dropped us off at my friend's house. I gave him a peck. I guess it wasn't that bad and besides, the old man was real nice and sweet. I just have a guilty conscience about getting his money."

I almost cussed the bitch out after she said that dumb ass shit. I remained cool and calm though.

"You shouldn't feel that way, baby. Our needs have to be taken care of just like the old man's does."

"Yeah, I guess you're right about that S.S. Boy."

I said, "Never sell yourself short to anyone."

It was on now. I will officially have my first hoe once she pays me hoe money, for my pimping and finesse. My goal was to get her in a whore house for months at a time. Plus Baby don't have any kids. There would be no need for her to come home in a hurry. I just needed to trick this bitch out of that square ass job or get her fired. Either way was fine by me. First, I wanted her to turn her first trick. I'll take it slow for now.

A week had passed and I had only made five thousand dollars with another five thousand out. That was better than nothing. I still had eighty eight pounds left at $850.00 a pound. This time I should make $850 x 88 = $74,800 + $10,000, leaving me a grand total of $84,800. That's pretty damn good. I just needed to take my time and get my money. I already had Timer's $10,000.

I wanted to pay off my house, which was thirty thousand, & plus having enough to buy another hundred pounds of sticky green. A hustler will be straight for a long time. I won't have to worry about paying the mortgage. Just the bills: water, electric, gas, insurance on the house, and car. I could handle that. If I never hustled again, I could just keep my little job and stay straight.

The old man took her shopping. The old sugar daddy bought baby an outfit for everyday of the week. That was cool for Baby, but I needed my money. I'll make her take all that shit back to the store next time, so I can get paid.

My clients were starting to blow me up for those pounds again. Some people out in Kansas were driving down for twenty pounds and I couldn't wait. I ended up giving them a good deal at $700.00 each. They loved it.

The K.C. players mentioned, "The cost doesn't matter as long as the quality is A1."

My man reached in his hidden stash spot and pulled out a bankroll. They had a paper sack full of money. Those Kansas City players peeled me off $14,000.00. I had to kick my home boy down a little something because those were his people. I gave him two pounds. He was a good hustler; and besides, I do my people right. That's the reason why they love me.

I had about sixty six pounds and about fifteen thousand plus Timer's ten thousand. I also had a woman trying to hustle.

Timer, Gator, and Pimping X were gone for almost two weeks. By then I had accumulated another ten thousand dollars. I got rid of another twelve pounds for ten thousand dollars. Still sitting on 54 pounds and twenty five thousand dollars in cash. My clientele saw that I had a solid connection and they started to inquire about kilos of cocaine. They were wondering if I could ask my people about the yola (coke).

Chapter 8

I told them, "I will check on it."

I really didn't want to fuck with the yola because its trouble. Besides it carries a lot of time. I did have five guys who wanted a key (kilo) at twenty thousand dollars each. That made it worth checking with Timer about.

Timer called, "Meet me at your house in twenty minutes."

That's what I did. I couldn't wait to hear what he had been doing.

He said, "My girls in Jersey had a nice little fifteen thousand for me to pick up. I found a little easy lick for Pimping X and his boys just for initiation to the game. I'm charging them, this nice Presidential gold Rolex with the diamonds & all the fixings. That's for introducing him to this nationwide game."

I rudely interrupted, "Hold on Timer."

Rushing into the bedroom to get the ten thousand I owed him. Now I didn't owe him shit. The rest was all mine. I still had 54 pounds and twenty five thousand cash.

I told Timer, "My girl hooked up with a sugar daddy. She been charging him for material shit; but I haven't received any money yet."

Timer said, "Well, it's a start. It's better than nothing. You will eventually have to get her out there. I'll turn you on to some good spots. You do understand pimping right?"

I ask, "What do you mean?"

Timer said, "Now you know other pimps will be shooting at your hoe trying to get her out of bounds? They'll try to peel you for your hoe. You need to thoroughly explain the rules to her about not speaking or smiling at other pimps. Not even me. Now she has opened up a new can of worms. See, I used to look at her as square; but I would never come to her unless she was out of bounds. She can't be all up in my face or inquiring about my business. There can be nothing of that nature. I mean no disrespect; but that's pimping. Pimps knock other pimps for their hoes. The game goes on and on. Hoes choose other pimps. An average hoe will run from pimp to pimp and then end up back in your stable. A true dedicated bitch will always stay down with her man until the wheels fall off. It's very few true ones out here. Let me ask you a question. If my bottom bitch presented you with a phat bank roll and said she is choosing you, would you take that money? Knowing that bitch makes five thousand a week or better would you accept her? You better because it wouldn't be nothing personal. Bitches like different forms and styles of pimping. My girl might like your pimping at the time or vice versa. Your bitch might like my style of pimping. That's why you never let your girl hang around ear hustling when real pimps and men are around talking."

I said, "Dig that."

"I feel you. So if your bitch come up to me skinning and grinning I would have to see what she can do for Daddy. I know what a good bitch can be worth."

I said, "That's right."

"So before you put her out there make sure she is ready. Your pimping better be tight. There are all kinds of game out there. So be about your pimping. You don't want to send your bitch out to get peeled. She will be gone if she re-chose on you with a flyer pimp spitting paralyzing venom at her. That would make her leave you. You would hate to get out on the highway several states over and she run off on you. Bitches will leave you high and dry. That shit will have you fucked up. It'll make you want to kill that bitch whenever you see her."

I appreciated Timer's schooling a great deal.

He said, "It's good that you made it to first base with her."

I asked, "What's up with that yola? Could you get me some?"

Timer answered, "Yes I've got that too. Are you sure that you want to graduate to that level? You will have to look out for the fiends, the police, the bandits, and robbers."

"Yeah, I know. So how much would you charge me for a kilo or two Big Bro?"

"I'll charge you fourteen thousand dollars each. However, I don't front the coke (cocaine). You must have the cash."

I said, "Okay, I might have a bite for five of them."

Timer said, "That's cool. When?"

"Maybe this week Big Bro. How long will it take to get them?"

Timer said, "Forty-eight hours or sooner, as a matter of fact, I only have about eight left. So handle your business and page me in the next two hours. Let me know something before I leave town."

Okay, "Cool, I'll get on it right now."

We both left heading in different directions.

I was checking in with my homies on the North Side. They were some little Bloods out there that handled big business. These brothers were about their paper.

I also got back with my homies on the East Side. That was Crip territory. You had the Hoover 107, Shot Gun, neighborhood and the Rolling 60 Crips. They all had big cheese (money), & were ready with $100,000 in cash.

The Bloods told me, "We will get with you next week or so because we're still straight for now."

I paged Timer and said, "Get me five of them ASAP."

"Alright, I'll get on it now lil bro."

Three hours later, Timer was calling me back saying, "I'll be at Jimmy Johnson restaurant on Lincoln Blvd. I need for you to come now."

I jumped in my Monte Carlo SS. Smashing out toward the East Side to the former Dallas Cowboy's head coach Jimmy Johnson's restaurant. I fell up in there and pulled up a chair. Timer handed me a set of keys to homie's old pickup truck from Dallas with the lawnmowers in the back.

"How long would it take to handle your business?"

Well Timer, "About 45 minutes to an hour."

He said, "Cool, you know where everything is. It's five of them in there. My homie will ride shot gun with you. I'll be right here watching Sports Center and eating my fat T-bone steak. I'll wait for an hour at the longest. Handle your business. My Texas homie is ready to kill on sight if things aren't right; so be smooth. Homie don't give a fuck and neither do I about that money."

"Cool, I'm with you Timer. They better not try anything because I would have to smoke them personally or get smoked."

Timer said, "That's right. You know the rules, the seriousness of the yola, and the game."

So we rode out to handle our business. Me, & homie dropped off the five kilos that I sold for $20,000 each. We counted one hundred thousand dollars and everyone was happy.

They were asking, "Can we do it again when we're done with these?"

I told them, "We should since everything went smooth. I'll let you know what's up later."

They all noticed the homie from Texas with the two automatic .45 pistols. He never smiled or said one word. He was just watching, listening, and ready to kill something.

All I could do was calculate the profits in my head. Making thirty thousand dollars profit in one hour. Man that was cool. No wonder people prefer to deal with the yola (coke). I just made thirty thousand dollars in less than an hour and that's exactly what I owed on my house.

The homie from Texas and I were smiling while giving Timer the good news. We went to my house to count Timer's money and separate mine from his.

Timer asked, "Did you have a good day today?"

"Hell yes! It was my best day so far in the game."

I was now sitting on fifty five thousand dollars plus 54 pounds of sticky green. It was safe to say that I was balling now.

Timer gave me dap as he and the Texas homie rode off back to Dallas following each other. Timer was in the Rolls Royce and homie was in the old pickup truck with a hundred thousand cash inside.

Timer makes big money. I usually don't count any one's money; but I had to this time. Timer picked up fifteen thousand in Jersey, ten thousand of what I owed him and seventy thousand on what I just made him. That was a total of ninety five thousand dollars. Timer does this kind of shit all the time, so it was nothing to him.

Before Timer left, he told me, "If it's on again like that do not hesitate to call me. I will be back next week. I'm riding out with Pimping X and his boys. We supposed to ride out and make something happen."

I went to Bryon's liquor warehouse and picked up two bottles of Don P. I also stopped & picked up Big Seamore; my right hand man. We went straight to my house to chop it up for a minute. While sipping on Don P., playing on the play station, talking about money and charging these square hoes. We even snorted some of that bomb yola, getting high as a mother fucker until my girl came home. We ended up going to Big Seamore's house to finish parlaying and getting our game plan together.

My boy Big Seamore had an old school ride too. He had the cleanest '85 four door Olds 98 in the city. It was brandy wine with the candy finish. With white guts, wine trimming and wine buttons. It had the 455 big block motor with the 4 barrel carburetor. The motor was also wine colored. The chrome dual pipes poked from the ass. It was sitting on 15 inch chrome and gold Daytons wrapped in Vogue tires. The system was top of line and powered by Pioneer, with remote controlled detachable face unit. The amps pushed the four 12 inch audio woofers, the tweeters, 6x9s, and the 200 watt 4 way pioneers. That ride was most definitely a hoe catcher.

We hustled just alike as far as selling weed, charging bitches, dressing, and hitting the highway. I took the game and ran with it though. He was still my boy. We had been down since the late 70's together. We did our first quarter pound together on foot with my other partner Eagle.

I was fronting my boy Big Seamore 20 pounds at a time, & he was handling up. We had plenty of fun all through the years. Making plenty of money together, but for some reason, he just couldn't graduate to the next level of the game as quick.

The next day, I called Mom.

I asked her, "Would you pay my house off for me? Your name is on the loan."

She said Boy, "I don't have thirty thousand dollars."

"Mom, don't worry about that part. I'll be over there in a few minutes."

I counted out thirty five thousand dollars and took it to her house. I gave Momma thirty thousand for my house mortgage and five thousand for herself. That was for her troubles. She was so happy that she didn't ask any questions.

She just told me, "Be careful. You should chill out with whatever you are doing. You've got the majority of your worries covered, now."

Momma, "How soon will it be before they send you the deed with a zero balance?"

"Well Son, It will be paid off in big payments. I'm going to make five payments of six thousand dollars each week. I will be sure to ask them how long it will take before we get the deed. Alright?"

I said, "Cool, I'll talk to you later. I'm out. Love you Mom, & thank you very much for everything."

I jumped in the SS. Racing home to recount my money, stash, and smoke an Indo blunt. I had twenty thousand and 54 pounds of weed, which was still good. Plus I paid off my house.

The following week, Timer was back in town in the 'Burban flexin. He still had the 600 V-12 Benz and the Double R. This nigga was doing way too much and having a fun time doing it, at the same time. I loved his style. He was still down to earth, even though he was rich. Well, I considered him to be rich.

Timer asked, "Can I leave the Suburban in your garage for a week or so?"

I answered, "Yes sir, I'll sport it, flex, and check some hoes."

Okay, "Cool. Just park it in the garage every night from the haters. I'm riding with Pimping X in the big body. His boys are following us in a K-5 Blazer. We shouldn't be gone long. I'm taking four of my boys. One of them pop (steal) cars and drive. The other three get down as well. It's just a simple lick to see what they're made of. See how well they can follow instructions. Don't be driving my truck around to the hot spots selling dope out of it either. Don't get my shit (truck) hot. You really don't need to drive your shit anymore. You need to buy you an old bucket with tinted windows or something."

I said, "Yeah, I thought about that. I need an old car or something new. I just haven't figured out what I want yet. You are right Timer about a low key car. I need one of those in my life. I'll start looking for an old bucket with a tight motor in it starting today."

I dropped Timer off at Pimping X's condo out by Lake Hefner. Then started flexing in the Burb immediately. Timer had that new Aaron Hall and was jamming on it. I put in some of that new Snoop and the East Sidas along with Roger and Zap's greatest hits. His surround sound system sounded like the artists were directly behind and in front of us.

A young hustler headed straight to the East Side. I had to go see what was happening at the barber shop. Also had to straighten up a bit and shoot the shit with the homies. We stayed until the shop closed. I decided to go to the black strip club to do some light prospecting on some potential hookers.

I flexed in Timer's 'burban all night, & started drinking on that Remy Martin. Twisted up a blunt, and it was on. I started falling in love with Timer's Suburban. I could see why he was always in it. It was roomy, spacious, and fun to drive. Timer had a built in ice chest between the two front captain chairs. That helped keep our drinks nice and chilled.

Chapter 9

I fell in the strip joint and was treated like a celebrity. The girls were all over me; but I wasn't in to all that free fucking. I've got a bitch at home for that. I was spitting pimping and trying to knock me a hooker. A dancer was cool, because if a girl will dance butt ass naked, she will sell some pussy. That's just the way I looked at it.

They would always say, "I'm not a prostitute. I'm a dancer."

All the while they would be fucking for free. I take that back. They would fuck for a blunt and a ride in Timer's 'Burban. One of them listened to my pimping though.

I told her, "We can hit the highway and get some real money. Fuck stripping butt naked while a person gives you a dollar tip. How far can one dollar take you?"

We exchanged numbers.

She said, "I'll call you tomorrow to take you out to eat or something."

I answered, "Cool, Just give me a call. I won't sweat you like the average brother. You are fine and thick though. And I do want to see how interested you are in having nice shit. Do you like that 'Suburban?

I had the bitch turned up, amped up & on super charge. She was ready to show me that she was willing to do whatever. There was also two other hooker's ear hustling on our conversation. I really wanted some snow bunnies. Tricks love to fuck with white girls; but two crows (black girls) will be just fine for new pimping. I could totally feel what Timer was talking about on the pimp game. These hoes need guidance and instructions; because they're running like Fred Flinstone, in one spot. These girls most definitely need some pimping behind them because you just can't be nice to the average woman. She will take your kindness for weakness.

Just like this bitch I used to fuck with for years. I charged the shit out of her. She took care of Daddy. When we broke up, I always told myself that I could never deny her of anything if she needed my help. The broad finally bought a house, but it had fucked up plumbing. It was a nice house, so I volunteered to get it repaired.

She wasn't use to a pimp giving her anything. She always paid for my shit. The bitch got a whole different attitude toward me. She thought I was a trick and even tried stealing a kilo of cocaine from me. I started to kill that hoe. I would have if her and her nigga would have stolen my shit. I was at least two steps ahead of her in the game. I was so hot that I wanted to kick the bitch's door down, tie her up, and unload her whole house. I would've taken every piece of furniture; big screens and everything. Then I would've beaten the bitch to death, with my ski mask on and never said a word.

My little homies and I felt that I bought that on myself. I made the mistake of being nice to a hoe.

You know the old saying, "You can't change a hoe into a house wife."

That is so true. I should have never given the bitch shit but more pimping. I should've just kept it pimping.

The next day, at twelve noon, the little broad from the strip club called me just like she promised. She was on time & was a business inspired woman & I liked that.

Little mamma asked, "Can you come pick up my friend and I? Let's go to lunch."

A hustler answered, "Cool, I'll be there in an hour after I rap up and finish my business."

I didn't want to tell the girl's that a pimp had a square job. I wanted them to think that a pimp, was pimping full time. The girls already thought Timer's Suburban was mine. Female's thought that I really had it going on too.

I picked up those fine ass hoes, & they were dressed in some revealing shit. 'Bitches had navel and tongue rings in, & was pretty from head to toe just like I liked them. I popped in that old Keith Sweat and Gerald Levert. Those bitches went off. They loved that Suburban sitting on twenty inches. Really they loved all the attention we received while rolling down the street. I fired up a blunt so we could get mellow.

Little mamma's friend was inquiring about me & shit. While all up in my face every time I looked in the rear view mirror. Smiling & blowing kisses, winking at me, and just smiling up a storm. She knew that I was a pimp because that's all I was spitting.

We fell up in Joe's Crab Shack off of Northwest Highway. With good drinks, having lobster, steak, and all that good shit. We had a good time. Little Momma's friend was just all up in my grill.

Little Momma asked, "Do you like my friend?"

I answered, "Yes. I think she's cool and she's most definitely good looking."

"Well, remember what we talked about last night S.S. Boy? You were talking about hitting the highway."

"Yes mam' & I mean it."

Little mamma said, "Well, I would really feel comfortable if she went with us."

Okay Little mamma, "Well what is she planning on doing?"

I already knew the answer to that. She was going to work with me.

"That's right. Two heads are much better than one. How can a man go wrong with two beautiful women?"

They both just blushed and laughed.

I said, "Well, let me explain something to you so we won't have any problems. I feel if I have to fight you, I don't need you. Two things I can't tolerate are for someone to lie or steal from me. Are you both choosing me?"

Both of them looked at each other and answered, "Yes."

"Well ladies, where are my choosing fees?"

They said, "We don't have too much right now; but, we are ready to go and get your money."

"Well when you do, that's when I'll consider you two as my girls. It will be on from there. You know those strip clubs aren't shit. We are going to hit those truck stops and a couple of other good spots before we hit the highway."

I was feeling like the biggest pimp in the world. I almost fell out my chair. I couldn't believe this shit was working. Timer said it would. We finished our drinks and they paid the hundred dollar tab along with the tips.

The girls asked, "Will you take us back home and smoke another blunt with us?"

I answered, "Sure."

A young player already knew what they wanted to do. They wanted to get freaky with me. Don't get me wrong; I wanted to get freaky with them too, but I had to keep it pimping. At least until I get a phat bank roll from them. No free dick was my motto.

We jumped in the 'Burban and were ready to go. I had to put in that RR, (Richie Rich) about pimping hoes and the track. I was rapping to them along with RR. We made it to their apartment and they invited me in.

Little Momma asked, "Why don't you have a seat? We'll be right back."

I started rolling a blunt. They came out the bedroom with their negligees on. Their titties were everywhere. Their high heel shoes exposed their pretty toes.

They asked me, "What do you think? Do you like us?"

I quickly answered, "Yes, you two have got it going on. Now I see why the other girls don't like you two."

They sat down on each side of me. I fired up the blunt. They just giggled and smiled the whole time we were smoking. Immediately after we smoked the blunt, they tried to seduce me. One thing about pimping, you have to control your dick. I couldn't fall weak. It was hard to resist after they stripped down to nothing and were all over me. The girls were also touching on each other. They tried several times to unzip my pants and taste this joy stick. But, I held strong and refused to fall weak.

I told them, "I'm going to save the best for last. Let's just handle business first. We need to get my choosing fees handled first before we get intimate. Let's get paid, take pussy out of the equation, & go to work tonight at one of my spots and get some money. We can have some big fun. My dick won't get hard unless I know that you two are down for me Baby. So what time will you two be ready for work tonight?"

They thought about it and said, "We'll be ready at about ten o'clock."

I suggested, "How about seven thirty when the sun goes down?"

They answered, "Okay, it's on. We will be ready by seven thirty. Just don't forget about us ladies."

"How can I forget about two beautiful creatures who want to choose up with me? Well, I have to go and handle some business."

My pager went off for a bite of sixteen hundred dollars. I left them enough weed for another blunt.

I told them, "Make sure you're looking as sexy as possible. Be prepared to do a lot of walking and fucking. This is a cool spot. It will be on tonight. You two will be the best looking ladies out there."

They both kissed me on the cheek and said, "Okay, we will be ready."

So I hurried to answer my page & returned the call.

"I'll be there in thirty minutes, I'm on my way."

I went home to get my old lady's Honda Accord to drive to my hiding spot in the country. Then grabbed two pounds and shot to the East Side to get that sixteen hundred dollar bite. I had fifty two pounds and $21,000.00. With two possible hookers on my team. My woman was still fucking around with that sugar daddy. That situation wasn't making any progress at all.

While I was on the East Side, I stopped at Big Seamore's house to chop it up with him.

Seamore, "I got these two potential hookers that I came across. I'm supposed to drop them off at the track tonight. This will be my first time ever dropping hoes off at the track to get my money."

Afterward I made it home about six o'clock that evening. A young freshman pimp had to shower, get dressed, and go pick up his girls. My pager blew up with the code 2-7-3-0. I dialed the number back using *69 so who ever this person was couldn't get my home phone number. There was a sexy sounding broad who answered the phone.

In her sexy voice, she asked, "Is this SS Boy?"

I ask, "Who wants to know?"

While laughing, "SS Boy, this is me, little momma. We fooled you didn't we?"

"Yeah, what's up, girl?"

Little mamma said, "I'm just calling to remind you to pick us up at seven thirty. Did you see the code in your pager 2-7-3-0? That means two women at seven thirty."

I said, "How could I forget Baby? I'm looking forward to seeing you two this evening."

She laughed and said, "You are such a gentleman. I see why ladies love you."

"Well, unfortunately I'm not looking for some ladies to love me," I said.

My old lady was in the next room probably ease dropping. I hoped that she was listening. Maybe she would make something happen and get off her lazy ass to make some real money.

I told Little Momma, "I haven't forgotten about our date. I need to get in the shower so I can get dressed. That way I'm not late."

She said, "Okay."

So I rushed into the bedroom to get some fresh silk Polo underwear from the dresser. I got in the shower, while singing and feeling good knowing that I had two dedicated hookers. I loved it when they called to remind me, to work them. I was still singing when my woman came into the bathroom.

She asked, "What are you so happy about?"

"Life, I quickly answered."

"Are you going somewhere S.S. Boy?"

"Yes I am."

She asked, "Where?"

Fuck it, I just told her the truth, "A manager knocked two hookers, & tonight will be our first night on the job."

"Yeah right nigga."

So I continued singing.

Then the bitch said, "Well, I'm going too."

"You can go if you plan on going to work with them. I'm not bullshitting."

The bitch said, "I just want to ride with you while you drop them off @ the track."

"Baby what you fail to realize is that if you ride, when I drop them off, I'm dropping you off as well. I don't need you with me cock blocking and running the hoes off. So just chill unless you plan on getting down tonight. Besides, you need to learn how to work the track anyway. You really need to go; as a matter of fact bitch, get dressed."

She suddenly changed her mind about riding with me that night. Deep down inside, I believe she thought that I was bullshitting.

I got out the shower and looked in the closet. And grabbed my freshly starched Polo shirt, slacks, boots, jewelry, and safari jacket. I sprayed on that Herrera cologne; which had me smelling like a million bucks.

I told Baby, "That job and that old ass man ain't hitting on shit. You need to put some serious consideration on hitting that track or a whore house. It's plenty of bad bitches out here trying to take your place."

I left out the door after leaving something on her mind again and jumped into the 'Burban. I was jamming on that old Dru Hill (love train). She just stood in the door way speechless while I backed out the driveway. I was now headed to the East Side.

When I pulled up to Little Momma's apartment, they were peeking out the curtains watching for me. I got out the Suburban and walked to the door. Before I could knock, Sunshine opened the door. She greeted me while admiring how well I was dressed and how good I smelled. Little Momma was also admiring my taste.

They were also looking hotter than ever with them little silk coochie cutter outfits and high heel shoes on, with no bras. Their nipples stood at attention; front and center. They looked great.

I knew if it was hard for me to resist, I know a trick couldn't refuse. We left the apartment and jumped in the Suburban. Punching out toward the highway down NE 23rd street, headed toward Guthrie, Oklahoma, but first I had to stop @ the store. Guthrie was about twenty five or thirty minutes outside the city.

I stopped at the Iranian store on MLK and purchased a box of extra lubricated Trojan condoms and a box of Optimo green leaf blunts. Then went back out to the 'Burban where the girls were. We were talking while I rolled a blunt and put my pimping down.

I was explaining the pimp rules to them, "You can't be out of bounds talking to other pimps. A girl can knock another girl quicker than a pimp can sometimes. If anything, you need to knock me some new girls. You feel me?"

They replied, "Yes."

The girls were listening & paying attention, while admiring and enjoying my pimping.

Chapter 10

I said, "About these rubbers. Each one is worth no less than forty dollars. Whatever you do, don't lose one. I might think that you're trying me or testing my pimping. If you lose one, you will be held accountable."

They said, "Okay baby. We won't lose any."

"At least I won't," said Little Momma.

I dropped that Twista in the CD changer and fired up another blunt. I put the big 'Burban in drive and drove off the store parking lot. The little neighborhood Crips peeped my game and observed Timer's clean ass Suburban with the Texas license plates. I pulled off slowly and did the Cadillac turn. The homies just stood there serving dope while checking me out with these two fine ass bitches. Needless to say, the truck and I were clean as hell.

The girls were on super charge. They were ready to prove that they were capable and ready to get down (get my money). Since this was my first night as a true pimp, I decided to sit at the rest area for a while just to see what's happening.

I told them, "As soon as we pull on the parking lot of the rest area, get out my truck very discreetly and low key. Just walk as sexy as possible in front of the long line of 18 wheelers."

They loved every minute of it.

I said, "The average price is forty or fifty dollars for a half and half. (Half blow job and half pussy). I'm going to be sitting over here. If I happen to leave and you need me, just page me. Just put that same code in there. I'll be back shortly. Both of you look out for each other because people get crazy sometimes. I don't want to hear anything about someone stole my money or robbed you. I ain't taking no shorts Baby. Be real with me and I'll be real with you. Also, this is your first night down."

I didn't let them know that this was also my first night pimping. I kept them in the dark completely; like a new pimp is supposed to do.

I pulled off the highway and on to the truck stop parking lot. I noticed Big Pimppin's big body Fleetwood and some other pimps' cars. I met them that night on Robinson Street with Timer. I saw them sitting at the picnic tables. They were waving and signaling for me to come over. They must've been thinking I was Timer, since I was driving his shit. I parked the 'Burban amongst the row of pimp cars and as soon as I put the truck in park, my new turnouts jumped 0out the truck almost running toward that long line of diesel trucks.

I got out and walked toward the pimps to chop it up with them. As soon as I got in clear sight, they could see that I wasn't Timer. A couple of them remembered me from the distance. As I got closer, they all remembered me as hustling SS Boy, with the bomb ass weed.

They all stood up and we shook hands. While greeting each other and they passed me the blunt.

They asked, "SS Boy, what do you have there?"

I replied, "I knocked me a couple bitches and I'm putting them down just to see how things will turn out."

One pimp said, "It will turn out pimping. It looks like you have two fine ass thoroughbreds."

I answered, "That's right."

All the pimps asked, "Where is Timer? Is he coming out tonight?"

"No, he is on the highway putting it down baby. He's rolling from state to state, pimping up a storm."

They all laughed and said, "Dig that. SS Boy, we have one more question for a new pimp on the block."

"What is that?"

"Do you have some more of that bomb ass weed? S.S. Boy we need some more of that sticky green?"

Answering with the quickness, "Yes sir you know it", but unfortunately I don't have anything with me except my personal stash. Hold on. Let me go over to the truck and get a little of that sticky green and the Optimos. I'll be right back."

I came back to the picnic table and threw my personal stash on the table with two sticks.

I said, "Whoever wants to twist a couple up, feel free."

It had to be about ten hookers out there running from truck to truck. It looked like it was trick or treat or something. Big Pimppin had some ice cold Coronas. We popped pimping and got fucked up while our girls were busy selling pussy. 18 wheelers were steady pulling in and out of the rest area.

Pimping Phoenix Rainbow told me, "This kind of action jumps off all night; but sometimes the sheriff comes through. You have to tell your hoes to hide in the 18 wheelers whenever they see the sheriff. We most definitely won't be around."

We finished the second blunt and I saw my girls running toward the 'Burban. I excused myself from the pimps for a minute so I could see what was going on. I hit the remote control alarm to unlock the doors.

They got in with the quickness like they had stolen something. I got in on the driver's side and closed the door. These bitches were on super charge. They reached in their pants and pulled out a bank roll. The bitches had already clocked about two hundred and twenty five dollars each. They handed it to me which was four hundred and fifty dollars.

The girls asked, "Is this enough for our choosing fees?"

Well, "It's a dam good start ladies."

They both said, "SS Boy, it's on out here. Those other bitches are getting upset with us because all the tricks want us."

I said, "Fuck those bitches. Tell them to re-choose and get on our team. Then they can turn some tricks and make their new man some money."

Afterward they counted their rubbers to show me that everything was right. The girls jumped out the 'Burban with big smiles on their faces." They didn't know how much their pussies were worth until I opened up their eyes. I got back out and went back over there where the big pimps were. I had a smile on my face as well.

A couple of pimps left, but Porter House sat there until about midnight checking hoe money. Porter House was getting bites, but my bites were just a little bit bigger because I had two young fine bitches. Porter House had one veteran bitch out there that night. That old veteran bitch knew how to work her jelly though. She had more experience than my girls.

My girls now had given me about twelve hundred dollars. This was before midnight.

They came to the truck saying, "Things are kind of slow now, but if you want us to keep working, we will."

I told Porter House, "I will get with you later. I might go over to the Robinson Street track to see what's cracking."

I jumped back in the 'Burban. With blunts already rolled for us. There was no way that I could smoke after them right now, especially after they had sucked all those dicks. If I did happen to smoke behind them, that would make me a second hand dick sucker (lol). I threw in that old Biggie (Life after Death) and played (The World is Filled with Pimps and Hoes).

We rode off getting back on the highway, headed south toward the city.

I asked them, "Are you ladies hungry?"

"Yes S.S. Boy."

"Well ladies. What would you like to eat?"

"Let's stop at the Waffle House off the highway, S.S. Boy. We can go in the bathroom and brush our teeth and wash our hands."

Okay, "Dig that. It's on. My girls can have whatever they want to eat."

They went on to say, "It was easy to get money out there. It was also alot of money out there too."

I had to let down the windows for a little bit. I couldn't smell nothing but pussy; but for twelve hundred dollars, it was worth smelling. We had the all you can eat buffet at the Waffle House and headed to the Southwest Side of Oklahoma City.

Before we got to the track, we needed to stop at the store again for more Trojans (condoms). I dropped the girls off on the track, & had Timer's 'Burban washed and the tires dressed with black magic tire dressing.

I couldn't wait to see Timer so I could tell him that I sent two hoes out the door with instructions. The track was slower than the truck stop. We stayed out there until about three in the morning. They only made about three hundred dollars and some change while on Robinson Street combined. I gathered them up and we called it a night.

On the way home we stopped at the bootlegger to pick up a bottle of Hennessy. I took the girls home so they could clean up and rest for tomorrow night. They loved my pimping. The girls also inquired about their reward; which was for me to sleep with them. They didn't pursue it though, nor was a new pimp hyped at the moment to lay pipe in those hoes anyway.

I wanted to keep pimping until the sun came up; but it got slow out on the track. Besides, a fifteen hundred dollar night wasn't no punk money. That was a nice little lick.

My pager was blowing up and guess who it was?

It was my square girl at home asking, "What time are you coming home?"

"I'll be there when I get there. Don't sweat a pimp."

& hung up in her face.

I told Little Momma and Sunshine, "Rest up and keep your mind on the prize."

They told me, "We want some twin super Beetle Volkswagens."

Okay ladies, "We can get them with no problem. Just stay down and be about your paper."

What was so raw about the game is I would buy those bitches cars as long as they brought me fifteen hundred dollars or more every night. Some pimps might not see the situation like I do, but I'm a halfway decent guy. I'm not a doggie dog. If a girl makes me fifteen hundred dollars a night for seven days a week, that's ten thousand five hundred dollars a week. That's a total of forty two thousand dollars a month. I wouldn't have a problem with buying two Beetles after three or four months of making forty two thousand dollars. Now that's pimping, you feel me?

I went home to this square broad that was in the bed playing possum with all the lights out like she was asleep. I emptied my pockets and laid my fifteen hundred dollars on the dresser. Just so this girl would see it whenever she got up. I proceeded to get undressed, & climbed into bed.

Then, all of a sudden, I heard a voice giving me the third degree about my where about's.

Girl, "I've been pimping."

Then I got out of my bed to turn on the lamp.

& pointed, "Look on the dresser."

Her next question was, "So you've been out all night with some dam hookers?"

I said, "That is right and that's how it's going to be from here on out. And if you can't accept that, I'll holler at you. If you don't shit you are going to have to get off the pot."

Baby asked, "What does that mean?"

Chapter 11

I said, "That means you need to do something like get my money or you'll have to move your square ass out. I have a three bedroom house and I can fill up those other two rooms with hookers. Women would love to live in this new crib with their own rooms. See, as of now, you're holding up progress and you're hoe blocking. I guess you thought I was bullshitting when I told you that there are plenty of hoes who would love to take your place. Well I wasn't bullshitting and you really need to get with the program or get the fuck out."

She sat there and cried because she didn't know how to handle the new me.

"Just like I turned those girls out on pimping, I also turned myself out. I rather not accept a square. I want bona fide hookers. You need to come go with me tomorrow night to contribute to that bank roll on the dresser. I would be wrong if I spent their hard earned money on you."

She said, "I'm not asking you for anything."

"Baby you don't have to in order for you to be taking part in me and my girl's money. See, just you living here and not selling pussy is a no-no in a hooker's eyes. How would you feel if you were selling pussy for me from sun up to sun down, and I was tricking the money off with a square bitch? You wouldn't like that would you? Besides that's against the pimp rules, Baby. I love you, but maybe you need to find you a square motherfucker or a full time sugar daddy. I'm not firing you; I'm just trying to get off skid row. I thought that's what you wanted."

She was just sitting there crying and sucking in snot from this pimping I was spitting at her. I knew that she was now seeing that S.S. Boy was no joke. Now she was putting some serious thought into what I was saying to her. While baby was sitting up in the bed crying. A pimp turned the lamp off, climbed back into bed, and went to sleep. The next morning, she was gone. I got dressed and headed to the barber shop. Thinking that baby was just gone to work, but I noticed her shit was gone. I guess she decided to get off the pot and she left.

Little Momma and Sunshine paged me at noon saying, "We just woke up and wanted to see you and get something to eat."

Okay ladies, "I'll be over in about twenty minutes. Be ready because I'm just going to blow the horn."

That's what I did and they came out with the quickness. The girls hugged and kissed me on the cheek. We went out to eat some lunch, & they were still charged up about last night and ready to go again.

I told them, "We are going to work in Oklahoma City for a month. Then we'll hit the highway to get some real money. I'm going to drop you two off at the track tonight. Every time you make two hundred and fifty dollars each; call me to come pick up the money. You don't need to be working and handling money too. Shit happens."

They both said, "That's right."

& I took them home where we blew a blunt.

My pager blew up at the same time as yesterday with a bite. This time it was a bite for three pounds at twenty four hundred dollars. I had to dismiss myself from the ladies.

I told them, "Be ready about seven thirty. I'll be here."

Okay, "SS Boy, please don't be late."

After a hustler served the weed. Now I had twenty four thousand cash; plus the fifteen hundred from last night. Still having forty nine pounds of weed left. I was doing well, but I felt bad about losing my square bitch. When it was all said and done, I did love her.

Later on that evening, a player hit the showers and proceeded to get dressed. I didn't want to be late for my date with Sunshine and Little Momma. We had a big night ahead of us. When I picked them up in the drop top SS, they loved it.

"Is this yours too S.S. Boy?"

Yes ladies, "That's right."

They replied, "We see this car all the time in the city. We always wondered who the owner was."

I said, "Now you know."

We stopped at the same store on MLK, next to the car wash. I went in to get the same thing, a large box of Trojan condoms and a box of green leaf Optimo's. I twisted a blunt in the parking lot and Cadillac turned off the store parking lot. Banging on some of that old Isley Brothers (Choosey Lover).

Us three got on the highway and headed to the truck stop in Guthrie. When we arrived, it was no competition there yet.

Ladies, "Hurry and get on the grind before a lot of competition arrives."

We weren't the first ones out there, but there were only about two or three wore out hoes there. I let my girls out and I got back on the highway headed to my boy Big Seamore's house.

Big Seamore was on super charge after I told him that I knocked two hoes and checked hoe money yesterday. As soon as I pulled up, he was standing outside in the yard with a double breasted suit on. Pimping had on his brim with the red feather, a phat blunt in his mouth, and was waving at every female that drove by (soliciting).

I said, "What up Bro?"

"I got my sign up accepting all applications for all mislead hoes and women who needed guidance."

I said, "That's right. Dig that."

Big Seamore also had the '98 Olds parked front and center. It was cleaner than a mother fucker too. It looked like he had been waxing on it all day because there wasn't a speck on it. I must admit that everyone was looking at this down ass hustler standing in the front yard on the East Side. Then Big Seamore put the icing on the cake. He went in the house and came out with an ice cold bottle of champagne and popped the cork. We then blazed up the blunt. Seamore was downer than four flat tires and was determined to knock him a hoe. I started drinking and getting high with him, & I was feeling him all the way.

"I'll be right back Big Seamore."

I jumped in the Drop Top S. and went to the floral shop and purchased two dozen roses. Then came back to the set and started soliciting with him(lol). I was passing out roses to every pretty woman who drove down the street.

Spitting pimping and letting them know, "We are accepting applications and in high pursuit for a prostitute that will get on the highway."

One thing about it, the women we encountered knew that we weren't bull shitting.

I told Big Seamore, "I need a stable with five bitches; instead of just two. As a matter of fact, my two girls are out right now as we speak getting Daddy's money."

He couldn't say nothing but laugh and give me dap. Ten minutes after I said that, my pager blew up with the code 2-250.

"Feel that. I got hoe money to go pick up. Let's ride Big Seamore."

"Dig that S.S. Boy. Let's take the '98; so I can expose some new pimping to those hoes on the track."

So we jumped in the '98 and he threw in the Isley Brothers. We got on the highway and headed toward the truck stop in Guthrie Okla. When we arrived, I didn't see my girls. I did see plenty of others.

Big Seamore stepped out with the double breasted suit on; trying to pass out roses to hookers. I know a couple of them wanted to accept the roses; but they couldn't. They knew that they would be out of bounds and their pimps would beat the fuck out of them.

Now my hoes finally noticed me and came over to where we were sitting on the picnic table. I knew that it would take a minute for them to notice me since I wasn't in my vehicle. They reached in their panties and pulled out bank rolls. The girls still had plenty of work left to handle.

I asked them, "Do you need some more condoms?"

They replied, "No, not yet, but probably in a little while."

Big Seamore was standing there smiling and loving this pimp shit. He was hungry as ever for a hoe, so he could do the same exact thing.

My girls ran back toward the 18 wheelers with big smiles on their faces, after I congratulated them on their success.

Me, & Seamore sat on the picnic tables for another ten or fifteen minutes soliciting before we jumped back in the '98 and headed back to the East Side. I saw in his eyes that he wanted to pimp so bad that he could taste it. I pulled out the two stacks that my girls just handed me. I proceeded to straighten out my money all nice and neat to count it. It was a little over five hundred dollars.

Big Seamore, "I have pimped over two thousand dollars out of them in less than twenty four hours and the day is far from over."

He said, "Feel that."

I wanted Big Seamore on super charge & turned up so he could pick up on his pimping.

Big Seamore then told me, "I want to buy ten pounds. Can you front me ten?"

I answered, "Yes, we can do something. When you want to do it?"

"Yesterday, He replied."

Okay Big Seamore, "I'll give you a good deal. I'll sell you ten pounds for seven hundred dollars each and on the ones I front you I need eight hundred and fifty dollars each."

He said, "Cool."

I then told him, "Meet me at my house in thirty minutes. If I'm not there, just hold tight and I'll be there shortly."

Immediately a hustler headed to the stash spot and grabbed twenty pounds of that sticky green. Big Seamore was sitting in the driveway waiting on me.

Okay, "You owe me eighty five hundred dollars Big Seamore."

He answered, "Cool, I got you."

We went into the garage where I popped my trunk. Seamore popped his trunk and we took the pounds from my trunk and placed them in his. I had twenty nine pounds left and thirty one thousand dollars. With about ten thousand dollars out and two thousand dollars in hoe money. My house was also fully paid off. I was doing ghetto fabulous and feeling hella good about my stack.

A hustler often thought about his girl. I kind of missed her being around the house, but I refused to call her. A pimp had to stand firm on his pimping. First I had to make her break. If she call me first, that meant that she was ready to see things my way. While sitting at my crib all alone twisting up about five blunts. I was thinking about getting my game plan air tight.

My pager blew up again. This time it was from one of my little Blood homies named Redrum. He was upset because he fucked up some money and took a major loss. Redrum only had about five thousand dollars left to his name.

I told him, "I will be at your house in about forty five minutes. Stay there until I get there."

Redrum lived on the North Side. I quickly jumped in the SS and headed to my stash spot, & grabbed nine pounds for him. Redrum and a few of his homies were standing in the front yard. I got out the car and left the nine pounds in a duffle bag in the back seat. Redrum and the 456 Blood Posse greeted me with open arms and dap. We went inside to talk and I laid out my proposition to help him.

I told him, "I brought nine pounds and I'll sell them to you at eight hundred dollars each. If you have five thousand dollars, you'll only owe me twenty two hundred dollars."

Redrum replied, "That's cool, but I really need to sell one of my old buckets."

I quickly asked, "Which one?"

"My old Plymouth Barracuda."

"Where is it, Redrum?"

"It's in the back yard."

"Okay let me see it."

We went into the back yard and there it sat. It was an old 1975 Plymouth, nor was it the prettiest car.

Redrum stated, "It's got a new motor, transmission, and rear end.

I asked him, "What do you want for it?"

He answered, "I have over two thousand dollars tied up in it, & it runs like a stripped ape."

Oh Yeah, "Start it up and let me hear it."

Redrum went inside and came back out with the car keys. It started up on the first crank.

I ask, "Let me drive it."

Redrum pulled it out the back yard, and got into in the passenger seat. This was a standard shift car too. It sounded good and ran damn well. I punched out in the Hemi peeling both tires with that positive traction rear end. I got on the highway and reached a hundred mph so quick that I couldn't believe it. I had to have it. Now we had to renegotiate on the twenty two hundred that he owed me.

I asked him, "Do you have the title?"

He quickly answered, "Yes, it's at home."

I asked, "Do you have any of that good powder (cocaine) left as well?"

Redrum answered, "A little."

I said, "Here is the deal on the twenty two hundred dollars. I'll give you two thousand for the car. That will leave a two hundred dollar balance. You can give me a quarter ounce of powder for the remainder."

Redrum said, "I doubt if I have a quarter ounce left. I only have about five or six grams."

I said, "Cool. We can work. I'll give you nine pounds for the car. You give me the five thousand dollars and the 6 grams."

Redrum said, "Bet."

We went to his house to do the deal. I needed Seamore to ride back to Redrum's house with me so I could pick up my new car. I had twenty pounds of sticky green, thirty six thousand in weed money, two thousand in hoe money, and ten thousand out on credit. I purchased a nice bucket to handle my business. My crib was paid for; which I was very proud of. I felt great.

I called Big Seamore and told him, "I'm coming to pick you up right quick. I need your help bro."

I had Seamore follow me in the Drop top SS while I drove the four speed Barracuda to my house. Before I made it, my pager blew up with the code 2-250. Those were my girls with more grip for Daddy. Everything was going my way.

We jumped in Timer's Suburban and rode to Guthrie again. I still had the five blunts I had rolled at my house a few hours ago. Before we arrived at the truck stop, I stopped at a store off the highway to pick up more Trojans. I figured that they were probably out of condoms by now. When we pulled up to the rest area, my girls came running to the 'Burban. The girls got in handing me two bank rolls. Seamore sat there in the passenger seat taking notes.

The girls were telling me, "SS Boy, it's on out here. We should have a good night. It's only ten o'clock and trucks are pulling in left and right."

I said, "Here, I'm sure you need these then."

They replied, "Yes we do. You handle your business don't you, daddy?"

"Yes, just like my ladies do."

They instantly told me, "We're running back and forth across the highway working both sides of the truck stop. It's working out just fine."

Little Momma said, "The only reason we went across the highway was because the sheriff kept riding through sweating the girls. They took a couple of them to jail."

I said, "Don't you two get caught up. We don't need that kind of shit right now."

They replied, "I know that's right."

Chapter 12

I let the girls out after I counted and straightened out my money. It was a total of five hundred and seventy five dollars on this rip. I had already pimped eleven hundred dollars out of them today. And the night had just begun.

Seamore was just sitting there laughing and giving me my props. While firing up a blunt from the ashtray. Seamore had a couple of square girls with jobs who he was charging, but that wasn't enough.

I told him, "I can feel you on that shit. That's why I fired my square bitch at home. I gave her, her termination papers. You are no longer needed around here, unless you get with the program."

We went back to my house where I had a bottle of Remy Martin and six grams of powder. We chopped it up and popped pimping until one o'clock am in the morning. We even took it a step further by cooking a couple of grams to lace a few joints, primos. We got tore up from the floor up. I was numb as hell from snorting that bomb yola. I put it on my gums and tongue. Big Seamore was fucked up and steady spitting pimping, hungry, and starving for some hoes.

My pager blew up again with the code 2-250.

I said, "It's time to ride and check some hoe money."

We punched out in Timer's 'Burban and I put in that new Snoop and the Eastsidas. Pounding down on the highway. Just like clockwork, my girls came running to the truck to hand me two more bank rolls. They were starting to get a little tired, by their conversation.

I told them, "Get down until three in the morning and I'll come and pick ya'll up for the evening."

"Okay S.S. Boy."

& the ladies got back out there & continued getting my money.

Me, & Big Seamore got back on the highway headed to the city. We ended up at the black strip club where I knocked my first two bitches. Seamore was still clean as a mother fucker in his double breasted suit and brim. I was dressed casual as usual, in Polo or Nautica.

I ordered us some drinks, & went into the restroom to count my money the hookers had just handed me. It was four hundred and eighty dollars. The total for the day so far was One thousand five hundred seventy five dollars. With my girls still out working. My goal was to pimp one thousand dollars each out of them tonight. So far it was looking pretty good.

I went back to the table and Big Seamore had two dancers giving him a lap dance. He paid them once they got finished. That shit fucked me up.

I said, "How do you expect to knock a hoe if you are tricking with them?"

"I'm putting my pimping down S.S. Boy. I slid those hoes my pager number."

I said, "Dig that."

And I saw one of the little bitches who was in the 'Burban with me a couple of nights ago. Then she came over to the table.

& asked, "Where is Little Momma and Sunshine?"

I replied, "They're out getting some real money just like your ass should be doing."

Big Seamore said, "That's right. What is your name?"

She replied, "Special K."

Seamore said, "Well I'm special too. We have something in common. Do you know what that is?"

"No, she answered."

"You're a money maker and so am I, special K. Can I pick you up after work and take you to breakfast?"

Special K answered, "Yes & that would be nice."

He had action at a real hooker if he could flip her from dancing to selling pussy full time. We sat there and solicited for a while. While watching his new friend work her jelly. I dropped him off at his car so he could pick Special K up from work.

I needed to pick up my hard working girls. I got on the highway and headed to Guthrie for the fourth or fifth time of the day. I sat in the parking lot waiting on them for thirty minutes before they could get away from the tricks. My girls got in the 'Burban and we rode out. They handed me my money; which was about four hundred dollars. The total was nineteen hundred and sixty five dollars for a single nights work.

I knew that I had to pay the piper, & really didn't feel bad about freaking with them if it came down to it. We stopped at the Waffle House to eat. Then went to their apartment so they could clean up and smoke a blunt with me. I believe those two freaky hoes took a shower together. They came back at the same time ready to smoke one.

Little Momma told me, "My rent is due in a couple of weeks. But, I have a few other bills that are due now."

Okay, "That's no problem baby. It's on."

They both smiled. I believe they were testing me to see if I would leave them hanging high and dry; but I stayed true.

I ended up staying all night with them. We freaked up a storm. There was fucking and sucking going on until the sun came up. I did put in much work. They loved this dick like it was laced with crack cocaine. Those bitches swallowed everything. I had to cum twice so they wouldn't fight over whose turn it was to taste and swallow a pimp's cum. The third time I was almost shooting blanks, it was barely any cum left. The fourth time I shot blanks in both of their faces, & they loved it and so did I. I had both of them sucking each other's pussy, & I slept like a baby. A young pimp was fucking the shit out of them like a real stud. Plus I had been doing cocaine and drinking all that evening. It took a long time for me to cum. Bitches love that shit. They hate it when a nigga cum quick.

Ladies, "I'm a real one. I lay pipe all night; all nine inches."

While talking shit I was late to work that following morning. A young pimp quickly jumped out of bed and got dressed. Those hoes were still passed out. They didn't even hear me leave. I left them twenty dollars on the dresser; so they could get something to eat once they woke up. Punching out in Timer's 'Burban headed to the barber shop to check in. After clocking in I could go home, clean up, and go back to work. But once I got to work, the owner looked at me and started laughing.

I said, "What up?"

He said, "It looks like you had a rough night."

"Yeah, it was pretty rough. You know me. If it's not rough it's not right. I'll be back in thirty minutes to an hour. I'm going home to take a shower, brush my teeth, and change clothes."

"Alright S.S. Boy, hurry back so we can chop it up. I want to hear what you did last night."

I said, "Okay."

A hustler went home, cleaned up, and came back to work in my new old school Plymouth Barracuda. I made it back to the East Side in less than five minutes. I enjoyed driving that four speed car. It ran good as hell. It just needed new tires, paint, and some tinted windows. I stepped inside the barber shop and the homies started giving me dap and props on my pimping.

I grinned & asked, "What are you talking about?"

They said, "Don't play us like that. We already heard about you baby. You got two fine hookers, don't you? Two pimps came in from Dallas last night."

They told us, "You were pimping up a storm at the truck stop in Guthrie."

I could no longer hold a straight face.

I confessed, "I am now an official pimp, but I plan on keeping my job. I have to keep the hot boys (police) off of me."

My boy was just sitting there smiling. They all thought Timer put me down or introduced me to pimping. Which happened to be true. What I did learn is that pimp's gossip. Those guys are in Dallas and heard about me here. Well since they know that a new pimp was on the block, it's about time for me to take my pimping across the state line. My first stop will be Dallas, TX.

The other barbers stated, "SS Boy, I heard you knocked two hoes from the strip joint."

I said, "Yeah, me and my homie."

They said, "You didn't tell us about that."

I already knew how they found out about me knocking hoes.

One of the homies named BZ was trying to get my attention. BZ was also a barber.

He asked me, "Do you still work your other job?"

I answered, "Yes."

I already knew what he was inquiring about that sticky green.

Well, "I need to holler at you before you get out of here."

Okay BZ, "Cool."

BZ said, "I might need a few pounds from you later on tonight if my homie isn't bull shitting."

My girls paged me.

& asked, "What about lunch?"

"Order a pizza or something ladies with that 20 dollar bill on the dresser. I'm handling business right now and will not be able to get away until later."

I thought they were going to cry how they were moping and carrying on & shit.

Ladies, "I will call you in a few hours or so. Just be ready and rested up for tonight."

Later on that evening, it was the same action as the last two nights. The truck stop was treating me swell. I clocked another fifteen hundred dollars with ease.

I talked to Big Seamore and he told me, "I ended up staying all night with Special K after we had breakfast last night."

By the end of the week, I had clocked over eight thousand dollars in hoe money. Plus ten pounds of weed and forty four thousand dollars in weed money. I still had a ten thousand dollar credit out.

Now I started to worry about Timer. I hadn't heard from him in a week & couldn't wait to tell him the good news. So I paged him.

"I will be back tomorrow S.S. Boy. I can't wait to get away from these bandits."

"Is everything alright Timer?"

"Yeah, it's cool. I'm just tired."

I went to Bryon's Liquor Warehouse for a few bottles of Don P; which costed me two hundred and fifty dollars. I was walking out the electronic doors and guess who was coming in? It was Baby whom I served her walking papers. I stopped and gave her a hug.

"How are you doing?"

She said, "Good. My sugar daddy has been coming through for me. I still work at the same place. I'm going out tojnight with a new friend. He's waiting for me so I better go now."

I said, "Is that right?"

She said, "Yes. There he is over there."

I looked in the parking lot and saw a brother in an SS Impala sitting on twenty inch rims. Baby kind of smiled and walked into the liquor store. She was trying to make me jealous. A pimp must keep his composure @ all times, and continue being a gentleman. I had seen that SS before in the metro plex. Homie was a big dope boy. He had to be a trick or my ex-bitch wouldn't be fucking with him. I turned her out on getting paid for her services. From a player's perspective, I was crushed a bit. It does hurt when a person plays with your heart; but as long as I was sitting on a bank roll, the bitch couldn't hurt me. Fuck that bitch!

I went home and put the Don P in the refrigerator, & was keeping them until Timer returned. The next day, Timer showed up before day break. He walked in wearing a brand new platinum Rolex with the diamond bezel. I pulled out a bottle of Don P and retrieved a few champagne flutes from the cabinet. I poured some drinks while listening to Timer about what happened while with Pimping X and his boys.

He said, "Those young gangsters have plenty of heart, but they're dumb as a box of rocks. Pimping X and I sent them in the store with instructions. It was worth about sixty thousand dollars. Those bandits couldn't follow them. They bashed the wrong case & came out with a big bag of bull shit. I just looked at Pimping X and shook my head like hell no. I thought Pimping X was going to shoot those youngsters. We talked so monkey to them that they wanted to go back into the same store, and do the job over again. We had to search for another lick until we found one with their name on it. This time they followed instructions and bashed the right cases. That's where I got my new platinum Rolex. Pimping X got a gold Presidential Rolex. I think they will be ready after a couple more licks to get some big money. When a person who never had any big money before get a little piece, you have to analyze that person just to see if they can handle money. That's how the average person gets busted by either flexing or running off at the mouth. We gave them five thousand dollars apiece just to see how they would act. Five thousand dollars was a lot of money to them. Now we have to see if they can manage their money, make it grow, or if they will brag about where it came from. My boys would run circles around them without them even knowing it. Pimping X wants me to go out with them once more, just to make sure they have it down. I told him we can ride out again in a couple of weeks. Gator, the old man, is down. We showed them how real niggas get down and have fun doing it. Then he flew back to Chi-town with a bank roll."

I told Timer, "I got two hookers working on the track as we speak."

Timer said, "I already know about you pimping SS Boy."

I said, "How do you know?"

He said, "I heard about you on Robinson, mainly at the truck stop, working those two pretty black hoes out my 'Burban. That's why we are drinking Don P. right?"

I answered, "Yes. & I pimped eight thousand dollars straight out the womb of those bitches."

Timer looked around and said, "You better lower your voice before your bitch hears you."

I said, "Timer, you didn't know? I fired that bitch and sent her packing with her square ass, & haven't looked back since. I'm sitting on a bank roll and ready to re-up. I only have ten pounds left to my name."

Timer said, "Damn, you been getting down."

"Let me go home and see what's happening at the mansion. I let my little cousins stay with me all summer while on summer vacation from Grambling University. I know they've been parlaying, having pool parties, and all that. Everything will be cool as long as they haven't fucked with my baby grand piano or my white Polar Bear rug in the living room. I'll call you in a couple of days after I rest up S.S Boy. It takes a lot out of you to coach some crash dummies; not knowing what they will do next."

I rolled Timer a phat joint with the Zig Zag papers. & rolled an Optimo green leaf blunt for myself. We sat there drinking Don P. and chopping it up until the bottles where empty. Timer jumped in his Suburban and punched out to the mansion in Dallas, TX.

Chapter 13

Before leaving, Timer asked, "Whose old school is that?"

"It's mine and I'll put up whatever if somebody wants to race."

Timer laughed and said, "Dig that. I might have to test drive it next time I come back to OKC."

Okay, "You can get it anytime Big Bro."

By the way, "Thanks for babysitting the 'Burban. You took good care of her. Thank you for the full tank. You're alright SS Boy."

"You are too Timer. I appreciate you giving me game and putting me down on some real money."

Timer said, "SS Boy, I appreciate you for being real. You were real before I put you down. Whatever you do, stay down. If you ever get busted and can't pay your way out of it, always remember to keep your mouth shut and do your little bid (time). Real people will be out here waiting on you to touch down. I've been to the penitentiary three times and I have stayed down. That's why real people come to me. The SAs (Mexicans) with the drugs, my crew, my hookers, and the list goes on. You know why they love fucking with me? They all know that if shit hits the fan, I'll sit there with my mouth shut. Just take care of me while I'm doing this bid. Even if a weak snitch implicates you on some wicked shit. You'll just have to deal with him or her, after you get released. You might run into him in the penitentiary. If you're a true hustler, you can reach him regardless of which institution he is in. He can be touched by me or any true hustler."

I said, "Dig that."

Timer punched out in the big 'Burb. Leaving some real shit on my mind once again.

I continued doing my thing with the girls and the sticky green. Always keeping my guards up.

My bitches and I were spending more time together after they got down for a few more nights. I made them a player proposition, & took them to my crib. It was a brand new, three bedroom, two bath, with a fireplace, patio, cathedral ceilings and a double car garage. The girls really thought I was balling after seeing this shit, & they loved it. That made it even easier for my proposal.

"I want my girls to live just like me. I feel that you two are worth much more than a rundown apartment on the East Side. Don't get me wrong, your place is nice. You two are some damn good house keeper's too."

I showed them around the house, & showed them the two extra bedrooms. The whole house was completely furnished with leather, wood, big screens, an eight piece Pioneer house stereo, and a load of CDs both old and new.

Then I asked them, "So do you two want to move in with me? My house is yours. We must pay for this every month."

That was my little game because my house was already paid for. I just didn't want to pay their rent and bills every month out of my hoe money, you dig? Everything went as planned. They both agreed to move in with me.

"Let's be one big, happy family."

They both laughed & giggled while dancing to the old school grooves. Then they began negotiating over the bedrooms they had to choose from. I twisted up a big phat blunt and poured us all up a shot of Remy Martin. It was on now. That move alone would save me money and time.

Girls, "I want you to start packing your clothes and electronics. Leave the rest of that shit or give it away. From here on out, we are buying brand new Y2K shit. We deserve the best ladies."

I turned on that old Black Street (I Can't, Get You out of My Mind) and we started jamming while getting high. Pimping even gave them a day off, which is against the pimp rules. Rules are made to be broken though. I didn't have to, but I felt like I did. We went to the grocery store to get some large boxes and tape. I dropped them off at the apartment.

& told them, "Pack all your clothes and anything that has sentimental value to it."

They did just that with big smiles on their faces.

I headed over to Big Seamore's house to chop it up and see how his new career was going. When I pulled up, I saw him and that same bitch from the strip club. They were standing in the front yard laughing and giggling like they were in love or something.

I said, "What's up? Am I invited?"

Big Seamore looked at me and said, "SS Boy, this is the new love of my life."

He was hugging her with his right arm and winking at me with his left eye. She looked happy as a trick in a whore house. I guess he had to do what he had to do in order to get his pimping across.

My boy Redrum paged me.

"I need to holler at you S.S. in person."

Okay, "Meet me at Church's Chicken on 23rd St. in ten minutes."

I was already on the East Side. Redrum lives on the North Side. This young brother beat me to the spot. He was driving his clean ass dark green Millennium. Redrum was hype as hell.

He told me, "Three of my homies are ready to buy a bird each (three keys of cocaine). Do you still have the hook up?"

I answered, "Yes, but my people won't come unless it's five or better. You only have three sold. You need two more in order for them to come."

Redrum asked, "How much?"

I answered, "Eighteen thousand, but I know they go for twenty thousand all day long around here. You can make an extra two thousand off each one. That will be ten thousand for ten minutes of work."

"You know what S.S. Boy? In that case, I'll only have to come with eight thousand for one since I'll be making ten thousand."

"That's right, Redrum."

Okay, "Let me call a few more people right quick. Hold on SS Boy."

Redrum dialed some numbers on his mobile phone and talked to a few people.

As Redrum got off the phone he said, "Call your people and tell them it's on. I'll put it together. Let's do it."

I asked, "Are you sure? Because once I call my people it will be on in less than twenty four hours."

Okay "Call them S.S. We are ready."

All I thought about was making another thirty thousand if possible.

Alright, "I will call you either in a little while or later on tonight Redrum. To let you know whether it's a yes or no."

We dapped and pulled off going our separate ways.

I immediately called Timer.

"It's on again Big Bro. like at Jimmy Johnson's Bar and Grill. I'm ready to ride again. What's up?"

Timer said, "Is that right? I'm waiting on my friends now. I'll call you back tomorrow. Whatever you do, don't let that bite get away."

Okay, "Hurry up then."

Timer said, "I will little bro. Just be patient."

I called Redrum on his mobile.

Stating, "I will let you know what's up tomorrow. I'm pretty sure that we can make something happen."

"Cool S.S. Boy, that's good news."

I continued to kick it with my boy Big Seamore and his new love, Special K. Then I started paging my people to collect my loose ends. A hustler really needed that ten thousand I had out. A hustler had to leave after Seamore handed me five thousand dollars. Now he only owed me thirty five hundred dollars.

Now I went by the little homies weed houses to pick up another fifteen hundred, & took my stash home to re-count it again. A player had sixty thousand in weed money, ten thousand in hoe money, and thirty five hundred out. Along with two dedicated hookers. That totaled seventy three thousand, five hundred dollars. I was completely out of weed now; except for a quarter pound, which was my personal stash.

Little Momma and Sunshine paged me.

"We're ready S.S."

"Okay ladies."

So I borrowed a pickup truck and went to their old apartment. We loaded the back of the truck with boxes, & made about three trips to my house with the boxes, clothes, & dishes. I took my girls to their new home after we stopped and picked up some Kaluha, Absolut Vodka, & vanilla ice cream.

Ladies, "We are going to have a little party tonight. Unless you have more females to invite, it will be just us."

S.S. Boy "We might have a friend or two who may come and party with us."

Okay, "Well, invite them. It's cool. I'm going to turn everyone on to a drink that a female friend turned me on to. The drink is called a White Russian. It tastes like a chocolate shake and will get you ripped."

The girls chose their rooms. Both of them tried to move into a pimp's room with the eight thousand dollar bedroom suit.

Guess who they called? It was Special K, another dancer, and her boyfriend.

Special K fine ass asked, "Can I bring a male companion?"

She was unaware that she was coming to my house.

My girls asked her, "Who is this friend of yours? You can't just bring anybody to Daddy's house."

Special K., "It's a nice new friend of mine named Seamore."

Do you mean, "Big Seamore?"

She said, "Yes."

My girls said, "We know him. He is cool."

We all took a shower and got dressed. Our company arrived shortly afterward.

Special K couldn't believe how a pimp and his girls were living. She kept her eyes on me while Big Seamore was sleep to the game.

I pulled out an ounce of bud and he pulled out his stash. We started partying after I made everyone a White Russian. They all loved the way a pimp shook those drinks up. They played cards and watched freak videos while we popped pimping.

The other guy who came was cool and down. This brotha was working the shit out of his girl at the strip club. His game was tight as far as I could see. Number one, his girl never got out of bounds like Big Seamore's girl. Every time I looked up, her eyes were on me. I had to pull Seamore to the side.

I asked him, "What's up with Special K? She's all up in a pimp's mouth like a dentist."

"SS Boy, she's like that. I got the bitch in pocket."

I said, "Okay, now you know how pimps do it. If your bitch is out of bounds again, I need to check her to see if she wants to re-choose on some new Y2K pimping. If one of my bitches is out of bounds, you suppose to do the same thing."

Seamore said, "That's right. The out of bounds hoe will get checked and bow down to pimping."

I said, "Feel that."

Afterward we went back into the living room. I was starting to feel pretty good now. I had three White Russians and so did Big Seamore.

The other player's name was Crooks from the North Side. He was driving a Black 300 Benz with tan leather, sitting on chrome.

Seamore pulled Special K to the side. Hopefully he put her in check. I would hate to peel my boy for his future hooker.

Little Momma asked, "Can I have a moment with you in the bedroom right quick?"

I said, "Sure."

We walked into the bedroom and closed the door. That's when Little Momma began smiling.

She informed me, "Big Seamore's girl is really digging you and wanting to re-choose. And the bitch wants to get on a winning team."

I replied, "Is that right?"

Little Momma said, "Yeah."

Okay Little mamma, "It seems like you are doing a good job of building our team. Sometimes a bitch can knock another bitch quicker than a pimp can. Handle your business. I just don't want to bite her with this pimping in front of my boy. Is she trying to straight choose up and stay here with us?"

Little Momma kissed me on the cheek and said, "I'm falling in love with you more and more with every second. I love your style."

I grinned & asked, "Do you love my style or my pimping?"

The bitch couldn't take it anymore, & busted out laughing.

She asked, "Daddy, can I please suck your dick right quick?"

"Little Momma, you knock that bitch for me and I'm going to let you do more than suck a pimp's dick. I'm going to make you my bottom bitch. That means I'll let all the other hoes go before I let you go. You will have special privileges like sleeping with me every night, riding in the front passenger seat, and you get first dibs on everything. You have to work the hardest to make those other bitches want to keep up. I want you to coach Special K and make her get as much money as you are on the track."

We went back in the living room and Little Mamma sat at the card table with the girls. The fellows sat on the leather couch and kept chopping it up.

I asked Big Seamore, "Did you check that bitch?"

"Yes, I checked the broad."

I said, "Cool. But, if she gets out of bounds again, I'll have to pull her hoe card and see what's cracking."

We all laughed.

Seamore stated, "Fuck it if she re-choose."

We continued to pop pimping until four in the morning. Crooks and his girl left and Special K left with Seamore.

Little Momma said, "I guarantee you that she will be with us soon."

We climbed into my California king size bed; which sat about three feet off the floor. There were three or four small little steps you had to climb just to get in. Me, & baby got our freak on for a little while before passing out.

Chapter 14

The next morning, we all got dressed and headed to the grocery store. I bought about five hundred dollars' worth of food. We went home and the girls started putting up the groceries. I had to roll my morning blunt. All of a sudden, the door bell rang.

I told Little Momma, "Go and answer the door."

Guess who it was? It was my ex girl.

Little Momma, "Let her in."

She came in and I walked into the living room to see what was up.

She said, "I was just stopping by to pick up something I left."

I knew Baby was hurt from seeing that she had been replaced with the quickness. A player knew she was fucked up because number one, she didn't leave anything.

Sunshine came out the kitchen looking sexy as ever, & asked. "Daddy, do you mind if we roll us a blunt?"

I answered, "Certainly not. As a matter of fact, ya'll can have this one. I'll roll another one."

Baby was so furious that she had tears in her eyes while she watched me roll my blunt.

Baby said, "Oh, so you are Mr. Pimp now?"

A young pimp replied, "That's right. We clock eight to ten thousand a week. Now can you buy that? We are scheduling a trip to Hawaii next month. So what are you and your new friend doing?"

The bitch frowned and said, "We are just friends."

I said, "Baby, let's cut the games."

"Well, I just came to see how you were doing."

"Well I'm pimping and getting money. Pretty soon you will see three new vehicles in the driveway. Two Super Beetle Volkswagens and whatever else I decide to get. What's so cold is that, it could be a new Jaguar out there as well; but a certain individual chose not to earn it right now."

She said, "I'm leaving, bye."

"Well, next time you decide to drop by, would you try calling first?"

Baby left out walking real fast toward her car. I closed the door and fired up my blunt.

Little Momma and Sunshine came into the living room asking, "Daddy, who was that?"

"Just a square bitch who wants to take up a pimp's time for free."

They both said, "No, she can't do that. We can't do it. We have to work hard. If she comes back, we will tell her for you, Daddy."

Okay, "Cool, maybe she will understand it better coming from two fine ass women."

Later on that day, I received a page with the area code 214. I figured it was Timer and it was.

He told me, "The weather is fine in Dallas. It's sunny."

That meant it's on.

"How is it there in Oklahoma, S.S.?"

I answered, "Sunny."

That meant the money was here.

Timer replied, "Cool, I'll call you later on tonight or early in the morning."

"Okay Big Bro."

We hung up and I immediately called Redrum to confirm that it was on.

Redrum," Are you ready?"

"Yes, put me down for six S.S."

I said, "Radio station 108, meaning $108,000.00."

Redrum replied, "You know it."

Okay well, "I will call you as soon as I'm ready. So stay close by the telephone."

One hour later, Timer called from Will Rogers Airport in Oklahoma City.

S.S. Boy, "Would you come and pick me up?"

I rushed out to the airport to pick up Timer.

Timer said, "Let's grab a bite to eat."

Okay but first, "Let me drop my hookers off at the track."

That's, "Cool with me young pimping."

So I rushed back to my crib to pick up my girls. My girls climbed into the back seat and we punched out to the truck stop in Guthrie where I dropped them off.

Then me & Timer went to Red Lobster and ate an Ultimate Feast, stuffed mushrooms, and had two Blue Hawaiian drinks.

Timer said, "I am going to do you real proper this time so you won't have to re-up so often."

I said, "What's up?"

He said, "Here is the deal. I'll sell you a hundred pounds for forty thousand and front you another hundred for fifty thousand."

I said, "Cool, I have the forty thousand to pay for the hundred. With twenty thousand down payment for the other hundred. That will leave a balance of thirty thousand. I might not owe you that much depending on how this other deal goes."

Timer said, "We should find that out in less than an hour from now."

I said, "An hour?"

I quickly called Redrum and said, "Gather your people and get ready. I will be ready to shoot some ball in an hour or so."

Okay S.S. Boy, "I'll get on it right away."

Timer took me to one of his female's houses. Then pulled out a phat sack of Indo and we blazed up. His pager blew up and it was his boy in the old pickup truck. This time he was in a Toyota Camry. I jumped in the Camry with homie from Dallas. We followed Timer back to his female friend's house while he drove the Barracuda.

Timer stated, "Call your people and tell him to come on. He can bring only one of his homies."

I said, "Okay Cool."

Immediately, a hustler got on the horn and spoke with Redrum.

Redrum, "Let's meet at the spot. Only bring one of your homies. The one with the rims (money)."

"Cool, we'll be there in twenty to thirty minutes S.S."

I said, "Cool & we hung up."

Timer told me, "Keep your mobile phone on. I'm going to step out for a minute until ya'll are finished handling business."

The homie from Texas and I both agreed that Timer should leave. If it went bad; it's no need in all of us falling.

Timer gave us dap and said, "They will be here in about ten minutes so I better go. SS Boy, keep your phone on and give me the keys to the Barracuda. I'll call you in forty five minutes."

I threw Timer the keys and he left. Shortly afterward, Redrum knocked on the door. He was with his cousin, Chub Roc; who was also a baller in the city. They had a bag of groceries with two loafs of bread and some celery sticks very visible hanging out of the bag. I knew it was on now. I invited them in and they had a seat. No one said a word.

I pulled out six bricks and Chub Roc checked each one of them before handing me the sack of groceries.

Then he grabbed a pencil and paper.

Chub Roc wrote, "That's 100 G's and I only wanted five keys."

We counted that hundred thousand so quick that it was amazing. Redrum and I stepped into the kitchen where he handed me the other eight thousand dollars. He didn't want his cousin or his homies to know that he made a quick ten thousand dollars off them.

Now I had the $108,000.00.

I winked my eye at Redrum before telling him, "I will front you the other bird." We went back to the living room and I handed Redrum the sixth bird.

Redrum, "Get at me soon."

Okay, "Bet, we're out."

Redrum and Chub Roc got into a bucket and drove off very carefully and cautious. I just made me a profit of twelve thousand dollars. Homie and I were glad that everything went well again.

Timer called and told us, "Meet me at Jimmy Johnson's Bar and Grill so we can have a drink."

We both said, "Cool."

Me & Big Homie got into the Camry with $108,000.00 and went straight to Jimmy Johnson's Bar & Grill on Lincoln Blvd. Timer was sitting at the wet bar watching Sports Center, while drinking a double shot of Remy Martin on the rocks. As soon as he noticed us, he ordered two more doubles.

I asked him, "How long have you been here?"

He said, "I just got here. This is my first drink. I was right there with you two; watching everything, close by; closer than you think. How were those groceries?"

I said, "Good."

We finished our drinks and left the restaurant. Headed out to my house to count the ninety six thousand I owed Timer for the six kilos. He saw that I made twelve thousand dollars profit. Homie didn't follow us to my house. He branched off and we counted the money and negotiated on the weed.

Timer asked, "Are you ready?"

"Hell Yeah."

& Timer, "I have a proposition for you. How about if I offer you seventy five thousand for the two hundred pounds right now?"

Timer said, "I probably would take it right now, but right now only."

Yeah, "Okay let's do it then. When can I get my shit?"

Timer said, "Homie is on his way with it as we speak. Homie went back to the hotel room to get it."

I said, "Cool. Here is ten thousand."

I walked in the bedroom and grabbed sixty five thousand from my seventy three thousand to give to Timer. Shortly after we counted everything, homie from Dallas showed up. I opened the garage door so he could pull in. I pulled the SS Monte Carlo out and parked the Barracuda next to homie's Camry. We took the duffle bags from his car and put them in mine. Then we went back inside.

I had ten thousand dollars, two hundred pounds of sticky green paid for, and two dedicated hookers selling pussy for me.

Timer said, "SS Boy, you are balling whether you know it or not. You are most definitely a six figure nigga. Just stack your chips and stay low key. Stay away from off brand niggas."

I said Okay, "But, I've got to buy something new to ride in."

Timer said, "Yeah, but you don't need a new 600 V-12 or nothing like that. OKC police will definitely be sweating you, following you, and tapping your phones & shit. You don't need that. See, the reason I flex is because I live in the land of the rich, Dallas TX. There are a lot of brothers and Mexicans that make me look like a little boy. Oklahoma isn't like that yet. You can have all the money in the world in OKC; but can't flex hard unless you can legitimately explain your income. Your game has to be air tight in OKC."

I said, "I was thinking about getting a utility truck. Your 'Burban got me sprung, but I really like that Cadillac Escalade or that Eldorado drop top with the four tail pipes."

Timer said, "Something like that is cool. Just no Y2K 600 V-12 Benz. Keep it under fifty thousand."

I said, "Okay."

Timer got on his mobile phone and called Pimping X.

He told him, "Round up your crew and let's ride."

When he got off the phone, Big Bro. told me, "It's on."

Timer then called his crew and told them, "Get ready to hit the highway."

This nigga is down like a mother fucker. I just wondered how much was enough?

Timer said, "Since I'm out, I might as well grind for a minute. I'm going to get an all diamond necklace, with whole karats, and twenty five solitaire karats all the way around it."

I said, "Feel that."

Timer made $171,000.00 in a few hours. Now he was getting ready to go hit a lick.

Chapter 15

"SS Boy, you shouldn't have to look back for a long time with the product you have."

Timer and homie from Dallas left the crib with the $171,000.00.

I headed to my spot in the country to put my weed up and start sacking up pounds. A hustler was trying to imagine how much money I would have after the dust settle. I had twenty pounds weighed and sacked up.

My pager blew up with Little Momma on the line. She was sounding full of life and on super charge.

"S.S. Boy come out as soon as you get a chance."

"Okay give me about an hour."

"Also can you stop by the store for us, S.S.?"

A young pimp knew little mamma had to be fat if her, and Sunshine had gone through all of those rubbers (condoms).

I loaded the twenty pounds in the trunk of the Barracuda and punched out toward the East Side. Immediately dropping off ten pounds each to my weed houses. I also stopped by Big Seamore's house and he paid me thirty five hundred dollars.

A hustler punched out on the highway and headed back toward Guthrie truck stop to check my trap. It was a good trap to check too, & well worth it. There were so many trucks out there. I dropped them off more rubbers and a half a blunt, and punched out back toward the city. I left them hoes to continue getting a pimp's money.

With forty seven hundred in my pocket, & on my way home to drop it off.

I then got on my mobile phone and called a few of the homies.

"It's on, so get at me."

One thing for sure; I was tired of driving back and forth to the track every night. Two or three times a night. I had to figure out something new. Maybe I could get my boy Goody to drive them or buy them a nice bucket. In the meantime, I had to keep it pimping.

I was sitting on $14,700.00 with two fine bitches taking care of a pimp real proper. A hustler had a feeling that I couldn't explain. Only the real can feel me who have been there and done that!

A week had passed and my girls had me papered up again with another eight thousand dollar week. My weed houses were balling out of control. The homies paid me my seventeen thousand and got twenty more pounds. In one week, I was sitting on twenty nine thousand and seven hundred dollars. I had another seventeen thousand out to the homies at the weed houses and one hundred and sixty pounds left.

One night, while my girls were at work, Baby came over again. She wanted to come back home, now realizing how good she had it.

I said, "What up Baby?"

While smoking an Indo blunt mixed with sticky green and sitting on my throne in my little castle. I knew this bitch would come back damn near crawling on her knees.

She said, "SS Boy, I love you dearly. Basically, you want me to prove to you that I love you by selling my body."

I answered "Baby, can you sell dope or rob?"

S.S. Boy, "You know I can't do that."

"Well, what else can we do together?"

She said, "I wouldn't mind showing that I love you in that manner, but I just can't do that here in Oklahoma City. My family lives here."

"Well, there are fifty other states besides Oklahoma, Baby."

Baby then asked, "Where are those girls?"

"At work, where you should be instead of playing these love games."

"Love games?"

I answered, "Yes."

"I'm not playing any love games with you. I'm serious about how much I love and miss you, SS Boy."

"Well baby, let's get down in Nashville at this whore house named Meeko's."

I then grabbed, kissed, and rubbed her all over. A young pimp knew she was a freak, & wanted this dick; but never again for free. I unbuttoned her blouse and unsnapped that bra knowing her titties were her weakness. A player stopped everything while she was breathing heavily with her pussy soaking wet.

I said, "Baby, I do love being with you and making love to you, but you scare me because I don't know if you really love me. I don't know if you love someone else like that brother I saw you with at the liquor store."

"S.S., how could I love him? I don't even know him like that."

"I thought I knew you too but you packed your shit and moved out before I woke up, remember?"

"You forced me to."

"No baby, you chose to leave. I wanted you to stay and get that Jag. Now what's up with my idea on Nashville?"

Steady putting her directly on the spot again. Either get with it or get the fuck out of my house.

S.S., "Tell me about Meeko's in Nashville."

I said, "It's cool. You stay for a month at a time and get money with about ten other girls. Once the trick comes in, all the girls come out looking sexy. Then the trick picks which girl he wants to spend time with and that's it. In a month's time, we should have money. I will come see you every two weeks if you want me to."

Baby asked, "Would you do that for me?"

"Sure I will."

I couldn't let her know the only reason why I'm coming to visit is to pick up my money from Meeko's (the owner).

Baby asked, "No one will know? You won't tell anyone, will you?"

I quickly answered no, "Baby, it's nobody's business but ours."

"Daddy, I'm going to do this just for you. Just to let you know I love you and will do anything for you."

I said, "Feel that."

She asked, "What about my job?"

"Fuck that job". I'll take care of you Baby. I'm going to call Meeko's to find out if she has room for a beautiful, fine black woman as yourself. Start getting your shit together around here. Tie up all your lose ends and be prepared to be gone for a month."

My pager blew up with a bite.

I told Baby, "I will call you tomorrow while you at work. I have to go now."

She said, "I'm not doing anything. I will just sit here until you get back."

I answered, "Well, I want us to get close like that again, once we get money."

She asked, "Can I ride with you then?"

"No, I'm going to the track. I will get with you tomorrow, Baby."

I almost had to throw the girl out. I hated being like that; but women will make a brother act like that."

She left and I waited until her tail lights disappeared. I got in my car and headed to the country to get five more pounds. I had a bite on the South Side of Oklahoma City. I sold them at eight hundred dollars each, which totaled four thousand. That left me a hundred and fifty five pounds and thirty three thousand seven hundred dollars.

I paged Timer on his 1-800 number and waited for him to return my page. He called thirty minutes after I paged him.

He told me, "I'm sorry for taking so long to return your page. I was on the highway in a bad area. It was no frequency for my mobile phone."

I said, "Timer, what's up with Meeko's? Baby is ready to leave out the door with instructions."

Timer asked, "Is she ready?"

"Yeah, she is tweaking to get back with me and willing and ready to prove it."

Timer said, "I'll try to contact Meeko, but just chill until I get back in about three or four days."

Okay Big Bro., "Cool."

Timer said, "Keep that pimping on her mind. Don't let her cool off."

I said, "Bet."

& we hung up.

I kept mashing on the standard shift Cuda. With brand new low profile tires, got a master tune up, oil change, and a lube job. My old school was running like a champ and I was clocking major grip. I couldn't believe how smooth everything was going. A hustler had a few twos and fews still on the street. One thing about the dope game, you never collect every penny that's owed to you. Everyone takes a loss in the dope game sooner or later. The main idea is to collect more than you lose.

My girls were really getting down. They were not coming home with under seven hundred each and every night. I was tired of dropping them off and picking them up. I decided to buy them a 1992 Chevy Corsica to put them on automatic. I only paid twelve hundred for it from one of the homies. Now I could do my thing and not worry about waking up at five in the morning to pick them up.

I told them, "I will still come and check my grip while I'm out checking traps."

The next day, Timer showed up sitting even phatter, and telling me about his trip.

He said, "I think the diamond game is changing Pimping X. He has completely changed and is just money crazy now. He has the same tree in his backyard as I do. X would rather pluck his tree bone dry; instead of getting what is needed for the time being. X said that he and his crew are going on a robbing spree next month. He's not quitting until he get a meal ticket, (a million dollars). He invited me and my crew to ride. I told him thanks but, no thanks we will pass. We'll keep kicking it how we been doing it, what's not broken don't need fixing. Pimping X had a look in his eyes I had never seen before. His head had swollen up so big that it was unbelievable. He thinks this shit so easy. I had to tell him the same thing that will make you laugh will make you cry. I also could see that he had more up his sleeve. He doesn't care if anyone gets hurt or killed. He just wants dollars. SS Boy, this game isn't for everybody. Not everyone can handle big money like this at one time so quick and so fast. I refuse to lead my troops into an ambush. He doesn't care about his crew. I look out for my young gangsters like I look out for myself. If it's not a ninety nine percent chance we can get away with it, I'll pass it up until I find the perfect beat with my name on it. Pimping X will take a fifty fifty chance. Fuck that SS Boy."

I said, "I can feel you, Timer. & I don't blame you."

Timer then said, "I got in touch with Meeko and she might have an opening for your girl, but she needs to see & interview her first."

I said, "Cool. When?"

"As soon as possible."

"We are catching a flight to Nashville in a couple of days."

Timer said, "Let me call Meeko again to let her know that you will be there in two days with your girl."

Timer got on his mobile phone to call Meeko. He also got the green light for me to take my girl down there for an interview.

Timer asked, "How is everything else going?"

Timer, "I've got my hookers on automatic. I bought them a bucket to get around in. My weed houses are booming."

He said, "So you're still straight? You don't need anything do you?"

"No sir."

Timer gave me dap, & had one of his young gangsters take him back to Dallas.

Timer told me, "Call me once you are on your way to Nashville."

I said, "Cool, I'll have Baby Girl make us reservations and rent a car through Southwest Airlines."

Chapter 16

Two days later, we were in Nashville. Timer directed us to Meeko's. We finally found the private club. Baby was a little nervous. We had come too far to turn around now. We took a seat and waited on her. Meeko finally came out of her office. She was the most beautiful Asian woman that I had ever seen. All I could think about was knocking this bitch. Meeko introduced herself with much class. She invited us into her office.

Meeko explained, "This is a discreet business, & I run a tight ship. I have separate deposit boxes that only you two have access to. Baby is fine, but she could stand a little improvement."

Baby tried to get offended, but I wouldn't let her go there.

Meeko said, "It looks like Baby has class. That's what I look for, besides beauty."

I can't let my guard down to Meeko. She was a female pimp and capable of peeling me for my new turnout.

I asked Meeko, "How does the money work?"

She replied, "Every date is two hundred plus tips. I charge forty percent. The tips belong to the girls. The company receive eighty dollars from each date. One hundred and twenty dollars goes to your deposit box or she can hold it. I prefer that she put it in a safe place. I'm not responsible if something happens to it."

I said, "I don't blame you. So when can she start?"

"Well SS Boy, you might be in luck."

"Baby, are you ready to start immediately?"

Baby slowly replied, "Yes."

She was stunned at how fast things were going.

Meeko then asked, "Where are you from?"

Baby slowly answered, "Oklahoma City."

Meeko said, "Oh yes, I know a few businessmen from OKC. A couple of girls from there often come and work for me. How is Timer?"

"He's cool. Timer told me to tell you hello and he hasn't forgotten the bottle of Moet that was promised to you."

Meeko laughed and said, "Timer is such a fine gentleman; strictly business."

I whispered to Baby, "Try it out for a few days. I'll hang around here for a couple of days."

Baby asked, "SS Boy, do you truly love me?"

Yes, "I love you more than anything. I want the best for us and an eight to five won't get the things we like."

Baby gave me a big hug and said, "Okay."

I told Meeko, "It's on, but first we need to go to Victoria's Secret for some sexy lingerie. My baby need to look good."

Meeko asked, "Do you know where the mall is?"

I answered, "No."

She gave us directions on how to get to Rivergate Mall. Baby picked out seven sexy outfits and shoes. I purchased a nationwide pager, just in case Baby had to call me for some strange reason.

I asked Baby, "Are you hungry?"

She quickly answered, "Yes."

"Well sexy, what do you have a taste for?"

"I want you and a slice of pizza S.S. Boy."

"You and I have a life time of love making ahead of us."

"SS Boy, I want to make love to you now, today."

By the way she said that, I knew that she would probably renege if I didn't give her some dick.

I quickly said, "Baby, Meeko is waiting on us."

"Meeko can wait a couple of hours so we can have intimate time together."

I called Meeko, "We will be a few hours."

Meeko said, "I understand. I've been through this plenty of times. Just be here tonight by seven o'clock."

"Cool. She'll be there."

We left the mall and headed downtown, close to the Grand Ole Opry. I pulled into Motel 6 and got a room so she would quit tripping and get my money. A pimp went into the room, with strickly fucking on my mind. A player had to satisfy this bitch, and make her cum like a mother fucker.

I got her asshole naked before I started licking, rubbing, and playing with her clit. I sucked the shit out her pussy until she left a big cum puddle in the bed. Baby practically begged me to stop sucking her pussy. She was backing up like a crawfish trying to get away from me. My strong arms wrapped around her thighs so she couldn't get away. I was wearing her thighs around my head like ear muffs (lol). She started crying, & having multiple orgasms. I stopped licking and sucking on that little clit. I got out the bed, and stared at the cum drunk broad. She was shaking and shivering all over.

I didn't stop there. I unzipped my pants and shoved all nine inches of this big black Indian dick straight up in her. I was steady spitting in her ear that I loved her. She started cumming and crying all over again. I didn't last five minutes before my motor locked up (lol). I pulled my dick out her pussy and stuck it in her mouth just like she likes it. I came all down her throat then shot in her face. She loves that shit and will get angry if I don't cum in her mouth. We went at it until I was shooting blanks.

I said, "Baby, we better chill. I don't want you to get too tired to work."

I completed my task of freaking her the way she likes it. At six o'clock, we got out of bed and took a shower, then got dressed.

I asked, "Baby, are you ready to work and get that money?"

She answered, "Yes."

"Just keep that Jaguar on your mind and be sexy 24/7."

"Alright."

We left the hotel and stopped at Wendy's for a quick bite to eat. I wasn't trying to hear any excuses either.

I said, "Baby, you have the number to the motel room I'm staying in. I'm going to pay for two or three days rent, plus you have my new 1-888 nationwide sky pager number if there are any problems."

She replied, "Yes, I have it."

I pulled up in front of Meeko's and helped her with her bags of clothes, shoes, and make up. Then walked inside of Meeko's with her, trying my best to get rid of this girl. I needed to get on the phone to check on my other business, then I gave her a big hug and a kiss.

Then told her, "I'll pick you up tomorrow for lunch or something. Call me whenever you get a break to let me know how everything is working out."

I went back to the Rivergate Mall to solicit to some fine ass country girls I had noticed earlier.

I paged Timer and he called right back.

Timer, "Baby started work already. Meeko is a fine bitch that I wouldn't mind knocking."

"SS Boy, I've been trying to knock the bitch too because she makes plenty of money."

"Timer, I told her about the Moet."

"SS Boy, why don't you stop by the liquor store & buy her a bottle of Moet, a dozen roses, and a nice card? Show her that I appreciate everything she has done for me. I'll be there to thank her in person with another bottle of Moet soon."

"Cool. I'll take care of that Timer. As a matter of fact, I'll buy her two bottles of Moet to show her my appreciation as well."

I did all of my shopping and soliciting before I went back to my motel room. Rolled a fat one and poured a stiff drink of Remy Martin on the rocks. I got back on the phone to call home. No one answered and that was a good thing. That let me know that Little Momma and Sunshine were handling business. I knew that I had to get all of my girls a nationwide pager. They most definitely will be traveling state to state selling pussy.

I woke up the next morning and called home to catch my girls. Sunshine answered the phone.

"What up baby?"

"Hi SS Boy."

I asked, "How is everything going?"

She replied "Good."

"Where is Little Momma?"

"She's in her room asleep."

"Wake her up so I can speak to her."

Little Momma got on the phone.

"Hi Daddy. How are you?"

I answered, "Fine, how are you?"

She said, "Good. Everything is going fine."

I asked, "Do you miss me?"

"Yes, I can't wait until you get back."

"I will also be happy when I get back."

She said, "You sure will. We have a surprise for you, Daddy."

Yeah, "Cool. I hope it's a good one."

"It is, daddy."

Little Momma, "I will be home tomorrow night or the day after. Just continue handling business."

"I sure will, & will you hurry up home S.S.? We miss you."

I gave her my new pager number.

"Little Momma just hold tight. I'll be there."

I hung up and rolled my morning blunt.

Baby never did call me from Meeko's. That was also good news. I assumed she was working and making Daddy's money. About one o'clock in the afternoon, my phone rang in the room. It was Baby and she was ready for lunch. I quickly drove over to pick her up, & couldn't wait to hear how her first night as a hooker went.

Baby got into the car playing the mad role, but after ten or fifteen minutes, I could tell she wasn't going to die. In fact, I believe she enjoyed it, but she didn't want me to know that.

I asked, "What did you do last night?"

She replied, "The tricks didn't leave until nine or ten o'clock this morning. I was up all night and half this morning."

A pimp asked, "How many dates did you have?"

"I had five and a couple of them dated me more than once."

I said, "That's good Baby. That means they enjoyed your company."

"Well, you had a pretty good night then."

"Yes, Meeko was congratulating me on how well I did on my first night."

I said, "Shit. You keep this up and we'll have that Jag in no time."

Daddy, "We must have made about eight hundred and fifty dollars last night plus tips."

I said, "That's cool."

She couldn't believe how easy it was to make almost a thousand dollars in one night. We pulled up at Chili's Bar and Grill and had an excellent lunch with drinks. Plus we had to toast to our new success. Baby ordered the baby back ribs and I ordered the mushroom burger with Swiss cheese. We sat there for an hour talking, laughing, and having a good time.

Baby said, "Do you believe me when I say that I love you dearly?"

I said, "Baby, that's a damn good start, but I will really know it once we are rolling down the street in that Jag."

After we finished lunch, I fired up a blunt and took her back to Meeko's. Tricks come through 24/7 to get serviced. I picked up the little eight hundred and fifty dollars from the safe deposit box. Then headed to Motel 6 with intentions to leave Nashville and bounce back toward OKC. Baby insisted that I stay another night and take her to lunch again tomorrow. I already knew she wanted some more dick.

I laid up in the room thinking about my money and watching HBO until I fell asleep. The next morning, Baby woke me up about eleven.

She was asking me, "Can you come pick me up?"

Plus I got the green light from Meeko.

Meeko told her, "You don't have to return to work until seven o'clock this evening."

I said, "Cool."

I immediately got dressed and went to pick up my new turnout. She had another good night and made seven hundred dollars. That made a total of fifteen hundred fifty dollars in twenty four hours. That was cool coming from one hoe. Baby and I drove off from Meeko's.

I asked her, "What do you have a taste for?"

Chapter 17

She quickly answered, "You."

I wanted to ask her, "Do you ever get tired of sex?"

But, did not ask her anything.

We bee lined it to the motel room. I started putting down my pimping on her.

I let her know, "I believe in you to handle your business. Do not fuck with the money in the safe deposit box."

I didn't have a choice but to put the bitch on automatic, whether she was ready or not. Nor did I have time to baby sit the hoe and coach her 24/7. Now we will see what kind of woman she is.

I told her, "I must go back today to handle my business."

She said, "You're going back to be with those bitches of yours."

Bitch, "Don't even go there. Handle your business because it doesn't cost you a dime to stay out of mine."

That's why most pimps prefer snows instead of crows. A white bitch is less complicated than a black bitch. A black bitch has a smart mouth and loves to have drama in her life. I laid up with the bitch and made reservations through Southwest Airlines back to OKC.

I told her, "Give me your key to the safe deposit box. I'm the only one that needs to get into it. I'll be back in two weeks. Call me every Monday, Wednesday and Friday to keep me up to date."

She tried to cry and carry on because a pimp was putting her on automatic for a couple of weeks.

I had to go and attend my business. I still had one hundred and fifty five pounds of sticky green, thirty three thousand and seven hundred dollars in weed money, and seventeen thousand out on credit. No telling how much I had in my hoe trap from Little Momma and Sunshine. Also about two thousand cash in my pocket and a bitch on automatic. Pimping had come a long way in six months.

I gave Baby one hundred dollars and told her, "That's enough for food for a week, if not two weeks."

We jumped in the shower together where she sucked this dick for the last time, before my departure. Baby got dressed. I was clean as a mother fucker, knowing I had to catch a flight at 8:25 pm.

We arrived at Meeko's at seven o'clock that evening. I went inside with Baby to give Meeko two bottles of Moet, a sentimental card, and some roses. I also gave her Timer's message & she loved it.

I told her, "Thanks for everything. And I really appreciate doing business with you."

Meeko said, "I appreciate doing business with you and Timer."

I gave Baby a hug and kissed her on the cheek before walking out the door. I could feel my girl staring at me until I left out the front door. I jumped into the rental car and punched out. Leaving the bitch on automatic, & headed to Nashville International Airport.

I arrived back in OKC and got on my mobile phone. Instantly contacted my little YG's who were working the weed houses.

They told me, "Come by and chop it up."

I knew what time it was. A hustler had plenty of money to pick up, & the little homies had all of my money. They had seventeen thousand dollars in all. I picked up my money and chopped it up with them for a little while. Then proceeded to head home and see what was in my trap. A hustler had nineteen thousand in my possession and still hadn't checked my hoe trap yet.

When I made it home, no one was there. Little Momma and Sunshine were at the track getting Daddy's money. I went straight to my safe and pulled out all of my money, to re-counted it. I added more cash which totaled out to fifty two thousand, seven hundred dollars. A hustler was feeling real good now.

I looked in my dresser and had another stack from my girls. That was a total of six thousand and three hundred dollars in three days. I couldn't believe those girls had made almost sixty five hundred dollars in three days. I had a total of fifty nine thousand cash, one hundred and fifty five pounds, and three bitches.

A nigga had to roll an Indo Optimo blunt, and I poured myself some Remy Martin on the rocks. I had to pat myself on the back.

I also called Timer to tell him about Nashville.

Timer stated, "I'm in OKC, & on my way to the crib after I stop at Byron's to pick up a couple of bottles of Don P."

I said, "Cool."

Timer pulled up in the white on white Double R. Then stepped in cleaner than a mother fucker with a white Versace suit, white ostrich shoes, and a white brim on with a red feather in it. He had on thirty five karats with the Presidential Rolex watch and bracelet. Timer came in popping pimping on super charge. As he walked in the kitchen to place the two bottles of Don P in the freezer.

"SS Boy, get dressed. Let's see what's going on at the truck stop in Guthrie."

I said, "Cool."

Then I went and changed clothes. I put on one of my Italian cut Armani suits, a pair of crocodile shoes, my blue face Oyster Rolex, and some of my jewelry. I came back into the living room and Timer was rolling up Indo blunts. With one already blazed up. There were a couple of grams on the table and a champagne glass of Don P.

I told Timer, "Baby is at Meeko's, & she's already paid her choosing fees. That was fifteen hundred dollars. I'm three deep now, all crows and no snows."

Timer said, "Now that's pimping."

I sat on the leather couch with Timer and poured a glass of Don P and fired up an Indo blunt. With my Herrera cologne, & my Versace shades on popping pimping. We sat there until we finished that first bottle of Don P.

Timer said, "Now let's ride. Bring the champagne glasses and the other bottle of Don P. I'll finish rolling these indo blunts."

It was about midnight when we got into the Rolls Royce. We proceeded to cruise down 23rd street at about thirty or thirty five mph. Timer then played that Christopher Williams (Let's get right).The music was sounding just right in the Double R. The pimping was on tonight. Every bitch I encounter better bow down to pimping or don't look my way. That's how the game goes. If you got eyes, you got action, and young SS Boy is accepting all applications and choosing fees tonight.

Timer and I first went to the Robinson track on the Southwest Side of OKC. We were drinking Don P, smoking Indo blunts, and cruising about thirty five mph, flexing and flossing. We ran into ten other pimps from Dallas, Arizona, Kansas, and Memphis. Oklahoma City is the Southwest capitol for breeding pimps and hoes.

Young City was in his black Double R. There were Benzes, Rolls Royces, Lexuses, and Corvettes in the parking lot. There were also a few big body Cadillacs.

Pimping Cobra and Long Perm told me, "Your two bitches were out here earlier. They must have left. We haven't seen them three money makers in a few hours."

I heard them when they said three. When I left town, I only had two hookers. I figured those pimps made a mistake on the head count (lol), so I didn't mention it. I let them think, that a new pimp had three hoes around this camp now.

Pimpin Cobra said, "SS Boy, I see that you have thoroughly put your pimping down little brother. We tried to get at them before we noticed those were your hoes. Those hoes wouldn't even look our way while we were whistling and carrying on."

I replied, "That's right. They love my pimping, & love putting another true pimp on the map."

Timer and Cobra both said, pimping is putting pimping on the map but, "I feel you little brother."

Timer & Cobra gave me dap on my pimping.

Timer said, "Let's get back in the hoe catcher (the Double R) and do some hoe checking pimping S.S. Boy."

I said, "Dig that."

Me & Big Bro. jumped in the Rolls and pulled out playing that JT Money. While the other pimps were admiring Timer's clean ass Double R.

Timer said, "We can't knock any hoes hanging around a bunch of pimps. Besides, one of their hoes might want to re-choose with one of us. They most definitely tried to peel you for yours."

That's right, "Timer, I already know it, game recognize game."

Timer said, "That's right."

Then poured another glass of Don P. and we got on the highway headed to the truck stop in Guthrie, Oklahoma. When we got out there, it was plenty of action everywhere.

Timer even had a few of his girls out there getting his money. As soon as we parked, Timer's hoes came up to the car dropping off stacks. Big Bro. had three snows and one crow, of some fine dedicated hoes too.

I told Timer, "Ask them if they seen Little Momma and Sunshine."

"The girls who drive that little bucket over there?"

Timer said, "Come here bitch." Where is SS's crew?

"Little Momma is right over here in that blue 18 wheeler."

Timer said, "Tell the bitch that her man wants her."

That fine bitch quickly ran off toward the blue 18 wheeler.

Little Momma saw me standing outside the Double R. & came over to Daddy, with one of the biggest smiles I ever seen on her face. She was hugging on me and telling me what's happening around this camp.

"Baby, we have been busy, getting your money, daddy."

"Dig that."

Daddy, "When did you get back?"

I told her, "A few hours ago."

Little Mamma reached between her legs and pulled a condom full of money out of her pussy. Then she pulled the money out the condom and handed me a bank roll of seven hundred dollars.

I quickly asked, "Where is Sunshine?"

"She's over there. I'll go get her. I also have a surprise for you S.S."

Little Momma came back with Sunshine and this other broad who I couldn't see her face yet in the distance. Once they got closer, I could see that it was Special K, Big Seamore's ex-girl.

I said, "What up ladies?"

Timer had already broke his hoes and sent them back out the door with instructions. Now he was peeping out my game. I had to put it down and continue to keep these hoes broke.

Special K and Sunshine walked up to me and said, "Hi SS Boy."

Little Momma was standing in the cut winking at me. Sunshine reached in her bra and handed a pimp almost six hundred dollars.

I told Special K, "Break yourself bitch, drop it close up under you. & let a pimp see what you're working with"

The bitch reached in her bra and pulled out four hundred and fifty dollars.

"Plus I'll get Daddy much more."

I said, "So you finally decided to re-choose? What took you so long?"

The bitch said, "I was nervous and didn't know how to approach you."

I said, "It sure looks like you know how to approach a pimp. You do it with a new bank roll. I want it like this every day."

She smiled and said, "I can do that SS Boy. I just want to be on a winning team."

"As of now, you are on a winning team baby. It takes hard work, dedication, and loyalty. You feel me?"

"Yes S.S."

Okay well, "I'll be back out here in a few hours. Let me see you three get down and make a pimp even happier."

Chapter 18

Sunshine and Special K ran off back to work toward the 18 wheelers. Little Momma stood around until they left.

She asked, "Do you like my gift?"

I said, "I sure do, but no gift is better than you."

Little Momma smiled and said, "SS Boy, I'm deeply in love with you. I know we have been together for only a short period of time, but it feels like we been together for a long time. What's so real, I've never had a pimp before."

"Well Little Mamma you got one now, & there is no better relationship than a thoroughbred pimp and a true dedicated money making hoe. You feel me?"

Little Mamma replied, "I guess so."

I said, "If I don't make it back here tonight, I'll be waiting for you all at home."

"Okay SS Boy, I better get back to work."

I said, "That's right. Luv ya baby."

That bitch took off running across the parking lot like a Deer hopping across the highway (lol). I got back into the Rolls Royce. Timer gave me dap and put the Rolls in reverse. Then we proceeded to leave. I straightened out my money nice and neat and counted it. It was a total of seventeen hundred and fifty dollars and still more pimping to come.

Timer said, "SS Boy, I feel you baby boy. Pimp then young nigga! Let's fall up in the white strip club on the Northwest side of town and have us a drink."

He fired up one of his Indo blunts.

And said, "SS Boy, save your Indo blunt until later."

We fell up in the Million Dollar Saloon Night Club on Northwest Highway between MacArthur and Rockwell. Timer pulled up directly to the front door where the valet attendants ran to the doors of the Rolls. They opened the doors and Indo smoke rushed out the car directly hitting them in their faces. That old Rick James was beating in their ears. We got out like two macks. Pimp walking into the club clean as a mother fucker and high as hell. We headed directly to the VIP section and our ice was [diamonds] glittering everywhere. All heads turned and looked in our direction. Even the two white bitches dancing on stage had to take a double look at us. It seemed like everyone in there knew that we were pimps.

It kind of made me feel uncomfortable because I know how people feel toward real pimps. The reason I say real pimps is because this younger generation loves to use the word pimp and I don't believe they really know the true definition of a pimp. Most of the younger generation thinks that you're a pimp if you're free fucking a lot of hoes or shall I say girls. The older generation thinks a real pimp will sell his own ass if his girls don't. That sounds like a dope fiend to me, or a punk. The true definition of a pimp means you send a bitch out the door with instructions on getting a pimp his money. You are not pimping until a bitch breaks herself or relieves herself of your money every night. Pimping means you charge a bitch every day possible for your services and directions. Pimping is when you keep a bitch broke and she brings you new money every day. You have to keep her working 24/7.

You feel me? All of you square mother fucker's out there. I don't mean to bite some of my readers so hard, but I've got to be true and real with you. You wouldn't be reading this if you didn't feel me. Don't close the book if I bit you too hard [lol], just pick up on your pimping and charge a bitch instead of free fucking all the time.

I tell my hookers all the time, "I can jack off better than I can fuck, so go get my money. You dig?"

Now back to the story.

Timer and I sat in the VIP section that overlooked the whole club. Timer ordered another bottle of Don P. and we sat there campaigning with the dancers. Timer was passing out business cards that read: Nationwide Entertainment; State to State. There were dollar signs all around the card with his name and his 1800 pager number on it.

Girls were coming from everywhere to meet us. They even came out the dressing rooms to get action on what they thought were tricks in suits and ice. It was mostly white hoes and a couple of crows. We had some action. It was a damn shame because I had to write down my pager number five times that night. Timer passed out ten business cards. We were macking hard to those snow bunnies. We had five or six of them who wanted to take us out to eat and give us some free pussy on the house.

Timer quickly replied, "We appreciate the offer, but this good dick of mine isn't free. Now you can earn some free dick."

We stayed until the club closed. I had a pocket full of phone numbers and so did Timer. These bitches already knew we had money. I'm sure the owner of the club told the girls about us and had them to attack us.

We flipped the script on the hoes and the owner. If he wasn't careful, he would be losing some employees.

It was bitches all out in the parking lot watching us when the valet pulled the Double R up to us. Even men were standing in amazement with their mouths wide open. Four white bitches followed us out of the parking lot and down Northwest Highway. We were like celebrities.

I didn't know a Rolls Royce could run like that. He was jamming on Barry White and headed to the track to check more money from our hookers. I blazed up a fat Indo blunt, & was drunk and feeling good as hell. I even had to hit me a one on one (a toot of cocaine up each nostril).

We got back out to the truck stop and our girls ran over to the Rolls. I broke all three of my bitches for another seven hundred dollars, which was a damn good night. Timer broke his bitches for a phat knot (money). I had a damn good night for a total of almost twenty five hundred dollars.

I told my girls, "You can go home now."

Giving them fifty dollars, so they could go to the Waffle House and grab a bite to eat.

"As a matter of fact, I'm riding with you all. Timer, I will get with you tomorrow. I need to talk to them about a few things."

I gave Timer dap and jumped out the Rolls and into the bucket. The next morning, or shall I say afternoon. When a young pimp woke up, all four of us were in the California king size bed.

I paged Timer and he immediately returned my call.

What up S.S., "Meet me at the barber shop in about forty minutes."

I got dressed and rushed to my stash spot to pick up twenty pounds so I could drop ten pounds off at each weed house on the East Side. By the time I made it up to the barber shop, Timer was pulling up in the parking lot. He was still in the Rolls Royce, & I jumped in with him.

I asked Timer, "Do you have the hook up on vehicles? I'm ready for something new."

He replied, "Hell yes, I'll turn you on to my Iranian boys. They will hook you up real proper. They don't give a fuck where you got the money from either. They just want their money."

I said, "When can we do something?"

Timer said, "Yesterday, meaning now. They have Lexus, Benzes, Rolls Royces, Hummers, Suburban's, and Cadillacs. Whatever you want, it's on."

I said, "Timer you know what else I want?"

"What is it lil bro.?"

"I want some ice so, I can make me some nice pieces."

Timer asked, "How much did you plan on spending?"

"About ten thousand dollars."

Timer said, "I might be able to assist you in both of those areas."

I said, "Cool."

Okay lil Bro., "I'm leaving OKC after I get my hair cut; me and my girls. You can ride with me to Dallas. Then we can go to the dealership & see if you can't ride back to OKC in something major. Just bring about ten thousand dollars and you'll be riding in something phat."

I said, "Dig dat."

Me, & Timer both went inside the barber shop to get hooked up.

After our hair cut's, we both stepped outside & Timer said, "I will pick you up at your house in less than an hour, so be ready."

As soon as I left, I recieved a page from my boy, Big Seamore.

What up Seamore? "Stop by my crib for a minute S.S. I want to holler at you about something."

Now all kinds of crazy things were running through my head. I figured that Big Seamore wanted to talk to me about his bitch I peeled him for.

Once I got there, he asked me, "Can I get another deal? I need twenty pounds."

I asked, "What are you working with?"

"About twelve thousand dollars."

"Shit, Seamore you're straight. Here's the deal. I'll sell you twenty pounds at seven hundred each. Your tab will be fourteen thousand. You already paid me from the last round. You will only owe me two thousand dollars. When do you want to get down?"

"I'm ready now."

Okay but, "What's up with you and Special K?"

"I haven't heard from her. Fuck that bitch."

"Seamore, we are like brothers. We are pimp partners for life right? Special K chose up with a pimp. I've been working the shit out of the bitch."

I could tell by the look in his eyes that he was crushed, but I had to serve him about this bitch. Big Seamore took it like a champ though.

He said, "SS Boy, work the shit out of that bitch because I was trying to."

I said, "Bro, I'm rolling to Dallas tonight with Timer in the Rolls. I'll be back in a day or two. When I get back, we are going to drink a bottle of Don P and have a pimp toast. I peeled you for your bitch and you took it like a champ."

We both laughed about it, like true G's

I told Seamore, "You can meet me at the car wash in Midwest City."

He went inside his house and came out with a small paper sack, it was twelve thousand dollars.

"Be at the car wash in twenty minutes."

I was on a tight schedule and had to hurry so that I wouldn't miss Timer. A hustler had to rush to the spot & grab twenty more pounds, so I could met Seamore at the car wash. I punched out to the crib to get ready and pack my clothes. I had one hundred and fifteen pounds of weed, nineteen thousand out on credit, and seventy three thousand six hundred fifty dollars in cash. A young pimp also had four dedicated hookers in his stable. The only bills I had were utilities.

Timer showed up right on time. And I had plenty of time to put my girls on automatic while on the highway. A young pimp also packed for a couple of days. Took about fifteen thousand dollars with me, which left a total of fifty eight thousand, six hundred and fifty dollars in the safe.

We jumped back in the Rolls after I put my duffle bag, freshly starched slacks, and shirts in the trunk.

I asked Timer, "Where are your hoes?"

He replied, "They're right here at the service station filling up. In that brand new five series BMW Y2K."

I said, "I thought we were going to be jam packed in the Double R."

Timer replied, "A pimp can't ride like that. My hoes follow me from state to state baby. I'll never let these white folks split my wig for pimping, pandering, or white slavery for taking them across state lines."

We jumped on the highway headed to Dallas, Texas. It was a three hour ride. There was a car load of white hoes and a crow directly behind us. Timer pulled out an ounce of Indo and handed me the orange pack of Zig Zag rolling papers.

"Twist up a couple of fat ones lil Bro."

Then he put in that new Jigga cd and then that new Snoop and the Eastsidas. By the time we hit the Texas state line, we were banging on some old Ray Parker Jr. My neck was tired by the time we got to Timer's mansion.

We pulled up at the mansion with the four car garage, seven bedrooms, five and a half bathrooms, three living areas, a game room, two dining rooms, a breakfast area, two Jacuzzis, a large customized swimming pool, two fireplaces, and two staircases. This brother was living large. His house was about fifty five hundred square feet.

Timer showed me to my quarters.

"Stating, make yourself at home. Do whatever you want. When you finish hanging up your clothes, meet me at the wet bar for a drink."

I said, "Bet."

I hung up my clothes and put on a pair of gym shorts with no shirt or shoes. I headed to the pool and Jacuzzi after making a drink at Timer's wet bar. Timer's crib was huge. I got lost trying to find the wet bar, which was in the game room.

Timer was sitting at the wet bar with a silver platter full of Peruvian blue flake cocaine with a double shot of Louis the 13th cognac. He was enjoying life and his riches like any man from the ghetto would.

He said, "Help yourself."

I went behind the bar and made me a drink of Louis the 13th cognac on the rocks. Then sat next to Timer and snorted some of that bomb ass cocaine.

Timer asked, "Do you want to take this to the Jacuzzi?"

I answered, "Yes sir"

Timer got a smaller sterling silver plater; which was a saucer.

He told me, "Let's take this outside to the pool area and turn on the Jacuzzi & the outdoor stereo system. I will meet you out there in a few minutes young pimping."

Chapter 19

Me, & Timer popped pimping for a couple of hours in the Jacuzzi. We were snorting cocaine, smoking weed, and drinking Louie. Timer gave me a lot of game while I listened to him. There were alot of new avenues to explore on my pimping and hustling.

Timer said, "We'll go to my Iranian partner's tomorrow morning to see if you find anything you like."

I said, "Timer, whatever I roll home in has to be sitting on twenty inches."

"You ain't said nothing SS Boy, it's on."

I told Timer, "I'm going to take a pimp nap because I'm fucked up."

He said, "Cool."

His house was so large that I never did run into his hoes. They all had their own rooms.

Then my pager blew up. It was Baby calling me from Nashville. I called her back immediately to get the update on how everything was going.

She said, "I am doing well besides missing that dick and seeing my man."

I gave her plenty of pimping and encouragement to constantly keep that Jaguar on her mind. She was starting to get use to selling pussy. Baby enjoyed making tricks cum and getting paid for it.

Baby, "How much do we have in the safe deposit box?"

She replied, "It's about twenty five hundred dollars."

Okay, "That's cool Baby. Break those tricks and keep it coming."

She then asked, "When are you coming to see me?"

"Not this weekend, but maybe next weekend."

I was hoping the bitch would have ten thousand or better for me by the time I got there.

Baby said, "SS Boy, I love you."

"I love you too Baby. I do miss you dearly, but business before pleasure, you feel me?"

& I got off the phone with her and found Timer.

Timer, "My girl in Nashville is getting money, and she will probably average about five thousand a week. I broke her for twenty five hundred in Nashville. She already made twenty five hundred dollars in less than a week."

Timer said, "I told you that it was on in Nashville. I'll probably be sending one of my girls back to Nashville in the next week or so if the tracks slow down. I'm going to introduce you to one of Dallas's hoe strolls, Harry Hines Blvd. tonight."

I said, "Cool."

I knew I had to take a pimp nap now, so I would be rested up for tonight's action.

Timer, "Wake me up in a few hours because I'm tired as hell."

Timer was also tired. While we were talking, Timer was laying in his ten thousand dollar bed about to fall asleep. He was also fucked up. I went to my quarters and fell asleep with a smile on my face. I woke up at ten pm. Timer had just woke up and we were both rested up now and ready for action.

I asked Timer, "When is it enough for you and how much is enough? You're already rich, but you still hustle like a small guy on the totem pole, 24/7."

Timer said, "I don't count the money from state to state. I don't know when I'll be finished with the game. I hustle because I enjoy my job. I enjoy making deals, pimping hoes, and hitting big licks. If I had to put a price tag on my retirement, I would probably need about fifty million dollars to hang up my pistols & pimp cape."

By the way he said that, I knew Timer wouldn't quit until the casket dropped or prison cell doors locked. He was a true hustler in the game for life. Timer got dressed with his Versace jeans, crocodile cowboy boots, crocodile cowboy hat, crocodile vest, and no shirt under it. He had on a Rolex, phat necklace, medallion, and some big ass diamond rings.

He said, "This is Texas style baby boy. Have you ever seen the movie Vice Squad?"

I said, "Yeah, with a white pimp named Ramrod who pimped out of a clean ass pickup truck."

Timer said, "That's right, Pimping SS Boy. We will be in the truck tonight."

I said, "Dig that."

I put on Polo jeans and a Polo shirt to dress cowboy style since I was in Dallas. We rolled up three blunts and headed out the four car garage in the 'Burban. The 600 Benz and the Rolls Royce were parked inside. There were also two Suzuki motor cycles with double head lights on the front, fat wide slick tires on the back, back wheels extended, wheelie bars modified, and the whole nine yards.

We climbed in Timer's Suburban show truck. It had televisions, VCR, Play Station, leather and wood grain everywhere, interior lights on the door panels, and the head liners even had wood grain & lights. The thick pin stripe went down the side of the 'Burban with the ground effects and fog lights. It was sitting on chrome twenty inch Enkei wheels with rubber band low profile tires.

I asked Timer, "Where are your hookers?"

He said, "They on the track where they're famous at."

I couldn't do anything but laugh.

Timer said, "My bitches know to be out the house by sun down. I've got them on automatic rain, sleet, or snow."

We jumped on I-30 west to 635 west jamming the radio station 100.3 Jams and K104.5. That shit was banging in Dallas. You don't need to play your cassette or CD player because the radio station jams 24/7, even on Sundays. Dallas had four black radio stations. We stopped at the beer store and grabbed a twelve pack of Corona to load up the wood grain ice chest.

Bitches were steady checking us out in that hoe catching Suburban. They were skinning and grinning while the twenty inches kept spinning. We headed to Harry Hines, the hoe stroll. There were pimps and hookers everywhere. There was strip clubs and adults book stores. Timer and I pulled into the book store parking lot. I saw hookers sitting in trick's cars giving head and selling pussy. It was wide open and I loved it.

We pulled off and went to Momma's Café. In the parking lot were some of the same pimps from OKC at the truck stop. Pimping Cobra in his drop top 500 Benz, Long Perm in his Big body Lexus 400, Eyes in his 500 Benz two door coupe, and seven or eight other pimps from other states. It was a pimp reunion and convention. Pimps up and hoes down.

I immediately told Timer, "I need to bring my stable here."

Then a few pimps asked Timer and me, "Are ya'll coming to join us in Hawaii? We will be staying for a month or so."

Timer said, "I don't know, but it sounds good. I do need a vacation."

Everyone gave him dap on that because they could feel where he was coming from.

Long Perm invited us to come, stating, "I have a condo on the beach overlooking the ocean."

Timer said, "Now that sounds very inviting. I might have to buy a condo on the ocean front."

We popped pimping for hours while waiting on the hoes to break bread. We chopped it up until four am. Timer broke his bitches for over four thousand dollars that night. Each one of his hoes checked over a thousand dollars that night and that was cool.

Timer stated, "I won't let my girls come home unless they clock a thousand dollars or better each and every night. The other tracks are not as sweet as this one. When we work Harry Hines, they know not to come home with less than a thousand dollars each. This track keeps plenty of high rolling tricks."

We jumped back on 635 and headed back to the mansion.

All I could think about was bringing my hookers down here to let them get down. If I work four hoes at a thousand dollars each, that's four thousand dollars a night. At seven days a week, that's twenty eight thousand. In a month, I would have well over one hundred thousand. Now that's pimping to the highest degree. That's real money coming straight out the womb. If I'm getting money like that, I would not have to sell weed ever again, and that's real.

I couldn't even fall asleep. I tossed and turned all night, thinking about that one hundred thousand a month. I was laying up thinking in the bed until the sun came up. I finally fell asleep.

Timer woke me up at noon stating, "I talked to my Iranian partner at the car lot. We need to hurry over because they just got in some new cars and trucks."

I said, "Cool."

I jumped out of bed and got dressed before heading downstairs. One of Timer's hoes made us steak, eggs, potatoes with onions, and orange juice. Man was that shit good. I never met a white girl who cooked like a sister. I had to give her her props. We jumped in the 600 Benz and went to Baller's Unlimited car lot in Plano, Texas. It was on the outskirts of Dallas about twenty five minutes out.

As soon as we pulled up, I seen the cleanest 400 Lexus coupe convertible I had ever seen. He had the big body 300, 400, 500, 600 Mercedes Benz, Jaguars, Hummers, 'Burbans, Roll Royce, and Bentleys.

These guys had money. I liked every car I saw because each car or truck was top of the line and fully loaded. I still hadn't run into the vehicle with my name on it yet. I started looking at the Suburban show trucks. I liked those 'Burbans every since Timer left me his.

The salesman asked, "Do you like Suburban's?"

"Yes I do."

"I might have something for you. Follow me."

He took us back to their detailing department. There it sat, a 1999 white on white Cadillac Escalade, fully loaded, wood grain, leather, surround sound, VCR,TV, and Play Station hook ups. It only had sixteen thousand miles on it.

I asked the salesman, "Can we take it on a test drive?"

He answered, "Sure, but you'll have to excuse it because our detailer's haven't cleaned it up yet."

That's okay, "It's cool."

Before I test drove it, I already knew that this was what I wanted. We test drove it and I had to have it. The ride was so smooth.

I asked, "What are you asking for it?"

The salesman said, "$42,000.00, but since you are Timer's friend, I might can sell it to you for $37,000.00."

I said, "Cool, let's do it."

We went back to the car lot to draw up the paper work.

He asked, "How do you plan on paying for it? Are you getting it financed? Are you paying cash or do you want us to finance you?"

"I will spend my money with you & Baller's Unlimited. Could you finance me?"

I did exactly what Timer had previously told me to do.

The salesman asked, "How much do you plan on dropping for the down payment?"

"How much is required?"

He answered, "About four or five thousand dollars."

I said, "I'll tell you what, I plan on having this truck paid off within a year. I'll drop you nine thousand for the down payment."

You should have seen his eyes light up with dollar signs. He called back to the in-house detail department.

"Get that truck cleaned up within thirty minutes because a customer is waiting for it."

The owner of Baller's Unlimited came over to talk with Timer and myself.

Timer told the owner, "Hook him up with the same payment plan as mine. He will be dropping about eight or nine thousand every three months or so, instead of monthly payments."

Chapter 20

That way I'll have it paid off quicker without worrying about monthly payments every month.

I asked, "Can I come back next month to drop you a little something?"

"Sure, just as long as it's not over ten thousand dollars in less than twenty four hours. I don't want the IRS on our asses."

I said, "Cool."

He shook my hand and said, "Congratulations, that's a nice Cadillac you just purchased."

I replied, "Thank you."

While we waited on the detailers to finish, I told Timer, "Take me directly to the wheels and accessory shop. I've got to put some feet on him, (twenty inch rims), immediately."

Timer said, "That ain't no thang. We'll go directly over to B-Tec's."

Just as he said that, I saw my shit come from around the building. It was clean as a mother fucker and ready for a pimp to put foot in it.

Timer said, "That Cadillac Escalade is clean as a mother fucker. Just wait until you put those twenty's on it."

I asked Timer, "Let me bang on that Bucket-Loc CD until we stop at Block Buster's Music."

I followed him to Garland, Texas, to B-Tec's one stop shop. These three brothers had it going on. The oldest brother's wife worked as a secretary. They had ten employees, & did interior restoration, detailing, rims, tires, electronics, and hydraulics. These biological brothers had Y2K triplet Travel Time conversion kit Suburbans sitting on twenty inch rims. Their 'Burbans were cleaner than Timer's. These people were cool as hell. I see why people didn't mind spending big money with this family operated business.

They gave me high props on my new Escalade with the paper tag still in the rear window. Also they showed me so many sets of twenties that it was hard to choose from. I had to be different. I couldn't bite off Timer with the same rims, he had rims on his 600 Benz, the 'Burban, or the Rolls Royce.

I ended up buying some twenty inch chrome and gold Daytons, a Nardi wood grain steering wheel, and a gold package. The rims and tires cost me fifty five hundred. The wood grain steering wheel cost four hundred and fifty dollars. The gold package hit me for two hundred and fifty dollars. It consisted of the grill, emblems, and letters touched in gold with the gold plating machine.

B-Tec hit me for six thousand, two hundred and fifty dollars real quick. A Hustler had to borrow a couple grand from Timer. I had to pay for full coverage insurance and still have a few dollars left until I made it back home.

The manager of B-Tec told me, "Your vehicle will be ready in an hour and a half. Feel free to chill in the customer's waiting room or go and grab a bite to eat or something."

That was right up me and Timer's alley. We headed to one of Dallas's strip joints to do some prospecting on some dancers that needed guidance. Man, does the state of Texas have some fine ass women. I never seen white girls so thick and built like sisters. They could dance too.

We parlayed for a minute and had a beer or two. Then we headed back over to B-Tec. As soon we turned the corner to B-Tec, I saw my shit parked in front of their shop. I couldn't believe that that was my truck. It was most definitely a hoe catcher sitting on those big twenty inch chrome and gold Daytons with the gold touch all the way around it.

Timer said, "Damn SS Boy, you see what the game can get for you, if you play it right?"

I said, "Hell yes."

Well, "You deserve that little brother. That 'Lac is the cleanest I have seen. Those Daytons set it off. You got to let me sport that baby boy."

I said, "You can get it whenever you want to. I still want to roll the Double R to drop my hoes off at the track."

Timer replied, "The next time I bring it to OKC, you can. I did say once you knock some hoes, I'll let you drop them off at the track in the Rolls. You must stay one more night so we can flex this hoe catcher tonight on Harry Hines."

That was cool, but I couldn't wait to get back to OKC and flex this hoe catcher. I only owed about thirty thousand dollars more on it.

Timer, "That's cool, but I need to get back early tomorrow so I'll probably leave once I wake up in the morning. I got to check my trap and I'll be back next weekend. Take me to Block Buster music so I can fill up the ten disc Cd changer under my front passenger seat."

I followed Timer to Block Buster music. Everyone was staring at us and pointing at our clean ass vehicles. I bought ten cold ass CDs.

That night we got clean as a mother fucker. We had on linen pants and shirts. With our shirts buttoned up halfway, so the hoes could see the diamonds. I had B-Tec wipe my shit off, shine up the Daytons, and put black magic on the tires. A new pimp had intentions on knocking me a couple of those fine ass white and Mexican girls.

I told Timer, "All I need now is twenty karats and some pimp cards to pass out to these hoes that are misguided."

Timer laughed and said, "That's right."

We flexed and flossed all night with the AC blowing on high. We were soliciting to every woman we encountered: young or old, eight to eighty, blind, cripple, or crazy (lol). Then we went to Momma's Café where we were last night.

We ran into Long Perm, Eyes, Pimping Cobra, and Beale from Memphis. Those pimps loved my Cadillac and gave me my props all night. They checked it out from front to back, inside and out. Everyone looked under the hood at the motor admiring this new pimp on the block.

I ran into two of the finest Mexicans girls I ever encountered in Dallas. These Texas girls loved trucks, period. Any kind of truck or 'Burban, Dually extended cab, or whatever as long as it was a truck.

Timer said, "I told you this was a hoe catcher. That's all those two square ass Mexican broads are talking about.

They said, "We love his truck. Do you think that you can take us for a ride?"

I said, "Sure."

We exchanged numbers.

"We are going to call you SS Boy. Maybe it will be tonight or tomorrow."

Okay, "I'll be waiting on your page. What is your code ladies?"

One of them said, "I'm 69."

The other one said, "I'm code 68."

I asked, "Do those codes mean what I think they mean?"

Both of them answered with a smile, "You'll see."

They drove off in their new Chevy 1500 extended cab on chrome fifteen inch Daytons. It was probably their man's truck, but I didn't give a fuck. The only thing I had plans on was giving them some pimping and instructions.

Timer clocked another forty five hundred that night. His girls knew how to squeeze a trick for every dime. He truly had some veteran hoes, but he was also a veteran pimp, so I guess that had a lot to do with it. His girls drove BMWs, Volvos, Z28, Camaros, and Mustangs. Timer was seeing well over a hundred thousand dollars a month from his girls, & had a down ass team.

I was starting to consider moving to Dallas to buy a ranch or something.

Timer said, "I've also got the hook ups on the ranches and mansions."

For real Timer? "Dig that. I'll have to stack a couple hundred thousand before that happens."

We chopped it up until our eye lids were heavy. Then headed back to Timer's mansion at five in the morning. I had nothing but big faces on my mind. I fell fast asleep feeling good about my new hoe catcher parked outside. I woke up about noon after a monster night on the track.

Timer's girls had brunch prepared for us again that afternoon. There was lobster tail, dirty rice, and scrambled eggs. It was the bomb. Timer and I smoked an Indo blunt in a green leaf Optimo. He also gave me a blunt to ride with.

Timer, "I will be back next weekend."

Okay S.S., "Cool, if I'm still in town by then."

Timer, "I will call to make sure that you're still here first."

I proceeded to load my bags and clothes in the Escalade. My shit was looking like new money. It was real pimpish; sitting on those gold and chrome twenty inch Daytons with the two way spinners.

Timer said, "Your truck is clean. It's probably cleaner than mine."

I replied, "Not yet, but I'm knocking on your door. Thanks for hooking me up on the truck and everything big bro."

"Don't mention it, you're my little brother S.S."

I also told him, "I will wire the two thousand dollars to you once I get home."

He said, "Don't worry about it SS Boy. I'll get it next time I see you. If you decide to come back next weekend, you can stay here at the castle (mansion), even if I'm not here."

"No shit, thanks Timer."

I gave him a hand shake and a hug before I jumped in the Cadillac. Timer went back inside. I cruised off adjusting my music heading to the Chilly Mart. With plans to stock up on some of Texas's six and seven point beer, because Oklahoma beer content is three point two. It's nothing but beer tasting water, really fucked up in other words.

I got on I-35 north headed back to Oklahoma City to check my traps and recount my stack. I was going to charge this brand new Cadillac

Escalade to a bitch. It was most definitely a hoe catcher and only hoes could ride. No squares.

A young hustler cracked open one of those Coors light beers and blazed up my Indo blunt. I was rolling down the highway doing eighty and listening to Pimping Too Short. A pimp was ready to check these hoes and concentrate on pulling a grand a night out of each girl. I would pull it straight out of her womb, the same place where I pulled the 99 'Lac from. There would be plenty more to come behind it, maybe twins.

I made it to OKC in two and a half hours. There were bugs on the wind shield and the Daytons were a little dusty. When I pulled on to Twenty Third Street. I ran into my little Blood homie Redrum.

He said, "Nigga, for some strange reason I knew that was you. When did you get that clean mother fucker? Follow me to the car wash and let me check that hoe catcher out SS."

We fell up in the car wash. The little homies always tried to get their hustle on by cleaning pimps, hustler's, or baller's vehicles. I did the same thing when I was a youngster. I had to let them wash my shit while I talked to Redrum and one of his homies.

I asked Redrum, "Are you ready for some more birds (keys)?"

"Not yet, maybe in another week or two."

Redrum answered my questions, but I don't think he heard one word I was saying. He was too busy staring at my new truck. He was steady giving me props and dap.

Asking, "What year is it? Is that a Y2K model? Are those rims twenty inches? How much did it hit for?"

I couldn't do anything but start laughing at the little homies innocent curiosity. I chopped it up with him for about an hour while drinking a six point Coors light. I was waiting on the little homies to finish cleaning my shit, finally they were finished.

Redrum, "I will get with you later on."

He had a Nakamishi Cd /cassette deck, equalizer, tuner and remote control with two six hundred watt Phoenix Gold amps for fifteen hundred dollars. I really wanted it, but I had to check my traps before I spent another dime.

I went home to kick it with my girls.

"What's going on ladies?"

Little Momma said, "Daddy, I need to talk to you."

We went into my bedroom and closed the door

She said, "Check your trap Daddy."

Chapter 21

I opened my dresser drawer and grabbed what I thought should be a bank roll. It was only thirty five hundred from three hoes. The last time I left town, I returned home to sixty five hundred dollars.

I said, "Where is my money?"

Daddy, "Sunshine and I made seven hundred each for two nights straight."

I said, "That's fourteen hundred dollars each in two days. That totals out to twenty eight hundred. So you're telling me that Special K only made seven hundred dollars in two days?"

Little Momma just looked at me and threw her shoulders up.

She said, "Daddy, she's also been having some unexplained money lately too."

Oh yeah, "Dig that."

"Well she better not be stuffing (stealing) or she is going to be in big trouble,"

I told Little Momma, "You and Sunshine did good, but usually you two make more than seven hundred dollars a night."

She looked at me with those big pretty brown eyes and said, "Daddy, I'll never steal from you because I feel I don't have to."

I said, "That's right sweetness. Thanks for being true. That's the main reason why I made you my bottom bitch. You already gave the bitch Special K fair warning. Now let me handle it."

"Now get dressed. Let's all go get some lunch."

I left out the bedroom.

& told Special K and Sunshine, "Get dressed. I'm going to take you all out to lunch. Where do you all want to go?"

Special K shouted out, "Golden Corral!"

That let me see what level the cheap low budget bitch was on. Now I could see that the bitch was petty, tiny, (small minded) and capable of stuffing money on me. I still hadn't the time to chop it up with this new bitch to see where her head was yet, either. Now it was time for me to talk to the girl and put my pimping down on her.

We walked toward the driveway. The girls stepped around the corner to see that new 'Lac sitting on gold and chrome twenty inches. They immediately fell in love.

"Daddy that is so cute. We can't wait for you to drop us off at the track in it."

I said okay, "That might be tonight."

We jumped in the Escalade and went to Golden Corral. My girls nodded their heads and pussy popped while sitting on the leather. After we finished eating, I stopped at Auto Zone and bought ten Christmas tree air fresheners. Then went back to Block Buster music & bought ten more CDs and rented a few movies.

All of us went home to chill in front of the big screen. We smoked bud all day until it was time to go to the track. Later that evening, we all got dressed and went to the truck stop in Guthrie, Oklahoma. I gave each one of them twenty condoms each and sent them out the door with instructions.

I proceeded to flex and floss on the East Side while checking my traps. My main man Big Seamore had my two thousand. He jumped in the Cadillac Escalade and we headed up to Bryon's Liquor store and I bought two bottles of Don P. already chilled. With two champagne glasses to drink out of while flossing. Then we headed out to my weed houses so I could check my traps. It was five thousand in one spot and four thousand at the other.

Weed sells like hot cakes. It can sometimes be quicker than crack. We headed to my house so I could put up the eleven thousand dollars that was in my possession. Now I had almost seventy three thousand cash, one hundred and thirty five pounds of weed, and eight thousand out on credit. The stable was four deep. We rolled up a couple of blunts to go with the Don P. and got back into the hoe catcher to put our pimping down.

Big Seamore, "Here is a toast from one player to another. I promise you that I will keep that bitch broke. Plus keep a steering wheel in the bitch's back & drive her to the limit, as fast as she can go."

Seamore screamed out. "Pimp my nigga."

Big Seamore "We will always chop it up and be friends. I remember when you peeled me for a square bitch. Pimps always peel pimps for hoes, but the game keeps spinning. Now let's ride on Robinson Street hoe stroll to see if we can peel another mother fucker for a hoe."

Big Seamore gave me dap and we kept popping pimping, listening to JT Money, and sipping on Don P. Everywhere we rode, my hoe catcher turned heads. Even white folks were whispering and pointing at the 99 Lac. Our hair was blowing from the cold ass air conditioner.

My 1-800 pager blew up with the area code 214.

Wondering, "What up with Timer?"

I immediately got on the mobile phone assuming it was Timer, but it wasn't. It was those two fine ass Mexican girls I met in Dallas. They were ready to ride and do whatever. Thinking that I was still in Dallas.

Ladies, "I have bad news for you. I'm not in Texas, & probably won't be back until the weekend."

The girls asked, "What do you do for a living?"

Well ladies, "I'm a manager and money maker. What do you two do for a living? What were you two doing on Harry Hines?"

They replied, "We work off of Harry Hines."

I quickly asked, "What kind of work do you do?"

They laughed and said, "Well, you might not agree with what we do."

I said, "Maria tell me."

They both got quiet while on their speaker phone.

One of them said, "We entertain."

A player quickly stated, "That's lovely. I specialize in female entertainers."

S.S. Boy, "We are dancers and work at one of the strip clubs on Harry Hines."

Is that right? "Well that's cool, I bet you two make plenty of money, because both of you are so beautiful."

They both giggled.

I replied, "We are most definitely going to hook up now. I wasn't too sure about you two at first, thinking that you two were squares."

"Squares no. We are far from being squares."

I replied, "Is that right? Do you two have any friends just in case I decide to bring one of my partners?"

"We have plenty of friends S.S."

Okay, "Well pick up one of your friends, & page us back. So that my homie can talk to her, because both of you are for me."

The girls laughed and asked, "Can you handle both of us?"

"We'll see. Just page me back within one hour while me, and my home boy is still chopping it up."

Maria said, "Cool."

Now Big Seamore had a big smile on his face, thinking about them Mexican girls.

I said, "Nigga, quit trying to change a hoe into a house wife and stop talking love. Talk pimping to these hoes and let's flip these Mexican bitches. Let's keep it pimping."

We punched out on the highway headed to Guthrie, so I can check my grip. Little Momma came to the truck and dropped off two hundred and fifty dollars.

I told her, "Send Sunshine over here."

She came and I broke her for two hundred and fifty dollars.

Then I told Sunshine, "Send Special K over here."

Special K came and I broke her for every dime, which was only two hundred dollars. The bitch tried to act shy after she noticed Seamore with me.

She asked, "Why did you bring him?"

I said, "Bitch, a pimp can ride with whomever he wants. You don't need to worry about who I'm riding with. You need to be concentrating and breaking who you're riding with. Now get my money."

I jumped in the truck and headed back to OKC, East Side bound. I didn't try to bite my homie so hard by breaking his ex-bitch in his face, but

I had to check my dough and the bitch. How is she going to question a pimp?

I needed a snort now. I paged my boy Redrum for an eight ball of that powder. We headed to North Highland on the North Side of OKC. Redrum and his little homies were standing in front of his crib chopping it up, gang banging, and serving dope.

I told Big Seamore, "We have to hurry and get out of here. Redrum is doing way too much."

We did have to laugh and take our hats off because the little YGs (young gangsters) were getting money in a big way.

Redrum, I need about an eight ball for my own personal.

Also, "Can I see the car stereo and amps?"

Yes sir, "Yeah, come on in S.S."

Redrum pulled out that four piece Nakamishi car stereo and two clear Phoenix Gold amps. This shit was so clean and high dollar that I had to have it.

I asked, "What's the lowest you'll take for all this?"

Well, "SS Boy, since it's you, I'll take twelve hundred right now."

Alright "Cool, but what if I give you a thousand now and two hundred tomorrow?"

"SS Boy, we can do that. I'll call you tomorrow & meet you on the East Side somewhere, for the other two hundred dollars."

I reached in my pocket and paid Redrum with hoe money straight out the womb. Redrum pulled out a digital scale to weigh out an eight ball, which was three and a half grams.

He said, "That's for you OG."

Redrum and I walked to the Escalade to place my stereo equipment in it. I gave Redrum dap and punched out.

Big Seamore said, "Damn, that stereo is the shit. It has a remote control like my Pioneer."

We rode off into the night back to the East Side. All I could think of is to get my stereo system in and have it knocking. Then we headed to my house to get high, smoke blunts, and toot good cocaine. Me, & Seamore chopped it up for a couple hours. We killed the Don P. and started drinking my six point beers I brought from Dallas. We were fucked up. I took Big Seamore home and jumped on the highway to the track laying dead to catch any one of these bitches stuffing on me.

It was one thirty in the morning. They all got in the truck. I broke them all one at a time. Sunshine had another four hundred dollars and Little Momma had four hundred and sixty five dollars. Then Special K handed me another two hundred dollars.

The truck stop was full of plenty of pussy buying truckers. I hadn't questioned the little bitch yet. I decided to wait until I got home. A young pimp had a trick for all of them when we made it to the crib, tonight.

When we stepped foot inside the house, I told all three of them, "Stop where you're at and get butt asshole naked right now."

They all asked, "Are you serious?"

I said, "Hell yeah. This is penitentiary night, now get naked."

Little Momma and Sunshine undressed immediately. All of a sudden Special K. had to go to the rest room real quick like. Acting like she was about to piss or shit on herself.

I said Bitch, "You aren't going anywhere. Strip now, before I beat your black ass. Right now bitch."

The bitch got naked with tears falling from her eyes. She was already looking guilty as hell, giving herself away. I searched all their clothes, pockets, and shoes.

Then searched them one at a time. Little Momma was first.

I told her, "Bend over, spread your ass cheeks, and cough."

I stuck my finger in her pussy, and then her ass hole.

Now, "You can get in the shower."

Now it was Sunshine's turn. I did her the same way. Her pussy and ass hole were clean of any money.

Now it was Special K's turn.

She asked, "How can you do this to us, SS Boy?"

I said, "Bitch, I'm already tired of your mouth. You have one more time to open your dick sucking mouth. Now bend over, cough, and spread your ass cheeks."

I stuck my finger in her ass searching for anything, it was clean of money. Then I sat the bitch on the base of the fire place.

"Spread your legs."

Chapter 22

She was really crying and carrying on now. I reached deep off into the bitch's pussy with two fingers and felt something. As I started to pull this object out of her pussy, I noticed that it was a rubber condom with a nice little knot (money). It was two hundred dollars. Now the bitch was balling (crying) like a little baby and steady trying to lie.

Daddy, "I already had this money."

Before the bitch could get it out good, I hauled off and cold cocked her right in the nose, blacking both of her eyes. Then I grabbed the bitch by her hair and body slammed her on the living room floor. I started kicking and stomping her thieving ass while spitting pimping at her. This was the other side of the pimp game.

Special K. was begging and pleading, "Please stop beating my ass Daddy! I'm sorry!"

"Bitch, since you want to act like a slick kid and steal, I'll treat you like a kid."

I snatched the bitch up by the hair and drug her into my bedroom.

"Bitch, now lay on this bed."

I pulled off my thick wide ass Karl Kani belt and started beating the bitch like a child.

I beat the bitch so much she started screaming, "I love you SS Boy! I'm sorry! I'll never ever do it again!"

Special K. had tears and snot running down her face.

Bitch, "Get off my bed."

I grabbed her and threw her in the hot shower, & poured shampoo all over the bitch. That gave her a burning sensation from the whelps on her body from my thick ass Karl Kani belt. She was crying and screaming louder than any person I've ever heard before.

"Bitch, shut up and take this soap & towel. Also take a good shower."

I sat there and watched her take a soapy shower. She was crying all the way through it.

Steady saying, "I am sorry. I love you S.S."

Bitch, "Get out of the shower and dry off. Now lay down on my bed."

She was so afraid that her body was trembling all over. Then I grabbed my jar of Vaseline and greased up the bitch's asshole. A young pimp went up in her asshole real deep and hard, doggy style with this nine inch dick. I was pulling on her hair and slapping the bitch while spitting pimping at her.

She hollered and screamed out, "Daddy, you're going to bust my asshole! Please be gentle!"

I replied, "Bitch, you like putting things in you, so I figured that you'll like this nine inches in your ass."

I believe the more I slapped and fucked her in the ass, the more she liked it. And what was so crazy, so did I. I didn't mind beating the fuck out of her, then fucking her hard in the asshole.

She cried, "I love you!"

I put the bitch through turmoil all night.

I told her, "I'm putting you out because I would rather not be with you before beating you. This is not my style bitch."

She said, "SS Boy, I'm sorry. Please, whatever you do, please don't put me out. I don't have anywhere to go. You can beat me some more. Just please, whatever you do, don't throw me out."

I called Sunshine and Little Momma into the bedroom. I knew they were ease dropping and ear hustling anyway.

"Now bitch, ask Little Momma and Sunshine if we need you. All you're doing is making it tough on everyone else."

Quickly, Little Momma and Sunshine said, "Hell no, we don't need her. We were doing just fine before she came."

I said, "Little Momma and Sunshine look what happens to a bitch when she tries to hold out on me. Look at the bitch, two black eyes, busted lips, and whelps all over her body while she stood there with a busted ass hole."

They could clearly see because I wouldn't let the bitch put on any clothes. On top of that a busted asshole, feel that. Special K was standing there looking crazy as ever.

I asked, "How can we trust you on the highway? You might run off and leave us high and dry one thousand miles away from home."

Special K was steady crying, pleading her case, and stating, "I would never do you like that."

I said, "Bitch, pack your shit and get the fuck out of my house."

She was really crying now and begging, "Please give me one more chance."

Finally Sunshine and Little Momma said, "Daddy, maybe we can give her one more chance to do right."

I asked, "Why should I? You two work very hard to please me and we have never had any problems, like this. You know one bad apple can spoil the whole bunch."

Little Momma said, "I feel you SS Boy, but she said she was sorry and she'll never stuff on you again. Please give her one more chance."

I said, "I'll tell you what, since you two are cosigning for Special K, I'll reconsider the scandalous bitch. If she fucks up, I'm holding you two responsible as well. I want eight hundred dollars or more every night. Whoever doesn't make their quota cannot come home until you get my money. Understand me?"

All of them said, "Yes."

I slapped Special K one more time.

& told her, "Don't ever cross me again. Now get the fuck out of my face."

Special K. went into the bedroom with Sunshine. Little Momma stayed in the bedroom with me and smoked a blunt while I rolled Sunshine a joint.

Little Momma said, "Daddy, I'm going to watch every move she make. She better get your money like me and Sunshine."

I was starting to dig Little Momma more and more every day. She was down like four flat tires. After I took a shower & popped some more pimping @ her, I ended up with my dick in her mouth. The bitch fell asleep sucking this big black Indian dick. Little Mamma was like a baby with a pacifier in its mouth, jaws steady sucking even while she was asleep. She put me to sleep.

I woke up the next morning and my dick was still in her mouth. I never had my dick sucked all night before. It wasn't shit though, a pimp need his money.

Little Momma, "Wake up and prepare me some breakfast. Wake those bitches up also and tell them to help you. From here on out, I want breakfast every morning."

Just like my boy Timer, as I thought to myself.

I called Edmond Electronics to make an appointment to get my stereo system installed.

They told me, "You can bring it in immediately."

Sunshine, "Get dressed and jump in the Monte Carlo S.S. & follow me to Edmond."

I told Little Momma, "We'll be ready to eat once we get back."

She said, "Okay, I'll wake Special K and we'll prepare the bomb ass breakfast."

Me & lil mamma headed to Edmond Electronics. I ended up spending more money on eight 12 inch JL audio sub woofers, tweeters, and two crossovers. There was honey gold amps with white neon lights around the eight 12 inch woofers. My shit was going to be banging and hitting harder than thunder.

The manager said, "We'll try to finish today, but we probably won't be done until tomorrow."

I said, "Cool, I'll pay the tab once I come pick it up, alright?"

That was another two thousand and some change. I gave them my 1800 pager number and my home number.

I told them, "Contact me the second it is ready."

We rode off in the Super Sport sitting on all gold Dayton's. Then went home and ate ham and cheese omelets, hash browns, and pancakes. I must admit that it was pretty good.

Special K was acting humble as a little puppy, with two ugly black eyes that I could hardly stand to look at myself (lol). I had to keep it gangster though, and act like the shit didn't affect me at all.

I told the bitch, "You are getting out tonight and you better get my money. I don't give a fuck how ugly you look. You brought that on yourself, now deal with it."

"Okay Daddy, I'll put on plenty of make-up and wear my shades if I have to."

"You do whatever you have to do. Just get my money and no shorts."

Then I twisted up a couple of fat joints and smoked one. I gave the other one to my hookers. Shortly after, my local pager blew up with a page from Kansas City. I returned the call from a pay phone and it was my Kansas City homies who bought the twenty pounds from me a couple of months ago.

They asked, "Is it still on?"

I answered, "Homie, it don't stop. I wondered what happen to you and your home boy. I hadn't heard from ya'll in a minute."

"SS Boy, we are on a serious come up and trying to find a 50 disc CD changer."

I said, "Is that all? Come on with it."

Okay, "Bet, we are on our way, & will be there today sometime."

I decided to get out the house and go to the barber shop to do a little work or shall I say, hang out for a minute.

As soon as I fell up in there, the fella's said, "Nigga, we already heard about it, so where is it?"

I said, "What?"

"That mother fucking Escalade."

I continued, "What are you talking about?"

"SS Boy, quit bullshitting, I seen it. I just didn't know who was driving that clean mother fucker."

"Well, how did you figure it was me?"

S.S., "You know how these niggas in OKC be talking and shit. Now where is it?"

I started laughing and said, "It's in the shop getting some adjustments. I'm getting it ready for these hoes, so they can pay for it."

"Nigga, you have come up in the game over night. Are you sure you haven't bashed a couple of glass cases full of diamonds and Rolexes?"

"No, not yet, but who said I won't? All I need now is about twenty five karats or so."

They said, "Dig that. I need to ride with you SS Boy. When can we see the Cadillac and go turn some corners?"

I said, "Maybe tomorrow if he's out of the shop."

We continued to chop it up. Some boosters came through with several bags of clothes for ladies and men. They had top of the line Liz Claiborne, Coach, Louis Vuitton, Gucci purses, Polo, and Nautica clothes. They had a gang of shit.

I asked, "How much do you want for everything?"

All three of them said, "Hold on."

While walking toward a corner to huddle. The boosters came out with their price, which was eight hundred and fifty dollars.

I asked, "How many men outfits are in there?"

One of the girls said, "Fifteen Polo outfits and maybe ten Nautica outfits. It's even socks to match them."

I said, "I'll tell you what, I'll give you my pager number and eight hundred dollars right now, for everything. Every time you hit, you can call me and I'll buy everything you got, male or female. I prefer for you to get all the male clothes in my size."

They looked at each other and said, "Okay."

I quickly counted out eight hundred dollars. I even gave them a little sticky green, enough for a couple of blunts, just to keep them coming back. They left the barber shop and I carried all the shit out to the drop top Monte Carlo & threw it in the trunk.

My pager blew up with a ten pound bite from Redrum. I had to move around now & go and pick up fourteen pounds from my stash spot. First I had to stop at home and drop these clothes off and then jump in my old bucket to handle business. A hustler grabbed fourteen pounds of the greenery and headed to the North Side of OKC to Redrum's house.

Redrum told his little homie, "Drop the ten thousand dollars and I'll page you after he leaves."

He knew that I didn't like new faces.

I told Redrum, "I have fourteen pounds at seven hundred and fifty dollars each and they total out to ten thousand and five hundred dollars. You can tell him that he owes me five hundred dollars, but you can keep that. Subtract the two hundred dollars I owe you for the stereo equipment."

Redrum said, "That's cool, plus the homie got to drop me something anyway."

I said, "That's right. You should be making a little something from both ends."

Chapter 23

I punched out to the crib to count and restack my money, & neatly placed it in my safe. A young hustler had $82,000.00, 121 pounds of weed, three dedicated hoes, and one nickel slick ass bitch. Everything was going my way. I ended up chilling at the crib that day until it was time for my girls to get ready for work.

My local pager blew up again. It was my people from Kansas City. They were already checked into a motel off the highway.

I told them, "Meet me at McDonalds on the East Side off 23rd Street."

I'll never go to a place where another mother fucker wants me. I'll be setting myself up for a robbery or failure. I'm smarter than that.

Let's meet at McDonald's, Okay "Follow me."

I had them follow me to Big Seamore's spot on the East Side where we made the deal. Everyone left happy. I made them a cool deal. Fifty pounds for $32,500.00 at $650.00 for each pound. We all went our separate ways with big smiles on our faces.

I hurried up and went back home to put this bankroll in the safe. I now had the most money I ever had in my whole life at one time. It was $114,000.00, 71 pounds of greenery, and my bitches were on their way to the track to get my money.

I chilled out all night at home by myself. Getting my game plan together on what I was going to do with all this money.

At four am, Little Momma and the crew fell in, but Special K or no one else was smiling.

I asked, "What up?"

Little Momma said, "Me and Sunshine made our sixteen hundred dollars, but Special K only made three hundred dollars."

I asked Special K, "Bitch, where is my money?"

She cried and said, "Daddy, the tricks won't spend with me because my face and body is all beat up."

Then Sunshine and Lil Momma said, "She is telling the truth Daddy."

Then I told the bitch, "Strip again."

I searched her clothes, pussy, and asshole. She was clean this time. I looked at the bitch's face and body thoroughly and she was fucked up. Her eyes were damn near shut and black as ever.

Bitch, "Get one of those steaks out of the freezer and thaw it out & put that mother fucker on your eyes & face. Tomorrow night you better not come home without my money. See bitch, I'm an easy going fella, but once you make me mad it's hard to cool me off."

They all got in the shower to clean up, and then came back into the living room where I was. After giving them a blunt I went to bed with almost a two thousand dollar night, which wasn't bad.

At ten thirty am, my 1800 pager was blowing up. It was Baby in Nashville. I called her back to see what was up. She sounded even better now, & use to her new job of selling pussy.

I asked her, "How is business Baby?"

Baby answered, "Good."

I asked, "What has your average been?"

She replied, "It's about seven hundred to a thousand dollars a night."

"Baby, that's good. You are doing big things in Nashville."

She giggled and said, "Yeah. When are you coming to see me?"

"I'll be there this weekend or earlier."

S.S. Boy, "Earlier in the week is cool, because my weekends are very busy."

"Alright Baby, I'll be there. You just keep up the good work."

"I love you S.S."

"I love you too Baby."

My girls woke up and started cooking breakfast while I smoked my morning blunt. We ate a good country breakfast of fried chicken, eggs, potatoes, onions, and orange juice. Man that shit was good.

Then I finally remembered that I bought my girls a surprise. I went into the garage to open the trunk of the Monte Carlo SS, & pulled out the bags of clothes. Immediately I went inside and dropped two garbage bags of clothes on the living room floor. Then went back to the garage and grabbed two more garbage bags full of clothes and threw them on the floor next to the other two bags.

Little Momma, Sunshine, and Special K were just looking at the bags wondering what was in them. I pulled out those Nautica, Polo outfits, and those purses. Man those girls were going crazy.

I had to tell them, "Put down everything and step back. Now you three are going to take turns picking your shit. Little Momma, you're first since you are my bottom girl. Then you are next Sunshine. You're last Special K. You shouldn't get shit for stuffing, but I'm not that kind of guy."

She said, "Thank you Daddy."

They ended up with four or five outfits and a purse. I got a few Polo outfits.

The girls were hugging and kissing me & steady saying, "Thank you."

I don't believe Sunshine ever had Polo or Nautica anything before. Now a pimp wanted his surprise and that was my hoe catcher with the system shoving in it. We had to call Edmond Electronics to get the status on my 'Lac.

The owner Mike said, "SS Boy, what's up?"

"You tell me Mike."

Well S.S., "You can start heading this way. We just finished. They are adjusting the sound as we speak."

I said, "Cool, I'm on my way right now. Little Momma, hurry and get dressed so we can go and get my Lac. It's ready."

We were ready and out the door in less than fifteen minutes.

I told Sunshine and Special K, "Be dressed, because we are going to turn a few corners when I get back."

"Okay daddy."

Me and Little Momma jumped in the drop top SS and punched out headed to Edmond Electronics. I got there and heard a system out in the garage. This system had all the windows in the stereo shop vibrating. Finally, Mike came from out of the garage area.

I asked, "Whose shit is that banging like that?"

Mike answered, "SS Boy, that's your shit."

I couldn't believe it. I reached in my pocket and pulled out those big faces (brand new one hundred dollars bills). I noticed that Mike was really checking out Little Momma's sexy ass.

I said, "Mike, before I peel off twenty of these big faces, let me see my shit to check it out."

No problem, "Follow me."

We followed him into the five car garage shop.

I whispered to Little Momma, "He wants you, get at him girl."

We looked inside my truck and the Nakamishi system was sitting up in there so pimpish. Then I went around the back and looked at the eight 12 inch woofers in see through plexi glass. The speakers faced each other with the white neon light around each woofer. He hid the two twelve hundred watt Phoenix gold amps under the two rear captain chairs and the two small Phoenix gold amps under the passenger seat. My system lit up green and the in dash CD player held six discs at one time, with the remote. Mike turned that mother fucker on and I immediately knew that I had too much system. My shit was so loud. The bass was rich and hard hitting that it would practically make your heart skip a beat. That mother fucker was shoving.

Mike asked, "Would you mind if I entered your Cadillac in a car stereo contest?"

"No, it's cool. Do you think I could win something?"

Mike replied, I don't know but you'll have a damn good shot at it. What is your profession?"

I answered, "I'm an entertainment manager."

Mike asked, "Is that your wife?"

"No, she is a good friend of mine."

His eyes lit up with tricking on his mind. I peeled Mike off two thousand dollars and headed back inside the garage leaving him and Little Momma one on one.

I then left the shop shoving and beating on some old Eric B and Rakim, (I Ain't No Joke). My shit was hitting extra hard. You could hear me coming down the block on those gold and chrome twenty inch Daytons (100 spokes). I headed to the East Side. My truck was completely finished and there was nothing else to do to it. Anything else would be uncivilized and ghettoized.

I ended up @ home twisting a few blunts, then ate some leftovers from breakfast. Sunshine and Special K had on one of their new outfits I had bought them. Sunshine was looking good and so was Special K after she put her shades on. I beat the fuck out of that bitch, but she acted like the type who liked ass whoopings. I had to keep it pimping on her.

I said, "Bitch, you ride in the rear of the truck by the two back doors. If we were riding in the M.C. SS, I would put you in the trunk. Just like my old pimp partner Kojack use to do in his clean ass Thunder bird, (rest in peace Kody) and bang that system in your jaw. Feel that. Now let's go."

Sunshine jumped in the front passenger seat and Special K climbed in through the back doors. I pulled out the driveway with my gold Versace shades on. Banging H-Town's (Jezebel) in the bitch's jaw, while she was sitting right under those eight woofers. I was waiting on the bitch to ask me to turn it down, so I could pimp her out some more. But, we rode all over the metroplex, flexing and flossing.

I then went on the East Side to chop it up with my main man, Big Seamore. We drank six point beers from Texas and blew a blunt. We popped pimping in the front yard while looking at my truck. Big Seamore's ex-bitch was sat on the floor board in the back of the truck with two black eyes from trying to play a pimp.

Seamore said, "That's right, keep a foot in the bitch's ass. Keep her ass out on the track all night too."

Seamore, "I wouldn't have it no other way baby."

The bitch probably could feel that we were talking about her. She just laid down on the floor board.

I opened up the rear doors and said, "Bitch don't lie down in my shit."

I made her sit up straight to a pimp's attention.

We proceeded to drink our six point beers and smoke our blunt of sticky green with the Nakamshi shoving up a storm on some of that old Too Short.

Big Seamore replied, "My nigga, you're doing it baby. Keep it pimping and charge these hoes. Pimping ain't dead, just these square hoes been mislead."

"Big Seamore, I've got some new Y2K pimping for these mislead hoes. I'm going to show them affection, send them out the door with instructions, and directions."

"Dig that, my nigga. Pimp baby boy, we pimp from the womb in OKC."

I said, "Feel that. Oklahoma City breeds pimps and hoes."

By the way, "SS Boy, I just peeled a pimp for a hoe. I told the bitch to break herself and she did, that's my hoe now. She has already paid her choosing fees."

"That's right, keep it pimping Big Seamore."

We were feeling good from that good beer and weed.

He said, "I'm Pimping Seamore the pimpinest mother fucker from California to Oklahoma."

A young pimp couldn't do anything but laugh and give him dap.

I stated, "Seamore, you'll come up, long as you stay down you're bound to come up."

Yes sir, "Now SS Boy, let's ride over to this bitch's house."

"Cool, let's ride."

We jumped in the Cadillac Escalade. Sunshine sat in the captain chair directly behind me and Big Seamore sat up front with me where pimps belong. Pimps up hoes down. We jumped on I-35 south banging that Loose Ends (Slow Down). Leaning hard and soliciting to every hoe that pulled on the side of us. I'm sure those square hoes could see that we were pimps, real live pimps with two hoes riding shot gun. Exiting off the highway on SE 66th close to Crossroads Mall.

"Turn here S.S. in this residential area. Stop here."

Big Seamore got out and walked to this house. He came out with the prettiest little white girl. She was looking as innocent as ever. I saw her reach in her pocket and hand Seamore something. Then she went back in the house and Big Seamore came to the truck. Then he reached in his pocket to pull out a bankroll.

He said, "Yeah, I'm going to keep that bitch broke."

I had to put the Short Dog back in and listen to that pimp shit. With all of us headed back to the East Side to Seamore's house. We were putting some pimping down in OKC, leaving bitch's pockets looking like rabbit ears. With Special K riding shot gun in the rear of the hoe train. Steady holding her punk ass ears. The more I thought about that bitch, the angrier I became. If she wasn't careful I would be quick to knock her down again.

I stopped at my traps to pick up money. Everything was cool and steady rolling. Cars were pulling up left and right for the bomb weed! I left my hoes completely in the dark about my weed business, because I'll never trust a bitch and won't tell her shit. It's just better like that. A woman is a lot of hustler's downfall. My YG's had all of my money but a thousand dollars. They knocked their eight thousand dollar tab down to one thousand dollars.

I told the YGs, "I'll be back later on."

My crews were almost out of weed at both spots. After chopping it up for an hour or more. I dropped Seamore off at his crib on the East Side. Headed to my crib to drop the hoes off and to change vehicles. We pulled in the driveway and waited on the electric garage door to open. Little Momma rode up in the drop top SS, & was cheesing from ear to ear.

Little mamma "Are you just getting here?"

"Yes, I've been with the owner of Edmond Electronics."

Oh yeah, "So what's up baby?"

She reached in her pocket and pulled out five hundred dollars of my money. The same money I bought my stereo equipment with.

I said, "Damn, he tricks like that?"

"Yes, & he wants to date and take me out to dinner. I think he likes me."

"Mike must, if he peeled you off five hundred dollars. Five hundred dollars isn't shit to him anyway."

I congratulated her with a blunt and some more pimping.

Okay, "Rest up girls. It's almost time for work. Even you Special K, fuck that black eye shit. You brought that on yourself, now get my money and don't come home with anymore sad stories. Get my money."

"Okay Daddy, please don't get angry at me again."

I walked in my room and closed the door. Leaving them my weed box so they could roll them up one. I had seven thousand, five hundred dollars in my pocket. Having a grand total of $122,000.00 and four dedicated hoes. I still had 51 pounds of sticky green after dropping off the little homies another 20 pounds.

I left the house in the old school Barracuda headed to the country to pick up twenty pounds. Now I knew that it was about time to call Timer and arrange to re-up on some more weed. I hit him on his 1-800 from the pay phone with my code in it. It took him about fifteen minutes to call me back.

I told him, "It's about time again."

Chapter 24

I heard Mexican music in the background.

"Hold tight SS Boy, it's on but I'm in Mexico City right now. I probably won't be your way until early in the week."

Okay Timer, "Cool, be careful. The girls and I are headed to Nashville tomorrow night. I'm going to stop at every truck stop in between."

Timer replied, "That's right. I can tell you which truck stops to work."

I asked, "Which ones are cool?"

In answer Timer ask, "Are you taking I-40?"

"Yes." I replied

Okay first, "Stop in Shawnee, Oklahoma it's a big truck stop right off the highway. Then stop in Little Rock, Arkansas at the rest area to work those hoes. There are a few spots in Memphis to work. I would tell you where the hoe stroll is in Memphis. You do want to work the truck stops right?"

"Yes sir, this is a test run trip. I just want to see where my girls stand Big Bro."

"That's right lil Bro, once you get to Nashville it's on. You'll see several large rest areas and truck stops off the highway."

I said, "Big Bro., I really appreciate that game. Tomorrow is Wednesday and we are pulling out, & should be back Monday night."

Timer said, "I might be back in town by then. We'll go out to lunch or something."

After speaking with Timer I prepared myself a nice evening martini which was a double shot of Remy Martin on the rocks. Thinking about my trip that I was about to take with these girls. I was also wondering how much was in my trap in Nashville from Baby.

Early Wednesday morning, my three hookers came home from a long night on the track. It took them a little while longer to make their quota, but they seemed to pull it off. The girls handed me twenty five hundred dollars, & smelling like a pound of raw unwashed pussy.

I asked, "Special K, how much did you make?"

She hesitated and answered, "I only made six hundred and some change."

Little Momma and Sunshine said, "Daddy, that's why we are just coming home. We had to help her make her quota."

I replied, "Dig that, you two must really care about her. After all, you did co-sign for her, stating that you'll help her."

Special K was just standing there quiet as a mouse and hoping that I didn't lean into her with an over hand right punch to her grill (mouth) or something. I ended up letting the girl slide and dismissing her of all charges. I just had to put a little fear in the bitch and let her know and these other hoes know that I'm not playing games.

I told all three of them, "We are taking a little trip to Nashville TN. tonight so everyone needs to handle their business and get prepared. Ladies, be ready for work because we are stopping at every truck stop from here to Nashville. Plus doing the same thing on the way back."

All of their faces lit up waiting to get on the highway. They were looking for a change, besides OKC.

I said, "Ladies, it's time to see what you are made of. It's going to be a lot of pimping, pandering, and hoe handling."

Little Momma just sat there smiling, listening, and rolling up a joint @ the same time.

They said, "Daddy, don't go to sleep. We are going to shower and clean up. Will you smoke with us and feed us more game about the trip?"

"Yeah, but ya'll hurry up because I'm tired."

While they showered, I rolled three more joints. Now we all had a joint each. It's hard for me to smoke after a bitch that sucks dicks all night. That would make a pimp a second hand dick sucker (lol) and I'm not with that.

We smoked our joints and I laid my pimping on these hoes real thick.

Telling them, "Now don't make me look bad. I'm testing ya'll out here on this highway. If you fuck up, I might leave you out there in the middle of nowhere."

I was looking directly at Special K's slick ass.

They all said, "Daddy, we won't let you down. You have been by our side and we will stay by yours."

"At least I know I will Daddy", said little Momma.

The other two said, "& so will we."

Special K said, "Daddy, I'm not mad at you. A bitch messed up and you beat my ass real good. I also learned that you're not like my other boyfriends. I'll never stuff on you again. I never had a man beat my ass like you did. Most guys I can tell them whatever I want to."

"Well Special K, that sounds like you're learning the difference between a boyfriend and a pimp. I play hoes like you play songs on a CD. I've fucked with all types of hoes, like nobody knows sports like Bo. Nobody knows hoes like SS Boy, you feel me?"

I left them in the living room talking, then walked into the bedroom and laid down. Leaving some Y2K pimping on their minds. I woke up about one pm and headed to the barber shop, needing to prepare myself for the highway. Pimping got to keep his appearance together, by keeping his hair and nails done. I cruised to the barber shop while smoking my first blunt of the day. A player was shoving on some of that Tru and Master P. I was thinking about my riches. I pulled in the parking lot and all my homies came out of the barber shop to check out this hoe catcher and this pounding as Nakimitshi system. The fellas constantly gave me my props and dap.

They all said, "You got the cleanest truck in the city, hands down. SS Boy, you have come up baby boy. Pimping pays like that? I thought pimping was dead."

I said, "No, just these hard headed hoes been mislead."

They laughed, but were feeling me at the same time. All of them knew that I was serious about what I said. My barber trimmed me up and gave me a shave. I dropped him twenty dollars just because he was down like that and had me looking pimp tight.

He asked me, "When are we going out in the Escalade?"

I told him, "We'll chop it up once I get back from out of town."

Then gave him dap and jumped back in the 'Lac to fire up my blunt that I didn't get to finish, headed to my boy Big Seamore's house. As I turned on his block to see him and the whole Prospect Posse. These brothers were the definition of true to the game, some real O.G.s. Congratulators not haters. Even though they didn't have it like me and Big Seamore, they still showed much love without a speck of jealousy. As a matter of fact, they were having a little block party, with the barbeque grill blazing and the music bumping. Big Seamore was wiping off his clean old school Olds 98 with the chrome and gold Daytons sitting on Vogue tires. I pulled up and they really rolled out the red carpet for a player.

I asked, "What else do we need to throw on the grill?"

I reached deep in my Karl Kani jeans and peeled off two brand new big face's (hundred dollar bill). I had the ladies go to the store and get some t-bone steaks, a couple fifths of Remy Martin, and a couple of cases of beer.

Seamore said, "What up SS Boy?"

"I'm getting ready to put these hoes on the highway tonight."

He said, "Is that right, where are you headed?"

"I'm hitting every truck stop between here and Nashville."

"Shit, I might need to roll right behind you with my stable."

I said, "Stable, that's right. I'm two snow bunnies deep and one possible. I need a vacation, what's up? Big Seamore you ain't said nothing. Let's take our pimping from state to state then."

"Hold up SS Boy, you haven't said shit."

Big Seamore jumped on his mobile horn (phone) and called his girls and told them, "Get ready to take a fantastic voyage."

I couldn't do anything but laugh and say, "Pimp then my nigga. Big Seamore, tell your hoes to be ready to roll out by seven o'clock tonight."

I was puffing on a phat blunt that was just handed to me.

"Are you serious?"

He said, "Hell yeah, you know I love to hit the highway."

"SS Boy, we have been hitting the highway together since high school."

I told Big Seamore and the Prospect Posse, "I will be back before the steaks are ready. Save me a shot of Remy Martin."

I headed out to Redrum's house to get some more of that good ass powder. Really I needed about a quarter ounce (7 grams). Redrum was still infatuated by my truck.

Redrum asked, "Can I drive it around the block?"

"Sure, but hurry up, I'm in a rush."

That's exactly what he did and came back shaking his head.

Saying, "Damn that system I sold you shoves."

We went inside and weighed out 7 grams of that powder. As he was sacking my shit up, I saw the new Y2K Passport Escort radar detector on his table. I had to have it.

Redrum said, "Throw me a bill ($100.00) for it."

I hurried up and peeled him off a big face and he threw me the 7 grams.

He said, "O.G. SS Boy, you know I don't charge you for shit. Nigga, you put me back on my feet."

I gave him dap and pimped right out the front door with Redrum right behind me.

Okay, "Let me show you how this Passport works."

Redrum got in on the passenger side of the Lac, licked the two suction cups and stuck the Passport to the windshield. After that he plugged it into the cigarette lighter. That mother fucker started chirping &

shit. Redrum explained to me how it works and how to read it. I gave him dap, thanked him, and punched out. Then rushed to my house to put up the powder. I stopped at the pit stop to get an oil change and everything checked out.

They said, "Your shit is ready for the highway or where ever you are going."

I headed to the East Side after filling my tank with super premium unleaded gasoline, which cost me 100 dollars. Everything was jumping off on the East Side. The crew partying, kids playing, and eating burgers. I like to see that kind of activity. That's what having money is all about.

I told Seamore, "My shit is ready to eat up some highway."

He said, "A pimp stay ready to keep from getting ready. My baby, (his car) has already been to the doctor's office for a physical."

We ate our steaks and had double shots of Remy Martin. Nor did we drink too much or our trip would've been delayed until we sobered up. I had a good time.

Seamore, "I'll be back at about seven o'clock and ready to ride. I'm going home to take a pimp nap and get my clothes packed."

Okay S.S., "I'll be ready. I'm going to pick up my hoes about six o'clock."

At seven o'clock sharp, my girls and I were pulling up on the East Side at Big Seamore's house in the Cadillac Escalade. I didn't see my Boy or his Olds 98, & the Prospect Posse was still partying.

They told me, "Big Seamore said hold tight, he is on his way. He'll be here in less than ten minutes."

"Cool, I'll be right back. I'm headed to Bryon's Liquor store."

I had to pick up my own personal fifth of Remy Martin, & return back to the set in less than twenty minutes. Seamore and his two snow bunnies were right there waiting on me to Cadillac turn around the corner. I turned the corner into the hood and the kids looked up and seen who it was. They started doing the C-walk while I was banging that Big Bang Theory. I let down all the windows and kept the Lac running with the system still pounding. Now I had to get out and show the YGs how a pimp C-walk and do the pimp step.

I asked Seamore, "Are you ready?"

In reply, "A pimp stay ready to keep from getting ready."

Yes sir, "Dig that. Let's put these hoes on the highway. We need to be in Shawnee before the sun goes down."

Chapter 25

We gave everyone dap and I jumped in the Escalade with my three girls. He jumped in the Olds 98 with his two fine ass snow bunnies. Me, & Seamore punched out flexing and zig zagging in the hood and doing Cadillac turns and shit. When we passed our homies on 23rd street. People were hitting their horns and throwing up peace signs, giving a pimp support.

We jumped onto I-40 east bumper to bumper, with our Versace shades on. Seamore's dark candy 4 door Olds 98 was looking good with that sun light hitting on those chrome and gold Daytons and Vogue tires. He didn't have any tint on the windows either. That exposed those white leather guts (interior) with dark candy piping and buttons on the seats and door panels.

All of us arrived in Shawnee right on time. There were truckers everywhere. We stopped at the store and bought condoms & also grabbed two cups of ice.

"Seamore let's work these girls for a couple of hours then get on down the highway to Little Rock, Arkansas."

"Okay S.S. I just want to see what these white hoes are made of."

I told him, "Shit, let's go find out. I'm going to work my hoes until their feet look like deer hooves, you feel me?"

We jumped back in our separate cars and went down the street to drop our hoes off at the truck stop. Then parking directly across the street at the car wash, to keep an eye on our investments.

Both of us explained to our hookers, "Catch the train at ten o'clock, two hours from now."

We parked in the stalls at the car wash. I poured a couple of drinks, blazed up a blunt, and popped pimping. I was concentrating on nothing but pulling grands out of my bitches womb and coming up with a bank roll.

"Seamore, we'll probably take our pimp hats off in Little Rock and stay all night, & let the girls work until the sun comes up."

He asked, "Won't they be tired?"

"My hoes better rest up while I'm driving and be ready to hit the ground running."

Seamore said, "Feel that, they can sleep while we drive, that's right."

We continued to pop pimping until about ten o'clock. Our girls came from across the street with big smiles on their faces. They were being very discreet because the sheriffs had come out. It was time to dip (leave). We got back on the highway, I-40 east, headed to Little Rock, Arkansas. Little Rock was about five and half hours away. It was most definitely time to mash on these pimp wagons and get on down the highway.

I did alright for two hours of work in Shawnee. I broke Little Momma for one hundred and seventy five dollars, Sunshine for two hundred dollars, and Special K for one hundred and forty dollars. That equaled out to five hundred and fifteen dollars.

They said, "Pimping Seamore's girls were getting down and getting plenty of tricks."

I said, "Ya'll need to quit watching them and concentrate on your own money. Now handle your business."

I gave them a blunt and plenty more pimping while rolling down the highway listening to Changing Faces. While sipping on Remy Martin and loving the feel of this game in my new Cadillac Escalade sitting on twenty inches. My pimp partner was right behind me with a car full of dedicated hookers. We rolled up in Little Rock at about four o'clock in the morning. I had my hoes programmed to hit the ground running as soon as the pimp wagon stops.

Giving them strict instructions, "Do not stop until eight o'clock in the morning. You should have your quota. We are getting motel rooms right across the highway. It if gets hot (police) do not come to the motel. Hide until they leave and page me on the 1-800 if there are any problems."

I guess Big Seamore told his girls about the same. We headed across the highway to a little motel, & got two rooms with double beds. I pulled out a little powder. We chopped it up for a little while; while getting fucked up.

Seamore said, "I did all right in Shawnee. I broke my hoes for about four hundred dollars."

Before we knew it, it was seven forty five in the morning. Time to pick up the girls who had been out there all night. When we pulled up, our girls came to the truck. We all headed to the motel room. I wasn't even tired yet from snorting that good blow (coke) and I was really hype. I broke my bitches for another eight hundred and twenty five dollars. That gave me a total of $1,340.00 for the first night out on the highway.

Pimping Seamore was doing good too, he broke his hoes for another five hundred and fifty dollars, which gave him a total of $950.00.

I said, "See baby boy, I told you to stay down and now it's paying off. I'm going to put more pimping down on these girls and get me a little shut eye. Let's ride out of here about five o'clock. It takes about two and half or three hours to get to Memphis from here and we'll work them all night long in Memphis."

Seamore said, "Cool."

He went to his room with his girls and I went into my room where my girls were. My stable loved this new atmosphere and excitement. They were ready for the world and so was I. They all cleaned up and got into the other bed. I noticed Little Momma and Special K looking at each other crazy.

I asked, "What's up with you two?"

Little Momma quickly said, "Special K wants to sleep with you."

"It's cool since it's three of you in one bed."

"No Daddy, I mean make love to you. That's all she talk about."

I asked Special K, "What's up with you?"

"Baby, I just want to make love to my man. I've been doing the best I can for you."

I replied, "Dig that, now come over here."

Now Little Momma and Sunshine's eyes were fire ball red. I knew that I couldn't fuck this new bitch in their faces without any repercussions behind it. So I let Special K get into my bed and we hugged up while I spit pimping at her.

Then she asked, "Can I taste you?"

I said, "Why not? A pimp needs love too."

She got down on this big black dick like a champion head hunter (lol). That made Sunshine and Little Momma very jealous while they laid in the bed next to us watching in amazement. Special K could really suck some dick too. She swallowed every drop of a pimp's cum, just like I liked it. Bitch better not waste a single drop. Before I knew it, I was passed out asleep and so was she. About four o'clock, we all woke up from Big Seamore knocking on the door hard. I got up and answered the door.

What up? "We are up and we'll be ready to roll at five. I'm getting in the shower now."

I noticed that Little Momma had an attitude.

Little Momma, "Come wash my back for me while I'm in the shower."

I really needed to straighten her out & do some crowd control before things got out of hand with her and Special K, you dig?

Little Mamma, "You are my bottom girl, so quit tripping. You better not run Special K off or we will have some serious problems."

She explained, "I get so jealous to see anyone with you."

I said, "Baby you can't be like that. They deserve some love too every once in a while. If I never showed affection to them, they will feel that I don't care about them. Now would you want me to work the shit out of you and never show you that I appreciate your hard work & loyalty?"

She quietly answered, "No."

I could read the expression on her face that she was feeling me and slowly coming around again with a calm and cool attitude.

I said, "Baby, now let's get this money and have a good time. It's all going to pay off for us Beautiful."

I got out the shower and got dressed. The girls put on their sexy outfits and were ready to work Memphis. I put on my white linen Polo shirt, Polo pants, and my Polo shoes with the buckle across. With all my little pieces of jewelry, my blue face Rolex, and my gold Versace shades. I pimped to Seamore's room, & walked straight in. Big Seamore's girls were sitting there waiting to ride and get this money. Pimping had his girls turned all the way up, and they were also dressed nice and looking good. We were pimp tight and ready to take our pimping to a new city & a new level, Memphis, Tn.

Seamore had ten blunts rolled up already.

I asked him, "Give me a few blunts so we can ride out right now. Or do you want to wait for me to roll up a few blunts?"

He then handed me four blunts and said, "Bro, let's ride and get this paper."

"You haven't said shit."

I left the room to load up the Escalade with clothes and hoes. We were out of there in less than ten minutes. My girls were down, set, and ready to go. Little Momma jumped in the front passenger seat next to me, the captain of the ship. Sunshine and Special K were in the back captain seats directly behind me.

Ladies, "Tonight is an old school night."

I put in some of that old Morris Day and the Time (Don't Wait for Me, Oaktree, Color of Success). We made a stop at the store for gas and drinks. Pimping Seamore filled up the 98. It was now time to roll. My girls were really feeling that Morris Day after they smoked their first blunt of the day. We were having one big party while flossing down the highway. It was on.

Seamore would zoom by me on the highway throwing up the peace sign. He and his snow bunnies were leaning so hard that I could barely see them. I followed behind him for a while. He also had a top of the line Y2K Passport radar detector. There was no way my Cadillac Escalade could out run his old school 98 with the new 455 4 barrel motor in it. The glass pack dual pipes came out the rear, so I wasn't testing him. Seamore also loves to mash on that big candy catcher.

We were headed over the new bridge in West Memphis, which is really Arkansas, the home of former President Bill Clinton. Bill was a cool mother fucker in my books.

All we had to do now was pick out a Memphis or West Memphis truck stop or rest area. We ended up stopping at the truck stop off the highway in West Memphis. I had all three of my girls on super charge and feeling extra good. They were ready to break their backs for a pimp.

I told them, "I'll be back in a little while after I find us a motel room."

They said, "Cool."

My girl's opened the 'Lac doors and hit the ground running with a pimp's instruction. They were soliciting their services to the truck drivers. Big Seamore's girls did the exact same thing.

He followed me down the highway until we ran into a Motel 6 or Super 8. Soon we found a nice motel about four or five miles away from the truck stop. Both of us rented two rooms with double beds and extra towels. We unloaded our vehicles and I pulled out the Remy Martin and blow (coke). Big Seamore pulled out a couple of blunts that he didn't smoke from when we left Little Rock, Arkansas.

It was now about nine thirty in the evening or so. Pimping and I were having a good time. We were having a two man pimp rally getting turned up & putting each other on super charge.

I said, "Seamore, I should be sitting phat by the time we get back."

He replied, "So should I."

I said, "You know I put Baby on automatic in Nashville at the whore house."

Out of all the bitches in the world, I never thought she could be flipped and selling pussy."

"Conversation rules the nation. If a bitch listens to me for five minutes, I've got her."

Big Seamore gave me dap and said, "Dig that."

I said, "My bitch, Baby Girl, should have a nice bank roll for a young pimp. That's why I came to Tn."

Seamore said, "That's right, because time is money and money is time."

We chopped it up until midnight drinking, tooting, and smoking. My sinuses were draining with nothing but good cocaine. My gums and tongue were numb as ever. I was fucked up and so was Seamore.

Big Seamore, "It's time for me to go and check my trap."

"Me too S.S."

So we jumped in the 98, headed to the truck stop. As soon as we pulled up, we saw action everywhere. Pimps were dropping bitches off and picking bitches up. It was big shit popping and little shit dropping. Big Seamore's girls finally noticed him and came over to him.

I told him, "After you handle your business, tell your girls to go and get my girls bro."

Pimping Seamore broke his two snow bunnies and sent them back out the door with instructions. Little Momma and Special K came, but Sunshine was still busy with a trick.

Little Momma broke herself for two hundred and sixty dollars. Special K broke herself for two hundred and seventy five dollars. That fucked me up because she never made more than Little Momma. I guess all she needed was a little dick from her man and to be shown some affection. Finally, Sunshine came and broke herself of almost two hundred and fifty dollars, & it was on. I just broke those hoes for seven hundred and eighty five dollars.

I told them, "I'll be back in a couple of hours. I need a grand each tonight ladies."

Chapter 26

We pulled off and headed back to the room to finish parlaying.

"SS Boy, this is the life. We need to stay on the highway for months at a time."

"I just broke my hoes for almost six hundred dollars with more pimping to come."

Then I pulled out my brand new knot and threw it on the bed.

Big Seamore, "That's about eight hundred dollars."

Both of us went and got fresh ice. We were popping pimping all the way to the ice machine. Putting fresh ice in our cups and pouring up another double shot of Remy Martin, & had a toast to pimping.

Seamore said, "I'll be ready to re-up on the greenery once we get back to OKC. I'm ready for you Bro., it don't stop."

I said, "You should be ready to buy about fifty pounds."

"I'm going to try once I get finished with the five pounds I have left."

Okay Seamore, "Come with everything you can come up with. I'm going to make you a monster deal and put you down on whatever you buy."

Seamore just sat there smiling. I could actually see dollar signs in his eyes. Time was rolling by quick like it always does when you're having fun. It was now three o'clock in the morning and we were tore up from the floor up. We weren't staggering drunk, but real mellow from the powder and weed. It was time to go and check our traps again & break these hoes for every dime.

I said, "Seamore, let's switch vehicles this time and ride in the Escalade."

Big Seamore answered okay, "Let's ride."

We jumped in the 'Lac and drove off. Listening to Eminem and Dr Dre (Who's the real slim shady). As soon as we pulled up at the track, we noticed a sheriff's police car leaving with someone in the back seat. Little Momma and Sunshine came out of nowhere. They were running fast and breathing heavy. They got in the back seat and started telling me some bad news.

Daddy, "Some girls (hookers) robbed a trick for his money and got the whole track hot. Just so happened, Special K was getting out of an 18 wheeler. The sheriff pulled up, sees her, and then arrests her."

I said, "Damn, where is my money?"

They both said, "Oh."

While handing me the money. It was another five hundred and twenty five dollars.

I told Sunshine, "Go get Seamore's hoes for him. Call International Bail Bonding Company and get your wife n law out of jail."

Big Seamore's girls came & told him the same story and they broke themselves.

Explaining to Sunshine, "What's up? Keep working and be careful."

"Little Momma and I are going to get Special K out of jail. She is in the Memphis County Jail on Popular Ave."

Sunshine replied, "Okay."

My girl went back to work along with Big Seamore's girls. We took Little Momma with us and headed back to the room to find International Bail Bonding Company in Memphis TN. It was black owned and they were cool. They were just trying to make a living. I let Little Momma give them the information they needed.

They said, "Call back in ten minutes."

We did just that.

The owner told Little Momma, "Call back in twenty minutes this time. She just arrived at the jail and hasn't been booked in yet. We don't know what charges she has been arrested on or her bail amount yet."

Little Momma asked me, "Can I take a shower and get cleaned up?"

"Sure, you can't go down there dressed like a lady of the night."

Little Momma called back when she got out the shower and got dressed.

The bonding company told us, "Her charges were soliciting and prostitution, which isn't shit in Memphis. It's a fine really. Her bond is two hundred and fifty dollars. She had two hundred and thirty five dollars with her at the time of her arrest. Meet me in front of Memphis County Jail in twenty or thirty minutes."

Little Momma then asked, "What are the directions there?"

It was damn near in the heart of downtown Memphis.

He told her, "I will be in a black Cadillac."

Little Momma said, "I'll be in a pearl white Cadillac truck."

The bail bondsman was already sitting in front of the county jail when we pulled up, just waiting on his money. Since he looked cool, I walked over to greet him with Little Momma. I left Pimping Seamore in the truck. I know that bondsman knew, that I was a pimp and these were my hoes.

The bondsman asked, "Are you guys from here?"

"No sir, just passing through."

He said, "You can pay me five hundred dollars and never have to return for a court date or anything."

Okay, "Yes, let's do that."

I had Little Momma to hand him two hundred and sixty five dollars.

Also, "You can have the two hundred and thirty five dollars on her books."

He went in and came out with Special K. She was so happy that I stayed true. I immediately came to bond her out of jail. I must admit that Memphis has one of the most sophisticated jail systems in America.

Special K got in the truck all teeth and gums.

Stating, "I will make up that five hundred dollars bail money to you S.S. Boy. Thank you for coming to get me so quickly."

I said, "See baby, I stay true to you and I want you all to stay true to me. Ya'll don't want me to start playing games. I told all of you that I would make your bond before the ink dries on the incident report."

We headed back to the track and I let Little Momma out to work her jelly. I ended up giving Special K the night off, just in case that same sheriff comes through again and notices her. This time she probably wouldn't get out as quick, plus add a court date for sure this time. Special K got in the bath tub and soaked for a little while.

I told Big Seamore, "Let's pick up the girls from the track about six am or so."

Okay S.S., "Cool."

Big Seamore headed back to his motel room right next door to take a pimp nap. I laid down watching some weird ass movie on HBO. Special K came out of the bathroom ass hole naked and smelling good from the body lotion she wears. I must admit that Special K had a body out of this world and knew how to work it. She came and laid right up under me. Her fat ass was just wiggling, big titties jiggling and firm. Her nipples were rock hard.

I already knew what she had on her mind. I can't lie. She had my dick hard as ever looking like the Washington monument. It was harder than times in 1929 for a black man (lol). The cocaine and Remy Martin were behind this rock hard dick. Since little Momma and Sunshine weren't around, I might as well test out this honey hole.

Special K was all over me with her fine ass. She was unzipping my pants and licking on my chest. Then she pulled this hard black Indian dick out. Special K couldn't wait to put it in her mouth. She was sucking dick and playing with her pussy at the same time. While K. was sucking this dick, I pulled my shirt off. She helped pull my pants off with the dick still in her mouth. K. was a diabolical freak. I started licking on her titties and playing with her soaking wet pussy. She was fiending for me to lay this pipe in her. Steady trying to put it in for me and I kept resisting; making her fiend even more. Finally, I strapped up and rammed all 9 inches in her, hard and fast as I could. She grunted like I hit her with a Mike Tyson body blow to the mid-section or something (lol). I pulled out just leaving the head of this monster in her. Then I spreaded her legs as wide as they would go and lifted them up to almost my shoulder level and started long dicking this hoe. I had the bitch trying to back stroke through the head board as she was trying to push me out of her, while moaning loud as hell. Special K was definitely a moaner and a screamer and that turned me on even more.

I was steady long dicking and asking her, "How do you like this dick?"

She barely could talk but managed to say, "Oh, you got some good dick Daddy. You're fucking this pussy just like I like it."

I must have fucked her for thirty or fourty minutes straight without cumming. Thanks to the good cocaine. I turned her over doggie style and spreaded her legs as wide as they would go. I slammed this big black Indian dick in her with one of my fingers in her asshole. She came several times, multiple orgasms. After she finished trembling, yelling, moaning, and cumming, she just wanted me to lay still with this dick still in her. I could feel her pussy pulsating like a heartbeat. Her pussy muscles had contracted & extracted around my dick. For some reason, that made me want to cum. I rolled her back over on her back and lifted up those legs. I spreaded those big pretty legs again and started hitting that good pussy.

She said, "Daddy pull out when you cum, cum in my mouth please."

It wasn't five minutes later and my motor locked up (lol). I pulled out of her pussy. She immediately sat up in the bed and snatched off the condom. Baby girl grabbed my dick and put it into her mouth. I was now moaning. She swallowed every drop until there was no more. After she got finished, she licked her lips and fingers for extras.

Special K. said, "Um that was good."

We both got into the shower to clean up. K was a true diabolical dick sucker, and was one of the best I had ever encountered. After the shower, she climbed back into bed. I called Big Seamore to see if he was awake.

, "Hell yeah I'm woke, how can a pimp sleep next door to your room? You fucked the shit out of that bitch."

"Yes sir, I had to put in work."

Seamore said, "I'm listening to ya'll. I'm gonna have to fuck my girls early in the morning now."

I said, "Feel that. Let's go pick them up."

We followed each other to the truck stop to pick up our girls. Sunshine relieved herself of three hundred dollars and Little Momma made another quick one hundred and seventy dollars. I would have had a damn good day if Special K wouldn't have gone to jail. I grossed a total of two thousand and fifteen dollars. After jail costs, I ended up with about fifteen hundred dollars, which was still cool.

We went back to the room after stopping at the I-Hop to pick up some food. Special K was laying there sound asleep and asshole naked under the sheets. I woke her up to invite her to eat with us. She had a patty melt, hash browns, and orange juice.

Little Momma and Sunshine probably suspected something, but never let their suspicion out of the bag. They were real smart about that. Never question a pimp about what I do with my stable. Little Momma and Sunshine took a shower. I laid in bed with nothing but my silk Polo boxers, my robe, and medallion on around my neck.

Little Momma and Sunshine got out the shower.

They asked, "Can we lay down with you?"

"Sure ladies."

I'm also sure that they had freaking on their minds. Not tonight, or shall I say this morning.

Get some rest girls, "Go to sleep. We have a big day ahead of us."

I knew if I fucked these hoes frequently and allowed them to give me head that these diabolical freaks could and would turn me out. Then I wouldn't let the bitches work, because I would be a freaky sex addict. I had to keep my dick out of them and fuck them only when absolutely, positively necessary.

We didn't wake up until about six pm that evening. Seamore and his stable slept in also. I guess everyone was a little exhausted, but we finally got out of bed and started getting dressed.

I called Big Seamore's room on the motel telephone to ask him, "Will you be ready to pull out of here about seven o'clock?"

He said, "Hell yeah, I'm good and rested up now. Is it time to roll?"

"Yeah, I'm also rested up and feeling good. I'm ready for Nashville."

At seven o'clock sharp, we were in the parking lot with our vehicles loaded up. Ready for our three hour trip from Memphis to Nashville. I couldn't wait to get there so I could pick up my grip (money). I had already rolled two blunts, one for me and one for my girls. We made one last stop at the store. Pimping Seamore had to fill up again. My shit was still on three fourths of a tank, so I just filled my shit back up to the rim. The girls and I got soft drinks, gum, condoms, another box of green leaf Optimos, and a couple of lighters.

We were on the highway in no time. I put in some of that old ass Vanity 6 (Nasty Girls). My girls loved that song.

They kept asking, "Play it again Daddy."

Then I hit them with some of the old Cherrelle. We jammed all the way to Nashville, nonstop.

I said, "Ladies, after this last song, I'll have some shout outs on whatever you want to hear."

Now we were on some of that old Prince (Do me baby). Those hoes almost passed out in their seats. They were giving each other dap and shit.

The girls were saying, "That's the shit Daddy."

I had those eight twelve inch woofers shoving up a storm. The surround sound of the Nakimishi made the music sound like Prince and the Revolution were in the back seat. We had already passed up a nice rest area with plenty of truckers. We were looking for the ultimate feast; a shit load of truckers meant more money. So we kept rolling.

The girls made their request for a shout out.

They asked, "Do you have Melvin Riley? He is the lead singer from Ready for the World?"

I quickly hit them with some (Now who's is it). I let Melvin Riley's shit bang all the way through. Finally, we rode up on the mother load. It was a truck stop rest area with over one hundred 18 wheelers in a huge parking lot. I immediately got off the highway on the next available exit with Seamore right behind me. It also had several nice motels across the street. That was right up our alley. We could stand or sit on the balcony and watch all the action from across the street.

I told Seamore, "I'm going to rent two motel rooms."

I would get one for pimping (me) and one for the hoes and business. The main deal was I didn't want tricks or anyone else watching hookers come to a pimp's room. Some player haters might call the police on us.

Seamore said, "That's right, I'm doing the same thing."

We got the motel rooms and I explained the situation to my girls.

Chapter 27

"This is how we are going to work this track. Everyone needs to be discreet and low key because we are going to be here for a couple of days. Whatever you do, don't come to my room. I'll come to yours or you call me. You know my room number. Walk across the street to the track one at a time. I wouldn't want everyone seeing three women headed over there @ the same time. They will know what time it is for sure, if you did that. We will sneak up on the money and hit fast and hard before the dust settles. We'll be long gone with a fat bank roll before anyone knows it."

They were game for that plan.

I told Seamore, "Make your girls walk over one at a time too. Now that's what I call sending them out the door with instructions."

Before I knew it, they were all over there working their jelly. Every time they got two hundred and fifty dollars, they had to come and drop it off on the D L! I couldn't wait to call up to Meeko's and talk to Baby. I was able to talk with her for a brief second.

I told her, "I am in town. Here is my phone number and motel room number."

Baby said, "I'll call you back as soon as I get a break."

I said, "Come on Big Seamore. Let's find a liquor store. It's almost time to celebrate."

We jumped in the Escalade and found a nearby liquor store. I purchased two bottles of Moet champagne. Seamore bought a couple of bottles of champagne, not so expensive, just something to sip on. I also bought an ice chest for two bags of ice so we could chill our bottles, & head back to the room.

Everyone was paying close attention to us in the Escalade. It had a touch of gold, was sitting on chrome and gold twenty inch Daytons, and was beating up a storm. The ten thousand dollar Nakimishi sound system, Phoenix Gold amps, JL audio, eight twelve inch sub woofers with the Oklahoma license plates. We were clean as a white dove with money on our minds concentrating on nothing but keeping these hoes broke and full of pimping. I could really see myself getting rich in this game like big pimping Don Juan out of Chi-town (Chicago) or Benzo out of Kansas City.

I told Seamore, "If I had a stable of twenty hoes like Benzo, I could easily see ten thousand dollars a night."

Big Seamore was just sitting there jamming, thinking, and absorbing this game I'm putting him down on. He had dollar signs in his eyes. We got back inside the motel room and continued to chop it up and pop pimping. Seamore started breaking down an Optimo cigar and filling the green leaf paper with sticky green.

I said, "Hold up before you roll that."

I grabbed my little stash of that ether based powder cocaine and laced up that blunt with almost a fifty paper (half a gram). That left us with a couple of grams for the weekend, which was cool. Seamore popped open one of his less expensive bottles of champagne and we started drinking and smoking. Boy, that laced blunt had me higher than a mother fucker. I even broke out in a little sweat.

The telephone rang.

It was Little Momma asking, "Can you come see me in my room?"

I went over and Little Momma quickly relieved herself of two hundred and seventy dollars.

She told me, "It's on over there. Sunshine is on her way over as soon as I get back across the street, so wait here."

Little Mamma took off out the door to catch this trick. She claimed that he wanted to spend big money on her.

I said, "Go get him baby."

Ten minutes later, Sunshine came and I broke her for two hundred and sixty dollars real quick.

She said, "It's on over there. Hold tight because Special K is on her way."

As she was leaving, I noticed one of Seamore's girls headed our way.

I called him from my room and told him, "Go check your trap. I think you have a bite."

Special K came in with a big smile on her face. I broke her for two hundred and eighty dollars.

I said, "I thought I told you to come and drop off at the two hundred and fifty dollar mark?"

"Daddy, I had two hundred and thirty dollars and had to turn one more trick to get two hundred and fifty dollars. The trick gave me a tip."

I said, "Dig that. Keep up the good work. I want one thousand dollars or better out of you tonight."

She headed out the door and back to the track. I was having a good night so far. I already broke my girls for eight hundred and ten dollars in a couple of hours. Plus we still had six hours or so before the sun came up. Baby still hadn't called me. I guess she was busy as hell with those tricks. That was a good sign. We kept sipping and popping pimping.

Seamore stated, "I am also having a terrific night."

About two in the morning, my telephone rang again. It was Special K.

I told her, "I will be right over."

Big Seamore stood on the balcony waiting on his pigeon to land again. Special K relieved herself for another two hundred and sixty dollars.

She said, "The other two will be over here when I leave. I am going to make up the five hundred dollars from last night in Memphis, Tn."

Special K. left out the door again. Sunshine relieved herself of my money, which was two hundred and fifty five dollars.

She said, "Daddy, I'm waiting on my chance to be with you all alone."

I already figured out what she was getting at. She figured that I fucked Special K last night and now she wants me.

All I could say was, "Baby, you got that coming. We will be one on one."

She quickly said, "Okay."

Leaving out the door with a big smile on her pretty face. This time, Little Momma was the last one to make her quota. I broke her for another two hundred and sixty dollars and sent her back out the door with instructions. Now I just got paid a new bankroll of seven hundred and seventy five dollars. It was just a little over halfway to the three thousand dollar mark.

Seamore was back on the balcony. I thought he was still waiting on his pigeons to land.

He said, "I already broke my girls for a bankroll. I got over a thousand dollars."

"That's right. I broke mine for almost sixteen hundred dollars."

S.S. Boy, "It's time to pop my other bottle of champagne."

I said, "Dig that. Pimping is hard work. We deserve a drink."

We also laced another Optimo green leaf blunt with powder. It wasn't even two hours and the phone rang again.

I said, "Shit, it is on over there."

It was Baby this time calling from Meeko's stating, "I'm sorry it took me so long to call you back. I had about four clients in a row. I've got to get back to work. You know it's real busy on the weekends. I want you to come pick me up in the morning. I want to see you."

"Cool, just call me when you're ready. I'll be right there baby."

Baby asked, "Did you bring the key to the safe deposit box?"

"I sure did."

"Okay then, I'll call you at ten o'clock or once I wake up."

I said, "Cool."

As soon as I hung up, the telephone rang right back. I thought it was Baby again, but it was Special K.

Okay, "Here I come."

I went next door and broke her for two hundred and forty dollars more. Then breaking Little Momma for two hundred and seventy dollars and Sunshine for two hundred and fifty dollars. I then sent them back out the door with more condoms and pimping. That gave me a total of two thousand three hundred and sixty five dollars with more pimping to come for the evening.

18 wheelers were constantly pulling in and out of the truck stop. It was about six o'clock in the morning, with the sun beginning to rise. I looked out my motel window and the huge parking lot was still full of 18 wheelers. Seamore was sitting in the chair nodding, about to fall asleep. I was tired and fucked up, but I had to check my dough from these broads.

At six thirty in the morning, my phone rang. It was Little Momma.

I told her, "I'm on my way."

I broke her for another two hundred and sixty five dollars.

Stating, "You did a good job."

She immediately got prepared to take a shower. Sunshine came in and I broke her for two hundred and seventy dollars more. I congratulated her as well. Special K came and relieved herself of three hundred dollars and some change. I made them all feel good about their hard work. A good business owner congratulates his employee's whenever they do a good job. That gave me a record breaking high for one night of pimping of three thousand two hundred and ninety five dollars and some change.

"Rest up ladies, because it's on again tomorrow night."

I left them in their room, & went to my room so I could listen for Baby's call from Meeko's.

As soon as I closed my eyes, Baby was calling and telling me, "I am ready."

I asked her, "What time is it?"

She answered, "Twelve noon."

"Okay, I'm on my way."

A hustler got dressed, cleaned up, and called Big Seamore.

I told him, "I'll probably be gone all day."

Afterward I walked next door to my hookers' room and told them, "I'm going to handle some business. I'll be back later this evening before you go to work. Here is one hundred dollars. Call the pizza man or whatever if ya'll get hungry."

They said, "Okay."

Well, here is a hundred dollar bill on the night stand, and a hustler rolled out with the quickness.

As soon as entering the inside of Meeko's. I said, "Hello & asked, Will you please tell Baby to come down for me?"

I guess Baby heard me because she immediately came from around the corner with a big smile on her face.

Baby quickly said hello, followed by "Where is the key?"

I asked, "Where is the safe?"

We went directly to the safe. I opened it and saw nothing but brand new 20, 50, and 100dollar bills. I had to get a small paper sack to put all the money into.

Baby told Meeko, "I will be back before seven o'clock."

We headed out the door with gigantic smiles on our faces.

As soon as we walked outside, I heard Baby say, "Damn, that's a pretty truck sitting over there."

We were walking toward the truck which was mine, she just didn't know it.

I hit the remote control alarm and said, "Baby do you like it?"

"Is this yours?"

"Hell yeah. When you work hard you deserve nice things."

She was all teeth and gums after she sat that fat ass on the butter soft leather.

"SS Boy, I love this truck. This is one of those Cadillac truck's isn't it?"

In answer, "You know it Baby, I can't wait until we get that new Jaguar you've been dreaming about."

I had to keep her on super charge.

I asked her, "How much is in this paper sack?"

Chapter 28

She answered, "I know it's well over ten thousand dollars for sure."

I said, "Cool."

We headed to a nice restaurant that served breakfast. I ordered eggs benedict and a well done T-bone steak. Baby ate from the salad and fruit bar, because she was watching her weight & figure. Baby was happy that I came to see her, & I was happy to get my money. We talked, laughed, and had a good time in the restaurant.

Then the question came, "Can we just go to a nice place? Just you and I?"

Sure, "We can do that."

It's hard to turn a bitch down on some dick. I just broke her for over ten thousand dollars in two weeks. I rented a suite at the Marriot Hotel and had them bring my girl flowers and roses to the room.

I couldn't wait to pour that money out on the bed & count it. It was a total of eleven thousand, five hundred dollars.

I didn't fuck Baby, I made love to her. I caressed, held, and rubbed her back and pretty toes, & she loved it. All I could think about was that eleven thousand five hundred dollars I just cracked the bitch for. We laid up and watched movies butt naked all day until it was time to take her back to work. I dropped her off with another date planned for tomorrow which was Sunday afternoon.

Then I rushed back to the motel so I could send the rest of my stable out the door with instructions. Pimping Seamore and I sent our girls to the track with the same game plan as yesterday. I invited pimping to my room for a toast with one of those hundred and fifty dollar bottles of Moet.

I said, "Here's a toast to pimping and keeping these hoes broke."

We clashed our glasses together and drank up. I threw all eleven thousand five hundred dollars on the bed.

Big Seamore, "I pulled this out of a bitch's womb."

He said, "Damn, Baby doing it like that?"

I said, "Hell yeah, Nashville is like that."

We blazed up a phat blunt while I straightened out my money to put it in my stash spot in the Cadillac Escalade. I wasn't about to leave my money in the motel room for someone to rob me. Maybe room service or the police would peel me for it. Fuck that. I took my chances hiding it in the Escalade with the top of the line alarm and kill switch on it. I grabbed another fifty dollar paper of cocaine and made a few lines to celebrate.

It was on once again at the truck stop (track). I cracked my bitches for three thousand dollars that night. Pimping Seamore cracked his for eighteen hundred dollars, which was pretty damn good. The next day, I picked up Baby from Meeko's at twelve noon to take her shopping for some new lingerie, clothes, and shoes.

She told me, "I need to go home and check on my family soon."

I said, "Cool, no problem. In two weeks, I'll be back to get you."

We kicked it all day. She liked her new job, but still tried to act like she didn't. Baby was now a bona fide hooker. There was no turning back now. She was completely flipped and loving the life of a hooker.

"I am leaving tonight on my way back to OKC. Page me in a couple of day's baby."

She said, "Okay."

Her big pretty brown eyes were all watery, even though she was trying not to cry.

She was telling me, "I love you so much. I could never do anything like this for any other man."

I told her, "I love you too."

Then kissed her on the jaw. I pulled off, waving goodbye, headed back to the motel where everyone was.

I requested to Seamore, "Let's stay one more night. This is good money here. We'll pull out tomorrow afternoon or whatever."

We sent our hoes out the door for the third night straight. Sunday night was really on. We popped open my last bottle of Moet and laced another Optimo blunt. Both of us had a good time, popping big pimping all night.

I broke Little Momma for twelve hundred dollars, Sunshine for nine hundred and fifty dollars, and Special K for one thousand and fifty dollars for a total of thirty two hundred dollars. I was sitting real phat. Understanding now why international pimps travel from state to state pimping hoes, scoping new prospects, game, and spots.

We pulled out of Nashville late Monday afternoon and passed straight through Memphis, TN. My luck wasn't too good in Memphis. We stopped in Little Rock again on our way home. We got there at about eight o'clock that evening and the track was nowhere close to the truck stop in Nashville. It was slow money, but good money. It was better than no money at all. I ended up with a total of about eight hundred dollars from three hookers.

The next morning we rolled out, arriving back in Shawnee Oklahoma, at a truck stop.

It was still daylight but, "Fuck it, let's work now and head home Big Seamore."

We were only about twenty or thirty minutes outside of Oklahoma City. I was in a rush to get home, count my money, and check my traps at the weed houses. While the girls worked Shawnee for a couple of hours, Seamore and I went back to the same car wash. We cleaned off all the bugs, dirt, and dust on the windshields.

My girls came back in two hours with only five hundred dollars.

I said, "Seamore, I'm out of here. It's slow."

"I'm with you, S.S. Boy"

Big Seamore, "I'm headed to the crib to count my stack and check my traps."

He said, "I'll call you after I add up all my money. I want that deal we were talking about."

We took off toward OKC on I-40 west. I got off the highway on Air Depot and he kept rolling toward the East Side. We made it home safely. Everyone was a little tired, but feeling pretty good about themselves. I went straight to my bedroom and closed the door so I could open my safe.

Admiring my $122,000.00 and needing to add this new money to it. I counted my new money that I just broke my hookers for and it was a grand total of $21,835.00. I didn't know I had accumulated that much in five days. Baby gave me $11,500.00, so that meant I broke the rest of my stable for $10,335.00. That's pimping to the fullest you dig. I had a grand total of $143,835.00 and some change. S.S. Boy never had this much money in my whole life before. I also had fifty one pounds of sticky green and $17,000.00 out on credit. Advancing me closer to the $200,000.00 mark after the dust settles.

I blazed up a blunt with the girls and gave them the night off. They deserved it. The girls started cooking, dusting off furniture, and vacuuming. They were keeping a pimp's crib air tight and spotless, just like I liked it.

I paged my boy Big Timer to see if he was in town yet.

Timer called right back and said, "I been waiting on you."

Immediately I could tell something wasn't right by the sound of his voice.

He said, "I'll be over there in a minute."

In less than fifteen minutes the doorbell rang. I invited Timer into my bedroom so we could talk privately.

"SS Boy, my boy Pimping X is tripping."

I asked, "How?"

"He's got this funny look in his eyes."

"Why do you say that, Timer?"

Timer explained, "I had to park a rental van in Pimping X's girlfriend garage with over seven hundred pounds of weed and fifty kilos of cocaine in it. I thought Pimping X was use to seeing and handling big money. By the look in his eyes, I believe he and his boys want to kill me for it. They are at his girlfriend's house waiting to escort me to Denver, Colorado. I believe they are going to try something slick. I'm following my first mind like I always do."

I said Timer, "You haven't said shit. We are going to pick up that van and kill all those mother fuckers if we have to."

Timer said, "Dig that."

I said, "Hold on."

I called Big Seamore and the Prospect Posse. They lived for this kind of shit. We headed to the East Side to strap up and post up. Our posse was about four cars deep with plenty of fire power and ready to put in work if necessary.

Timer called Pimping X on his cellular and told him, "I'm on my way."

We pulled up and Pimping X had about five Crips standing around outside looking crazy & shit. Timer cocked his forty five automatic and stuffed it in the front of his pants, with the extra clip in his pocket.

He said, "If I'm not out in five minutes, come get me with the quickness."

Timer pimped on in the house. The five niggas standing in the yard followed Timer in and closed the door. I paid close attention to my Rolex. Timer had been in the house with no movement for four minutes and fifty three seconds. Then I saw the garage door raising up and Timer was in the van pulling out. We headed to the East Side following Timer with all this dope and weed in the van. The Prospect Posse never knew what was in the van. They just thought we had beef. Only me & Seamore knew what was up on the real. I pulled up on the side of Seamore and we let our windows down.

I told him, "We'll be in the hood in about an hour or less."

Me, & Timer branched off toward my house and the Prospect Posse headed back toward the eastside in the hood to put up the heat (guns). We got to my house and I let Timer pull the van into my garage. We went inside to my bedroom.

I gave the girls two hundred dollars each and told them, "Go shopping or something for a couple of hours."

They dropped everything and headed out the door, & left in their little bucket.

I said, "Timer, I thought Pimping X was cool."

He said, "I did too. Money will change a mother fucker. It will make a son kill his father, and also make a daughter kill her own mother. Its true what Notorious B.I.G. says, never let no one know, how much dough you hold (the Ten Crack Commandments). SS Boy, I could see death in the nigga eyes. He just hesitated to do it. Pimping X is a killer. If I was anybody else, he would have done it immediately without hesitation. He still would have done it if I had come by myself. It fucked him up that I was deep with killers too. I owe you this time SS Boy. I'm going to do something for you and the Prospect crew for having my back. I see why you fuck with those brothers. They are truly some real soldiers that will die for you, just like my crew. I could have called my crew, but everyone was out of town on a mission. So I decided to wait for you one more day before I called my Jamaican posse out of Dallas or my Mexican boys. If I called either one of them, somebody was most definitely going to die today."

Timer went to the van and came in with a duffle bag. The van was full of duffle bags and huge boxes.

Timer threw me fifty pounds and told me, "Give the Prospect Posse twenty of those pounds."

I said, "Bet."

He said, "I truly believe that you all just saved me from a kidnapping and murder. What were you trying to do?"

I asked, "What can I get for $125,000.00?"

Timer said, "Damn, I told you that you were a six figure nigga. I'll tell you what. I'll give you three hundred pounds. How is that?"

I didn't even answer. I just ran in my room to open the safe and counted out $125,000.00.

Timer said, "This will put you on top where you belong."

Timer sold me three hundred and ten pounds for $125,000.00. That was on top of the fifty one pounds I had left and the thirty pounds I had from riding on Pimping X with Timer. That gave me a total of three hundred and ninety one pounds of sticky green. You could smell it as you drove past my house.

Timer asked, "Can I borrow the old Barracuda?"

I said, "No, but you can drive the Escalade or the drop top SS."

He said, "Cool, I'll take the SS Monte Carlo drop top because I'm going to some spots where I might have to move around pretty quick."

I said, "Cool."

& threw him the keys.

Chapter 29

Timer said, "SS Boy, I appreciate you letting me park in your garage."

I said, "Don't mention it. Are you sure the van is locked up? Take the van keys with you. You never know what these slick mother fuckers might try to pull."

He said, "I feel you."

"I wondered why you didn't come here in the first place Big Bro?"

"You were out of town lil bro.."

I replied, "I could have gotten Mom to give you a key, better yet, you need your own key. My crib is your crib Timer."

He gave me dap and said, "I'll page you later on and hold this for me."

Then handed me back the $125,000.00 that I just gave to him.

Timer, "If you need to get in the house, look on the sun visor of the SS drop top. You'll see a garage door opener."

Timer pulled the S. out of the garage and I pulled the old school Barracuda in. I let the garage door back down to hide the rental extended Ford van. While I was doing all of this moving, I kept thinking about the Prospect Posse. Timer gave them twenty pounds to split, so I decided to give them ten more pounds. Thirty pounds should put them on their feet.

I loaded the Barracuda with my three hundred and ten pounds and headed to my stash spot in the country, to inventory my product. Then headed back home for the other fifty pounds before the girls came home.

I put the pounds in the trunk and headed to the East Side to reward my homies. When I pulled up in the old school, they were standing around hype as ever and hoping for some drama to jump off. I went into the yard where Big Seamore and the crew were standing.

I asked them, "Do ya'll want to make some big money?"

They got quiet and huddled around me with their ears standing up like German Shepherds.

Asking them, "How long will it take to pay me fifteen thousand dollars if I front ya'll twenty pounds of sticky green?"

The crew replied, "About a month."

You could see dollar signs in their eyes.

I said, "Okay, now are ya'll going to work it as a team or split it up?"

They replied, "Shit, we are a team."

"That's good. So you all shouldn't have any problem with splitting up thirty pounds."

"Thirty? I thought you said twenty pounds?"

"I did, the thirty pounds are for ya'll being down with me and Timer. You were ready to ride and handle your business."

They replied, "Yes sir?"

I said, "Yeah, so out of fifty pounds, you only owe me fifteen thousand dollars."

They all hugged me and gave me dap.

Stating, "SS Boy, you're a real mother fucker. The average nigga wouldn't give his crew shit but a high or something of that nature."

I walked back to the trunk and pulled out the fifty pounds, & sat it on the homies front porch. You should have seen those brothers. They were negotiating and debating on how they would distribute it.

Pimping Seamore said, "SS Boy, I broke my bitches for almost eight thousand dollars on our trip to Nashville. When this client comes to pick up my last five pounds, I should have about twenty five thousand cash. I'll spend twenty two thousand with you. That will leave me three thousand to play with."

I said, "Seamore, I'll tell you what. You're my dog and my right hand man. If I'm having money, then you should too. For twenty two thousand, I'll sell you pounds for six hundred dollars. That would be rounded out at about thirty seven pounds. I'll front you another forty three pounds making it an even eighty. For the forty three pounds, pay me seven hundred dollars each. Plus you got hands in the pot with the homies fifty pounds."

Seamore said, "Hell yeah."

I said, "You're getting ready to be a six figure nigga too, you dig? You'll only owe me thirty thousand dollars. That's not too much for you is it?"

He said, "That ain't shit. I'm going to start knocking that tab down, a.s.a.p."

Just as he said that, two brothers in a Lexus coupe pulled up.

Seamore said, "It's on now."

He went to the Lexus and kneeled down to speak with them. Seamore then went inside the house. They backed the Lexus coupe into his driveway. One of the guys went inside to talk to Seamore as the other one sat in the car. A few minutes later, the brother came out with a hefty garbage bag and threw it in the trunk. Seamore then came on the porch and called me into the house.

He counted out twenty two thousand cash and handed it to me, & talking cash shit.

I told Seamore, "I will be back in an hour or so."

I couldn't tell him to meet me at my house. I had too much shit jumping off. I wanted people to think that I'm strictly pimping and that's it.

The other pimps I know claim, "We don't accept any dope money or dirty money, only hoe money."

But, I feel most of them are handling though.

I punched out in the Barracuda spinning the rear tires. Headed home to put up the twenty two thousand and then to the country. I was back on the East Side in an hour and fifteen minutes. A hustler had to weigh out twenty nine pounds on top of the fifty one I already had weighed out. I dropped off his eighty pounds and jumped back in the Barracuda to check my traps at the weed houses.

I stopped at the first weed house to chop it up with the little homies for an hour or so. As a businessman I had to check out how everything was running. Everything was cool, but my first mind kept telling me to get out of there. The first rule of thumb for me, is to follow my first mind. They had forty five hundred dollars for me and I collected it.

I told them, "I will get with ya'll later. Call me when you're ready."

I pulled up at the other spot where they were conducting business in a major way. I wasn't about to stay and chop it up. People were coming in and out. The whole block was flooded with patients (customers) and runners (workers) were going from car to car serving ten and twenty dollar sacks. They had it going on, but they were wide open. I figured they wouldn't last much longer conducting business like this.

I suggested to them, "Ya'll should move because I'm sure someone has called the police with a complaint by now."

It went in one ear and out the other. The OG of the house was listening to me but he was infatuated by the fast money.

He said, "SS Boy, give me a ride to my crib so I can pay you your money."

"Okay I replied."

On the way taking him to his crib, I tried to talk some sense into him.

I explained to him, "In OKC, you have to change spots and get different locations every 60 to 90 days."

But, he was from California and thought that he was playing on the same ball field. If he didn't make a change very soon, he would have a rude awakening coming his way.

I told OG, "I would hate to lose you as a client and business associate. I feel that it's time for you to flip the script to a new location. Your same customers will come."

OG said, "SS Boy, I'm listening to you. I feel you, but I've got to get this cheese while the getting is good."

I said, "Dig that."

& left it alone after he said that. I did my job by giving OG some good advice. It's up to him now to use it.

Like Mom says, "You can lead a horse to water, but you can't make him drink."

OG went in the house and came out with the eight thousand and five hundred dollars that he owed me.

I told OG, "It's on in a major way and you need to put in your order while it's good."

OG said, "SS Boy, from all the times you have fronted me, I've been able to stack some money."

I asked him, "What are you working with?"

"About seven thousand dollars."

"Shit, you're doing alright O.G. I'll sell you pounds at six hundred and fifty dollars each. I'll front you ten more for eight hundred each. That will be a total of twenty one pounds coming your way."

OG said, "Shit, when can we do this?"

I answered, "Yesterday, meaning right now."

"How long will it take for you to bring them S.S.?"

"I'm leaving now and will be back before you know it."

OG said, "SS Boy hold on, let me get in here to get this other seven thousand."

I said, "Okay."

O.G. said, "I'll just stay here until you get back. I'm only allowing one pound at a time in the weed house anyway. I refuse to get robbed or let the police bust me with too much shit on deck."

"That's right OG, just chill for a minute and I'll be right back."

I made the four speed Barracuda fish tail and slide sideways. OG stood in the street laughing and watching me handle that bitch. I got to the country in ten minutes. I was constantly looking in my rear view mirror to make sure that no one was following me. I dropped my fifteen thousand five hundred dollars off at the crib. I then headed to my stash spot.

You have to watch your ass like that in OKC and Tulsa is just as rough, if not rougher. These bandits will rob and kidnap you in a New York minute. You really have to watch your back and your fronts around here. I kept my hand on the 9mm ready to dump at any given moment on these fools, busters, and haters. I never had a problem with squeezing the trigger (shooting someone).

I was weighing out twenty one pounds as fast as I could. My pager went off and it was Redrum from the North Side.

He was telling me, "I need to talk to you in a big way."

Okay, "I'll be out there in about an hour."

I moved fast because I knew when Redrum called its usually big cheese involved. I was back at OG's house on the East Side in an hour and a half with twenty one pounds of sticky green.

I flew out to Redrum's house. He sat in the old school Barracuda to spit game at me for more kilos. Redrum was ready to get another kilo practically for free again.

S.S. Boy, "My little Blood homies are ready to re-up again on some bricks."

I asked, "How many?"

"I don't know yet. I'll be able to tell you something either tonight or early tomorrow morning."

Okay but, "You need to tell me something tonight if possible. My people will be through here some time tonight. I wouldn't want to miss them."

Redrum said, "Okay, I'll call you tonight."

He jumped out the car and jogged into his house. I went home to count my riches and recalculate my inventory. When I got there, Little Momma and the girls were back from Heritage Park Mall in Midwest City. They had new clothes and big smiles on their faces.

I handed Little Momma the weed box and told her, "Roll up four big joints."

Quickly dashing into my room, closed the door, and locked it. They knew to knock on a pimp's door before entering. I opened the safe and counted $18,835.00 from the $143,835.00. I subtracted the $125,000.00 I paid Timer. That was a total of $18,835.00 in the safe. The $15,500.00 from OG was added with the $4,500.00 that I collected from the other weed house. That gave me a grand total of $38,835.00. I had to start all over on building my stack up again to six digits. I had two hundred and sixty five pounds of weed, fifty three thousand dollars out on credit, and four dedicated hoes in the stable. It turned out to be a damn good week.

I went back into the living room and handed everyone a joint. Then cracked open a six point Coors Light beer that was left over from the Dallas, Texas trip.

I told the girls, "You did a good job out there on the highway. We are going to Dallas for a week or so to stack some real paper."

They said, "We can't wait to go to Dallas. I know those tricks got plenty of money."

"That's right beautiful. No one should return back to the stable with under a grand a night."

They all replied, "We are ready baby."

"Good, you all need to relax and rest up tonight. It's back to work tomorrow night girls."

The telephone rang and Little Momma answered it. Timer was on the line.

Chapter 30

I said, "You have good timing because I was just about to page you. Why don't you meet me at KFC on 23rd street & MLK in ten minutes?"

He said, "Cool, I'm not far from it now. I'm on my way."

When I pulled up at KFC, Timer was already there in the parking lot. He was in my SS, eating a box of barbeque hot wings, and drinking a Pepsi, & had money on his mind as always.

"What's up S.S. Boy?"

I said, "My little Blood homies are ready again."

"They should be calling me tonight. How much can I get the kilos for?"

In answer, "Since it's you SS Boy, I'll give them to you today for fifteen thousand each."

I said, "Cool."

"I'll Call them and find out what's up."

Instantly calling Redrum's number on my cell phone while sitting in the SS drop top munching on one of Timer's KFC hot wings.

Redrum answered the phone.

I said, "What's up?"

Redrum replied, "Call me back in five minutes. I'm talking to Chub Roc right now."

I called him back in five minutes.

Redrum said, "SS Boy, meet me in the parking lot of Jimmy Johnson's Bar and Grill in five minutes."

I said, "Cool."

Timer told me, "Make the deal with only Redrum. His crew must trust him with the money. You and him one on one, can you handle it alone?"

"Yeah, why shouldn't I be able to? I will page you if it's on tonight."

Timer replied, "Page me anyway."

I punched out in the Barracuda headed to Jimmy Johnson's Bar and Grill on Lincoln blvd. Soon as I pulled up, guess who I saw? Redrum in his new Millennium Mazda sitting real cute and shoving something terrible. I sat in Redrum's car to talk with him.

Redrum said, "My boys are ready."

I asked, "How many?"

"They were talking about seven bricks; plus I want two this time."

I replied, "Dig that. The price is seventeen thousand dollars, since they are getting a few keys. The the only thing is, it have to be just you, and me to make the deal."

"SS Boy, I don't know if they will trust me with all that money."

"They will have to. My people trust me with all that shit."

Redrum replied, "I'm going to tell them the bricks cost eighteen thousand dollars. I will make seven thousand dollars."

"I don't care if you told them twenty five thousand each. All of the extras are yours."

Redrum said, "Let me call them. They are waiting at the pay phone for me to call and tell them something."

We rode down Lincoln Blvd. until we spotted a pay phone. Instantly we pulled over so he could make his call.

Redrum quoted, "The price is eighteen thousand dollars each &, you will have to trust me with the money."

He got off the phone and looked at me.

"SS Boy, I have good, and bad news."

Well, "Tell me the bad news first."

"They were real hesitant about doing the deal, but finally agreed to let me do it. I also have more bad news."

"What is it?"

"They don't like to do transactions late at night, so we'll have to wait until tomorrow sometime."

"Cool, so what's the good news?"

Redrum said, "They agreed to pay eighteen thousand dollars each."

"Damn, they bit for that?"

"Yes sir."

I got out the car and paged Timer with the quickness. Timer called right back.

"Timer it's a go but we will have to wait until tomorrow."

Timer replied, "Cool, I'll rather wait until tomorrow anyway."

I said, "Me too."

We hung up and I got back in the car with Redrum.

I explained to him, "Everything is cool for early tomorrow morning. How early can you have the money?"

He answered, "I can have it before eleven o'clock."

"You know nine bricks will cost you $153,000.00?"

Redrum said, "Yeah, the seven bricks will actually cost $126.000.00. I'll only have to pay $27,000.00 for two bricks (kilos) which will total $153,000.00. I'll be making a profit of about seven thousand dollars."

I said, "That's right."

Redrum took me back to the Jimmy Johnson's Bar and Grill to my car. We gave each other dap and he punched out.

I was thinking about the money I would be making, but I hate to count ghost money. I would rather wait until the money hits my hands. I ended up going straight home. I chilled for the rest of the evening with the girls in front of the Sony sixty inch big screen watching movies and getting high. With a new batch of sticky green. I was thinking and hoping everything went as planned tomorrow.

I told Sunshine, "Come over and sit under me on the leather love seat. I have spent quality time with Little Momma and Special K one at a time. Tonight is your night. You never complain about shit."

We hugged up and watched the movie, Big Momma's House.

I never knew that it makes a woman's day for her man to just chill, laugh, and hold her for a couple of hours. I noticed how relaxed and happy Sunshine was. We had a wonderful evening together. We smoked a quarter ounce of trees (weed) that night. I drank about three cans of that six point beer.

I was fucked up, & could tell by the look in Sunshine's eyes that she was ready to eat me up. After smoking, drinking, watching movies, and eating buttery popcorn. I grew tired and horny & so did Sunshine.

I told her, "There's a meeting in my bedroom and don't be late."

I walked into my bedroom and started to undress. Sunshine came in about ten minutes later with one of the sexiest lingerie outfits on I had ever seen. It was red and she had on red open toe high heel shoes on that exposed her beautiful toes that were painted red. Sunshine also had on some sweet smelling perfume.

I laid across the bed with my silk boxers on, flicking through the channels. I was acting like I didn't notice her enter the room. She came and posted up between me and the television so I would notice her and compliment her on how good she was looking. She knew that she was looking extra good. I sat up on the edge of the bed to grab her hand to pull her toward me. She quickly straddled me. Hugging me around the neck while staring into my eyes.

"SS Boy, I've fallen deeply in love with you and I can't ignore it any longer. You give me chills all over my body whenever you're near me. I want you to fuck me real good because I haven't had any dick in a while."

I had to ask the question, "What about your dates?"

She said, "I mostly give head. I try my best to save this good hot juicy pussy for my man. All real women do that. The only way I'll give those tricks some pussy is if they keep requesting it. I'll make them pay double for it. Nine times out of ten, they'll settle for a blow job."

I said, "Dig that."

She kissed me on the neck and rubbed the back of my head. That made her extremely hot. The way she approached me, my Johnson (my dick) started to wake up and stand straight up at attention. Sunshine started at my neck, but now she was licking and slowly biting my chest. I had an enormous erection. She slid those big, juicy red lips on this black night stick. Sunshine bobbed up and down on it. I laid back on the bed and let her do what she did best.

I tried to touch her clit, but her pussy was so wet & juicy that my finger slid right in her, & she loved it. She started jerking me off while she licked my balls. Sunshine went even further and licked my asshole. I never had a bitch do it like that before. It was awesome. I had butterflies in my stomach like I was riding a roller coaster or something. She had me running and trying to get away from her like a fish outta water.

I couldn't take it any longer. It felt too good. I had to grab her by the hair and pull her up out of my ass. Her snake tongue was still trying to lick me where ever it could. My dick was so hard. If I rolled over on my stomach, I would have broken it (lol).

Sunshine didn't waste any time mounting this nine inch black Indian dick. She rode me like a brand new Bentley fresh off the showroom floor. While on my back, Sunshine was on top of me riding this mule (dick). I reached behind her tight ass and got my middle finger soaking wet from her vaginal juices. I spreaded her ass cheeks wide as they would go, then ran my middle finger up in it.

Her big titties were right in my face. I had to suck them. Her nipples were as hard as an eraser on a fat husky boy pencil. My dick was deep inside her pussy. I was ringing that little bell every time she rode down on it with my index finger in her asshole. I could practically feel my dick through her asshole with my finger. Every time I pulled this dick out of her a little, I would shove my finger in her ass.

I called it, "The see saw tactic."

Sunshine still had on her high heels with her lingerie pulled up to expose her breasts for easy access. I constantly did the see saw tactic on her. She came all over me. Even the inside of her asshole was wet. Sunshine was shaking and shivering while dropping that load. She was holding on to me really tight, steady moaning and grunting. The bitch couldn't even talk at the time. When she was finished with her multiple orgasms, she looked at me with tears in her eyes. This dick and my see saw tactic felt so good to her that I really had her flipped now.

Now, it was my turn to cum. I can't cum on the bottom, & needed to be on top. I rolled her over and started hitting that pussy with this mule. The bitch was still cumming, shaking, and shivering every once in a while. I placed her feet on my shoulders so that I could watch this dick going in and out of that fat juicy pussy. I was hitting nothing but bottom ringing her bell every time I went deep. Sunshine was screaming and moaning so loud I knew that Little Momma and Special K could hear the bitch in the next room.

Sunshine practically begged me, "Please cum Daddy!"

I was knocking bark out of the bitch. Now my motor was starting to lock up (lol), & about to cum. I pulled out of her while she grabbed my Johnson (dick) & snatched my condom off. Sunshine started sucking it again while tasting some of her own pussy juice. She swallowed every drop of cum that came out of me, just like Special K. These hoes love to taste their own pussy. After it was all over, we washed up and passed straight out in my Cali. King sized bed.

That next morning, around seven o'clock am, my telephone rang.

I answered it was Timer, "Wake up, I'm on my way. Wake up SS Boy. Nothing comes to a sleeper but a dream. The early bird always gets the worm. I'll be there in ten minutes."

I got out of bed and Sunshine was still lying there sound asleep from that good fucking I put on her last night. I brushed my teeth, washed my face, and threw on my silk Polo robe. Timer was right on time as always. I opened the door before he rang the doorbell and woke up my whole stable.

He said, "SS Boy, I've got to roll out. I need to be in Denver by this evening some time."

I asked, "What about the nine keys I was going to drop for you today?"

He replied, "It's still on, I'll just leave you the nine bricks along with my $125,000.00 you're holding for me. I had a feeling that I would have to be out of here early this morning. That's why I told you to do the deal with only Redrum. Do you think they still want them?"

Chapter 31

I said, "Hell yeah. They should be gone before noon. I'll put the $135,000.00 up with your $125,000.00."

Timer asked, "Will you hold that for me?"

"Sure I will."

Timer said, "I guess that nigga Pimping X has got me real cautious now."

I replied, "Timer, you'll never have to worry about me. I feel I don't have to rob or steal from you. I feel all I have to do is ask."

"That's right SS Boy."

We walked into the garage through the kitchen. He unlocked his van and climbed inside to open up one of those big boxes with the bricks inside it. He counted out nine kilos of uncut powder cocaine. I hid them in the closet of my garage. Timer taped the big box back up. I let up the garage door as soon as he finished jumbling around inside the van.

"SS Boy, page me at one o'clock sharp this afternoon and tell me if everything went okay. I'll be back day after tomorrow."

We gave each other dap then hugged. Timer jumped in the driver seat of the van. Then closed the door and let his window down.

He said, "Oh yeah, I forgot to tell you that the drop top SS Monte Carlo of yours is a running mother fucker. I had a ball in it last night."

I threw up the peace sign as he pulled out the driveway. Then I pulled the SS inside the garage, went inside and turned on the Sony big screen. Afterward rolled up an early morning blunt. Watching the old school Looney Tunes: Bugs Bunny, Daffy Duck, Elmer Fudd, and the whole crew.

Shortly after Little Momma woke up, & came in the living room. She didn't say good morning or anything. Bitch just sat on the leather love seat. I knew that she was mad and jealous because I fucked the shit out of Sunshine without inviting her to the party last night.

I straightened her out by saying, "Bitch you better suck that lip in and quit tripping before you start something."

She quickly said, "What? What did I do? I'm not tripping, I just woke up."

I said, "Well, hook us up some breakfast while you're waking up. Maybe you'll learn how to speak when you enter a room with someone already sitting here. It won't hurt you to say good morning or something."

She replied, "Good morning SS Boy, what's going on?"

I said, "Little Momma, don't even go there trying to flip the script on me."

She started laughing and walked into the kitchen to see what she was going to cook. I sat there on the couch in my silk Polo robe, & smoked my morning blunt and watched Bugs Bunny run game.

Shortly after, Little Momma woke up Special K and Sunshine to help her cook breakfast. We had pancakes, eggs, bacon, sausages, milk, and orange juice. It was pretty good. These girls weren't just hookers and dancers, they were excellent cooks as well.

It was about nine thirty am after we ate breakfast. I was fully dressed and waiting for what lies ahead. Redrum hadn't paged me yet, so I decided to page him. I was trying to get rid of these bricks as fast as possible. I didn't want to sit on them longer than I had to.

Redrum called right back and said, "My friends are on the way now. I will call you after they arrive."

I said, "Cool."

He called back at ten thirty that morning asking me, "Are you ready to go and shoot some ball?"

I answered, "Yeah, if you come out here and pick me up."

He asked, "You're not coming this way?"

"No sir, I don't have any transportation right now."

That meant that he had to come to my house.

"Alright, I'm on my way."

Redrum showed up thirty minutes later ringing my door bell. He was wearing a warm up suit with Air Jordan's, a gym duffle bag around his shoulders, and a leather basketball in the other arm. Little Momma opened the door and he came inside to have a seat. I came out of my bedroom and that's when I noticed how he was dressed. I really liked his style. He was camouflaged down as if he was really on his way to shoot some ball.

I invited him into my bedroom, closed the door, and locked it. He unzipped his duffle bag and pulled out stacks of money. We started counting and it was exactly $153,000.00 on the nose. I placed the money in my dresser drawer.

Okay Redrum, "Follow me to the garage with your duffle bag."

I opened my storage closet door and counted out his nine bricks. Redrum cut one of the bricks open to look at the quality of the cocaine. He loved it. We placed the bricks in his duffle bag and zipped it back up.

He said, "I'm out of here. I'll get at you later."

I walked him back into the kitchen through the living room and out the front door. He had his basketball and duffle bag. I gave him dap as he got into his car and cruised off.

My girls never caught a clue as to what was really happening. That's how smooth it went.

My girls asked, "Are you going to meet him at the gym to play basketball?"

I said, "Not today."

Then went back into my room and closed the door. I separated mine from his. That gave me a quick profit of $18,000.00, which gave me a monster rush. Now I had a total of $56,835.00 in my safe, 265 pounds, $53,000.00 out on credit, and four dedicated hookers in my stable. I was also holding Timer's money which was a total of $260,000.00. I had well over a quarter million dollars in cash, & never had this much money in my possession before. I must admit that I felt a little nervous, but excited as hell.

I had Little Momma to go to the store and buy me a box of green leaf Optimos. When she came back, I rolled up one of the fattest blunts I possibly could, trying to put a quarter sack in one blunt. I rolled Little Momma and the others regular size blunts, while cracking open one of those ice cold six point Coors Light beers. Immediately turned on my Sony house stereo and jammed on return of The Mack. I had all the windows in the house vibrating while I chiefed on my Cuban size sticky green leaf blunt. Thinking about my ghetto riches while dancing with my girls.

At one o'clock sharp, I paged Timer. He phoned right back worried if everything went okay.

I said, "I can't wait until you get home big brother. We are going to drink us a bottle of Don P!"

When I said that, he knew that everything was alright.

He said, "Little brother, you're alright. I'll pick up a bottle on my way home."

His mobile phone faded in and out on the highway.

Later on that evening, I sent my girls out the door with instructions.

I told them, "I'll be at the track before midnight."

It was seven o'clock that evening. I couldn't wait to get rid of them so I could have some quality time to myself. As soon as they left the house, I jumped in the Escalade and headed to B.T.'s car wash to get my truck cleaned up. I had the vanilla flavored incenses sprayed on the inside with extra black magic on the tires. The workers were wiping and staring at my hoe catcher.

Finally the manager asked, "Can I take a picture of your truck & put it on the wall of fame inside of the car wash?"

I answered, "Why not?"

I thought about heading to the East Side or to my female friend Gina's house. She was a fine mother fucker with plenty of game. She paid me and I never had to fuck her. Everyone accused us of fucking because we were so close. I ended up introducing her to Redrum and they hit it off just fine. I wanted to see who would break who first .I was going to come out a winner regardless because they both had big cheese & much game.

Gina had a big brand new house fully furnished and a nice ass 300 Benz. She was breaking every dope boy that came through the city. I admired her for that. She would always run up on me hugging, kissing me, and holding my hand. I guess that's why people would accuse us of having an affair. I'm not saying that I wouldn't because any man would. If I fucked Gina, it could fuck up our friendship. Besides, she would give me anything I wanted or needed without sex.

I didn't have time to fuck with Gina today. She likes for me to stay around for hours or all night. When her boyfriend's come over, I would be lying in her bed with no shirt on. I didn't give a fuck.

My boy Redrum was putting some game down. I had taught him about the pimping and he had been successful at it. He didn't have the patience. He was sprung off the fast dope money. The hoes were just a past time for him. I couldn't lose because if Redrum cracked her I would get paid and if Gina cracked him I would get paid. I believe they knew that and therefore it was a Mexican standoff. Nobody got paid. It was just a lot of free fucking going on (lol).

I decided to go home & sit on my money like a chicken sits on eggs. Two days later, Timer was back in town with both of his crews.

He told me, "I dropped off the van in Kentucky."

I said, "I thought you were headed to Denver?"

He said, "So did Pimping X and his crew. SS Boy, you know that's a golden rule of mine. I never let anyone know where I'm going or when I'm leaving."

I smiled and said, "I feel you big brother."

Timer said, "I've got something for you little brother for being true to the game. I told my crews to go check in a motel some place and page me in forty minutes. SS Boy, we have to go handle something."

He got out the car with them and climbed into the Escalade with me. He had two big purple Crown Royal liquor pouches in his hands.

He said, "Let's head to the bat cave."

We headed to my house on the out skirts of Midwest City. I couldn't wait to see what he had in store for me. As soon as we got inside my house, I went and got his $260,000.00.

He asked, "Do you still want some jewelry?"

I answered, "Hell yes."

He grabbed the lighter of the two Crown Royal bags and dumped almost everything onto the floor. I couldn't believe the huge pieces I saw. It wasn't a ring in the whole pile with a price tag under five thousand dollars. There were quarter, half, and whole karat solitaires. Solitaire trillion cut, baguette cut, and marquise cut stones. It was well over two hundred diamond rings in that pile. Then there were about ten sets of diamond stud earrings weighing in at a karat each. A couple offsets were two karat studs.

Timer said, "If you broke all this shit down to make you some pieces, you would have some monster shit."

I replied, "You're damn right. So what do you have for me?"

He answered, "I'll give you all the rings and four sets of karat studs for fifteen thousand dollars."

I said, "Damn Timer."

He said, "You wanted big boy shit, well here it is. SS Boy, give me twelve thousand dollars right now. I can't go any lower. Add all that shit up. You're getting over a hundred thousand dollars' worth of jewelry."

I knew that he was telling the truth, so I bit.

Timer started singing, "All day, every day, hustling to get paid, fuck making minimum wage."

I peeled off twelve thousand dollars. I had to have that ice and get my monster pieces made up.

I asked him, "What is in the other pouch?"

He answered, "You don't even want to see this shit."

Chapter 32

Timer pulled out a couple of gigantic broaches. The first piece was a scorpion full of diamonds. It was the size of the palm of your hand with a price tag of seventy five thousand dollars attached to it. He also had a butterfly the same size as the first piece with ice and a price tag of $60,000.00 on it. Timer had a ladies diamond necklace made of fifty karats with a whopping price tag of $95,000.00.

I said, "Damn Timer, you and your boys hit the mother lode."

He still had a sack full of shit.

I said, "Ya'll got down."

While stating, "Pimping X and his boys can't do that."

Timer's pager blew up and it was his crew. He called them right back to find out what hotel they were in and also the room number.

"I'm on my way. SS Boy, put this jewelry in your safe along with the $160,000.00."

Timer took the other $112,000.00 to pay his crews for getting down on such a good job.

Timer then asked, "Can I borrow your old school Barracuda again?"

I threw him the car keys and tried not to count his money. I couldn't hold it in no longer.

I asked Timer, "You stacked a half mill this week didn't you?"

He said, "Not yet. Maybe by the time I get paid by my Mexican partners for driving the van to Kentucky. I need to sell this jewelry to make my profit. I should be real close to $500,000.00 for this week."

I said, "Damn, you're getting money in a major way."

Again Timer left me with something on my mind.

As he was leaving, he said, "Go pick up two bottles of Don P and put them on ice. I'll treat tonight."

Timer pulled off in my four speed 'Cuda. I had to reevaluate my grip now. Immediately headed to my bed room to count my money since I just spent a bankroll. I was still doing alright. Still sitting on $44,835.00. Since I was in a spending mood, I figured I might as well drop $9000.00 on my truck to knock that tab down a little bit. That left me a total of $35,835.00.

I felt foolish for buying all that jewelry. But, I looked at it as an investment. I came up with the conclusion that I haven't really lost anything. If bad came to worse, I could sell the jewelry & get my money back. I left the house after I quit tripping on that little money, then stopped at three different banks. I purchased cashier traveler's checks until I had three cashier money orders for three thousand dollars each. Quickly stopping at the post office to mail nine thousand dollars to Baller's Unlimited overnight.

Now I owed twenty thousand dollars on my truck and it would be paid off. I proceeded on to Bryon's Liquor Warehouse and purchased two bottles of Don P with Timer's money and went home to place them in the freezer.

As I closed the freezer, the telephone rang. It was Mom, the first lady in my life. She was on super charge about something and didn't want to tell me what she was hyped about until she saw me in person.

I said, "Well, come on over, let's kick it."

Mom was so hyped I believe she hung up in my face before I finished my sentence. Mom pulled up about thirty minutes later and so did Timer. They both came in and I introduced them to one another. Timer immediately thought that my Mom was the coolest woman on Earth right out the gate. I pulled out a bottle of Don P and three champagne glasses. I popped the cork on the Don P and poured us up some drinks.

We sat down at my dining room table and started conversating. Later in the conversation, Mom told me what she was so hyped about.

She told me, "I found this car that I like and I have to have it. It's winter green with tan interior. It's fully loaded with an electric sunroof."

I asked her, "What kind of car is it Mom?"

She answered, "It's a four door 400 Lexus Sedan."

I had to take another sip of Don P after she said that.

Mom then finished by saying, "It only cost about sixty two thousand dollars."

I said, "Only? So you gotta have it?"

She said, "Yes, I deserve one."

Timer spoke up, "She does, so you might as well buy her one."

I said, "Momma, I don't have sixty two thousand dollars right now."

She answered, "I don't need it paid in full. I only need the down payment."

Well "How much is it?"

She slowly answered, "Seven or eight thousand dollars."

I said, "Damn."

Timer was juicing her up by saying, "Seven or eight thousand is nothing to SS Boy."

I finally said, "Okay, we'll go check it out first thing in the morning."

Mom said, "Okay, I'm going to wake you up about nine am or so."

"Okay mamma."

Then she hit me with another blow, "Do you have some money on you?"

I answered, "Yeah, how much do you need?"

Mom replied, "However much you can stand."

Mom is smart and she has a nose for money.

I said, "Okay."

Timer said, "SS Boy, let me have the honors of helping out. Your Mom is my Mom and my Mom is your Mom."

Big Timer reached into his pocket to pull out a fist full of big faces, all hundred dollar bills.

Timer said, "This is for your insurance, tag and a full tank of gas for your new Lexus mom."

Mom couldn't believe it and neither could I.

Mom said, "Thank you Timer."

She finished her glass of Don P and said, "Well guys, I appreciate everything. I'll let you continue with your evening. SS Boy, I will call you first thing in the morning."

"Okay Mom."

She hugged us and told Timer, "It was nice meeting you and thank you. I will invite you over for dinner the next time you are in town."

He said, "I'll be sure to be there. I've heard alot about your cooking and baking."

Mom laughed and waved us good bye.

As soon as she closed the door, Timer pulled out a fat sack of Indo and asked, "Why don't you twist us up a big blunt? I will pour us another drink of Don P. SS Boy, those brothers were happy when I threw them those thousands. My one crew who made the smaller lick ended up getting forty thousand dollars. It was only two people making twenty thousand dollars each, and my other crew got seventy thousand dollars to divide with three people, making it about twenty three thousand each. Everyone had big smiles on their faces. I should come out with a seventy thousand dollar profit from the lick."

I said, "That's big money. Let's toast to getting money and keeping bitches broke."

That was a player's toast. We smoked that Indo blunt and knocked off that first bottle of Don P.

I said, "Timer, let me roll another Indo blunt so we can ride in the Cadillac and sip on this Don P. Let me check my hoe money."

"Dig that S.S. Boy."

I proceeded to roll another Indo blunt. We grabbed the other bottle of Don P and headed to the Escalade that was sitting pretty on dubs. I had that Tru ready to bang on the Nakamitshi system for Timer, because that's what he was singing after we made that deal on the ice. As we approached N.E. 23rd Street, it came on (All day, every day hustling to get paid, fuck making minimum wage, I got the day shift, You got the night shift) with those eight twelve's shoving in the 'Lac.

Timer said, "Damn, what do you have in this mother fucker?"

I ran down the list of shit that I had installed in the Escalade.

Timer said, "Damn, your shit is hitting harder than my Suburban."

I said, "Your shit is banging."

We jumped on I-35 north headed to Guthrie truck stop area, shoving up a storm and sipping on the bubbly. We got there and my girls were doing what they did best. They were selling pussy out of both pants legs and getting a pimp his cheese. I broke those bitches for almost six hundred dollars and we jumped back on the highway and blazed up that Indo blunt.

Timer said, "See SS Boy, I turned you on to a million dollar game and a pimpish life style. The game's not to be told and half the time it's not to be sold. A perfect example is Pimping X."

By the way Timer kept bringing up Pimping X's name; I could tell that he hadn't let that shit go by a long shot. We headed to the Robinson St. track, now banging on some of that Goodie Mob.

Timer said, "SS Boy, you make me feel good. I feel that I gave some game to the right person who won't cross me out."

"Like I said earlier, Timer I could never cross you out or bite the hand that feeds me."

We continued popping game on our way back to the East Side.

Timer said, "You should be straight on the weed tip for a while."

I told him, "Yeah."

"I'm about to get on a serious grind. My crew and I probably won't be back in OKC for a while, unless I needed something."

Timer, "I should be straight for a couple of months."

He said, "SS Boy, buy your Mom that Lexus. You only have one Mom."

I said, "I feel you, I'm going to buy it for her and she knows it."

Timer said, "A lot of brothers claim to be ballers and won't spend a dime on their own families. Refrigerator won't have any food in it. Their Momma is living in the projects. Babies running around the house with runny noses and shitty pampers. These so called ballers are riding around in Benzes, buying everyone in the club drinks, and tricking big with the hoes. Then once they get locked down, (in prison) they wonder why their families or so called friends won't send them shit. You don't want to be like that. The man upstairs doesn't like ugly or selfish people. We're already doing wrong, so why not take care of your children, families, and love ones? That's probably why I've been blessed and haven't seen the penitentiary again or the grave yard. I've had a couple of close calls in my days, but always seemed to slide through."

I never heard Timer talk like that before. He sounded like he was getting religious on me or something. One thing about it, he made perfectly good sense. Timer then snapped out of it and was back to his normal self again.

Timer requested, "Let's go kick it with Pimping Seamore and the Prospect Posse for a minute."

I said, "Cool."

So we headed to the hood. As soon as we hit the corner, they were all outside as usual conversating and handling business. We parked and got out with our champagne glasses full of the Don P. Everyone was happy as usual to see us.

Timer asked us, "Roll up a couple of those good Indo blunts."

We quickly got on the job while everyone was conversating about the L.A. Lakers and Mike Tyson. Timer was right in the conversation with them because he and the Prospect Posse loved Iron Mike Tyson and so did I. He was a real mother fucker as far as I'm concerned. Fuck any negative thinkers about the brother. He is a talented champion and a major money maker. The boxing committee hates him, but they need him. He magnetizes money like flies are magnetized to shit.

Me and Big Seamore rolled two fat blunts and handed them to Timer. Timer started giving his speech like he was running for office or mayor or something. He blazed up the blunt, hit it a few times with a light cough, and passed it.

He told the homies, "I appreciated your assistance the other day. I am very thankful. You don't meet real brothers like you all every day. It was my pleasure to meet some more real OGs who still play the game by the old school rules. I just want to let you know whenever you finish with that product you have, just get with SS Boy and he will take care of you. If it's any beef, me and my crews will come running with the quickness."

Timer shook everyone's hand and we continued to blaze up.

The Prospect Posse told Timer, "The average person usually won't give a brother shit for putting his life on the line."

Timer said, "That's not how I view things, especially someone's life which they put down for me, you feel me? So that's why I gave you real brothers a little something to show my gratitude and appreciation."

They said, "We feel you Big Timer. From here on out, you're one of us. Whenever you hit town, come by and chop it up with us if you have time."

Timer replied, "I sure will. I only associate with the real. I see why SS Boy is always over here hanging out. He is staying sucker free and picking up game at the same time."

They all said, "That's right. SS Boy is smart and he is also a real brother and down to earth. Just because he has struck gold, he hasn't forgotten about us or looked down on us."

Chapter 33

I spoke to them, "I could never do that. I know how fast the tables can turn. You're never supposed to burn your bridges."

Z said, "That's right SS Boy. It's going to be my turn to shine one day and I surely won't forget you or the brothers who were down for me when I was less fortunate."

Before we knew it, we had smoked both Indo blunts. Everybody was fucked up and feeling good with money in their pockets. We gave everyone dap and jumped in the Cadillac Escalade to bend some more corners.

"Well SS Boy, it's time for me to go home and see what kind of money I have in my hoe trap. Will you take me to Avis so I can rent a vehicle?"

We headed to the Avis rental at the airport. Timer rented a customized van. Then followed me to my house so he could pick up his $160,000.00 and his Crown Royal pouch full of jewelry. As soon as we arrived at my house, I gave him all of his belongings and he tucked & hid everything away in that customized van.

Timer then said, "Call me if you need anything. Stay down and on the DL (down low)."

I listened to the game and advice he gave me. Timer rode out on his way to Dallas. I chilled out for the rest of the day. I thought about all the experiences we had been through and the knowledge that Timer laid down on me real thick.

Hanging with Timer was like going to a major college. You took honor courses where you had to keep a 3.5 or 4.0 g.p.a or get kicked out of college. I had to keep up and do my homework. If I wasn't listening and applying this knowledge Timer was putting down on me, he would feel like he was spinning his wheels and kick me out of class. I surely didn't want that to happen.

He hadn't told me anything wrong yet and plus he helped me get a six figure income. I would be a complete fool not to listen and observe his game & knowledge.

I had a lot to think about. Also having to write some more notes down mentally. I ended up falling asleep thinking hard about the game. I wanted to be rich and play with seven digits like Timer and the other hustlers in the game. The smoothest, goes the furthest.

I had a vivid dream, that I was the boss with the sauce with major strings to pull. I played my hand just like Timer played his. Nine out of ten hustlers in the game had a court date, but that was according to how well you paid attention and took notes. If you're one of the nine you could put that court date off for a long time if you stay sucker free and follow your first mind. Maybe you will never get handed a court date, you feel me!

I had to be resting well because I didn't wake up until my girls came home at five in the morning.

They were telling me, "We had a fairly good night at the track."

They relieved themselves of a pimp's money, which was about $2,500.00. I rose up off the couch and proceeded to my bedroom, to put up my money, & take off my clothes, then went back to sleep.

At eight thirty am, Momma called to remind me, "You know its car day. You can come pick me up to shop for my Lexus."

I arrived at Mom's house an hour later. We headed to the car lot to find her dream car. She took me to Bob Moore Lexus dealership and showed me her dream car. I must admit that it was clean as a white dove. She had been speaking with this black salesman. He ran out to greet us with dollar signs in his eyes.

I had to do some quick talking and fast dealing with this guy. We weren't about to pay the sticker price for this car. We ended up talking him down to $57,500.00, plus tag, title, tax, gold package, chrome wheels, CD player, and cassette with all the extras. It was fully loaded. Mom was drooling at the mouth and so was the salesman.

I asked the salesman, "How much is necessary for the down payment?"

He answered, "$5,000.00 will put her in it, but her payments will be extremely high. The more she put down, the less her payments will be."

I said, "Well, she is trading in a 1999 Maxima. It's fully loaded and worth $18,000.00. She only owes about $10,000.00 on it. That would be at least $7,000.00 toward the down payment. She'll probably put $8,000.00 down. That will give her a grand total of $15,000.00 and leave a balance of $42,000.00 to get financed."

The salesman replied, "We can do it. I'll get her financed with no problem."

He immediately got the paper work together and had the car sent over to the detail department.

After he finished, I said, "It's only one problem."

He asked, "What?"

I said, "She lives deep on the northwest side of OKC where her trade in car is. My bank is in Midwest City. It could take a long time before we make it back."

The salesman said, "Brother that's no problem. I'll personally take her to pick up her Maxima."

I asked, "Would you do that for me?"

He quickly said, "Ms. Harris, are you ready to ride?"

Mom, "I will meet you back here in about forty five minutes. That's about how long it should take you to get back with your car."

We went our separate ways.

I secretly asked the salesman, "Can you put a giant ribbon (bow) around the Lexus?"

He answered, "I sure can."

I rushed to the crib, opened the safe, and counted out $8,000.00. Then headed back to the Lexus dealership. They were already back when I pulled up.

Mom said, "We just pulled up right before you did."

The salesman quickly checked out her car to make sure nothing was wrong with it. I handed Mom the money and her and the salesman counted it out. I must admit that I felt good being able to pay some of the down payment for moms new Lexus. I still had a surprise for her after she drove off in that new car.

The deal was done. We were just waiting on the car to come from the detailing department. Fifteen minutes later, the car came out with the big ribbon across the top. You should have seen her face light up with joy. I believe that's what made me feel best about the whole deal.

I asked, "Mom, pick me up at my house. I want to ride in the new Lexus with you."

She came to the house to pick me up. That Lexus rode smooth with much power. We went to the mall so that I could get her fingers measured and mine.

I told her, "I am going to buy you four big diamond rings. Do you want a diamond on every finger? I mean, you are driving a Y2K 400 Lexus."

She replied, "I'm straight on diamonds."

I answered, "Not like the ones I'm going to put on your fingers."

She answered, "Well, if they are that phat, I only need two rocks (diamonds) on each hand. So buy me four rings all together."

After we left the mall, we headed to Block Buster's music where she picked out some oldies but goodies: Bobby Womack, Teddy Pendergrass, Spinners, Luther, Isley Brothers, and several other old school CDs. I taught her how to operate her stereo and CD player. It was on from there. We had a good time spending money and riding.

Afterward having mom to take me home. I had to go lick my wounds and count my stash again. I counted my grip & had a total of $27,835.00.That was still cool. Plus still had 265 pounds, $53,000.00 out on credit, and four down ass bitches.

A young hustler needed to find out who I could trust in OKC to take this jewelry and get the diamonds mounted. A player also needed the gold melted down into whatever I wanted without me going to jail.

I paged my boy Timer to find out a little information on that end, from a pay phone. Timer called right back as always.

Big Timer, "Can we talk?"

He said, "Yeah, I'm at a pay phone too. I knew it was you paging me."

I asked, "Who can I hire for my jeweler that won't turn me in?"

Timer laughed and said, "I'm glad you called because I forgot to tell you don't ever take any of that jewelry to a pawn shop or anything of that nature."

I answered, "You don't have to worry about that big brother."

Timer said, "That's good. I'm going to turn you on to my jeweler on the Northwest Side. He's a good solid brother named Rocky. He can make any design and he won't split your wig with high prices. Hold on for a second."

I heard him on his mobile phone talking with someone. Then he hung up with them and returned talking to me.

Timer told me, "I just got off the telephone with Rock. I told him that I have a friend who wants to do business with him. He told me to send you on over to his store. SS Boy, take your shit over there and let him check it out. Tell Rocky I said to make my pimp partner some monster shit. Big pimps deserve big shit."

I laughed and said, "Dig that."

Timer gave me the name and location of his store.

And told me, "Handle up."

I went home, opened the safe, and grabbed my jewelry, all of it. I was at Rocky's jewelry store in forty five minutes with my Crown Royal pouch full of ice and gold. Rocky invited me into his office in the back of the store. We shook hands and introduced ourselves.

I had already envisioned how I wanted my pieces made up. A huge three ounce medallion covered in ice with my initials in it. A two ounce, nugget bracelet covered in ice. Four monster rings as big as he can make them, covered with half and a whole karat solitaries. I was going to pick out four phat rings for my Mother. Rocky laid out a velvet cloth on his desk.

He said, "Pour it all out SS Boy. Let's see what we're working with."

I poured out all the rings and diamond studs on the table. I saw a glow in Rocky's eyes. He was obsessed with diamonds as I was. They were his world and I could read the look in his eyes that he wasn't bullshitting about that.

While he was inspecting the grade of diamonds with the loop, (magnifying glass) he was smiling and saying, "Not bad. You guys really hit them big this time."

I never said anything regarding his statement. He finished looking at each piece and wrote down their total karat weight.

I asked him, "How many karats is that all together?"

He said, "A whole bunch SS Boy. You have about one hundred and fifty five karats or more and over a pound of fourteen karat gold. You have well over a hundred rings here and four sets of one karat stud earrings."

I picked out eight two karat rings for my mother, since I had so much jewelry. I gave Rocky her finger size.

"SS Boy, I can quickly size those for you right now."

I said, "Cool. Do you have eight little ring boxes I can put them in as a gift?"

"Sure, let's put all this stuff back in the bag and I'll get right on it."

I told Rocky, "Thanks, I really appreciate that."

It took him thirty minutes to size eight rings and place them in separate ring case boxes.

After he finished that little task, he asked, "Now what do you really want me to do for you?"

I told him, "Well, I want some really heavy shit covered in ice."

He said, "Oh, you want some giant pieces like Timer?"

I replied, "Yes sir, you got that right."

Okay, "I'm the man who can cast and design any piece you can dream of. I made Timer's pieces."

I explained to Rocky what I wanted and the weight that I wanted for the medallion, bracelet, and four rings using all of that fourteen karat gold and all those diamonds.

He asked, "You want all that in those six pieces?"

I answered, "That's right, now how much will it cost me?"

He answered, "You want some extremely large pieces? That is time consuming. It will cost you eight thousand dollars and you can pay me in cash. You are a friend of Timer's and he is a close friend of mine. So you can also pay me in diamonds. That's half and whole karats, no quarter karats."

That gave me something to think about.

I said, "Okay, let me calculate. After I pick out the eight rings, I still have over one hundred karats left right?"

He said, "That's right."

I said, "I want all four rings weighing two ounces. That's sixty karats for the rings. I want my medallion to have thirty karats or more. That's a total of ninety karats and three ounces in gold. The bracelet I want weighs three ounces in gold with karats all the way around it. I want it to look like Puff Daddy's, you feel me? That's one hundred and thirty karats total with many karats left over. Can you add ice to my Rolex?"

Rocky said, "I sure can."

"Okay, well put ten karats in my Rolex."

Rocky said, "It's a done deal. When do you want me to get started?"

I answered, "Yesterday. You can have five solid karats, but the rest of the ten karats will have to be half karats."

Rocky answered, "Cool."

I asked, "How long will it take you to finish everything?"

He said, "A couple of weeks probably."

Rocky showed me a display of rings, medallions, and bracelets. He wanted me to pick one of the styles I liked. I liked all of them, so it didn't take long for me to choose what I wanted. We shook hands and I gave him my 1800 sky pager number and cellular number.

Rocky said, "Call me every week. I should have a piece ready every week or ten days."

"Cool, I'll call you next week."

So I jumped in the drop and punched out on the triple gold Dayton's. Calling to see if Mom was at home, and she was.

Mom, "Will you meet me at my house around eight o'clock tonight?"

Mom answered, "Yes, I'll be there. I need some where to drive my new Lexus anyway."

Chapter 34

I knew by eight o'clock my girls would be out of the house and at the truck stop selling plenty of pussy. At eight o'clock sharp, Mom was pulling up in the driveway in her new hunter green Lexus. I greeted her and she was clean as a white dove. She looked like a millionaire or some big business woman.

Mom was like, "What's up?"

I said, "Nothing, just have a seat."

She sat down and shortly after, I went into my bedroom and came out with four little ring cases.

I handed them to her and told her, "I love you mom. You mean the world to me."

Mom opened those cases and damn near passed out with joy. She was just fumbling around with those rings checking them out from top to bottom with amazement.

She said, "I don't know which finger these rings look best on."

I went into my room again and came out with the other four rings.

I asked, "Well, which finger will these rings look best on?"

She gave me the biggest and tightest hug ever and kissed me on the cheek.

"Mom, I decided to get you eight rings for eight fingers. I figured that you would have a hard time deciding which finger to put them on. Well, here is eight of them to decide on. I love you Momma."

She sat there fumbling around looking at those big rings. Mom was trying those rings on each finger. She had forgotten all about the ones I had sized for her. I started watching BET on the big screen and laughing at her underneath my breath.

I believe that saying now, "Diamonds are a girl's best friend."

Mom didn't leave until almost midnight.

She claimed, "I have to go to work in the morning. I want to be rested up and looking good without feeling all tired at work."

Mom gave me another big hug and a kiss.

And said, "Thank you for the Lexus and the diamond rings son."

"Mom, just look at it as if you owe me now."

But mom quickly straightened me out, "No, you got that wrong son. This is just a down payment of what you owe me. I gave birth to you boy (lol)."

With a big smile on her face.

I replied, "Yeah, you're right Mom."

She gave me another hug and said, "You'll always be in debt to me son, now where did you get all of this shit from (lol)."

I told her, "I know a guy who owns a jewelry store. He let me pick eight rings from his show case display to pay me back."

She said, "Good. I don't want any hot merchandise. I'm not ready for jail yet."

We laughed and walked toward her new Lexus.

The following weekend, I flew to Nashville on Southwest Airlines to pick up my bank roll and bring Baby home for a week's vacation. I picked her up and collected ten thousand dollars from her. I checked over twenty thousand dollars from her in one month. That was cool coming from a whore house. Once she came back to OKC, that's when the drama started in my stable. Baby was use to my house being our house without three hookers living with me.

I said, "Baby, you knew they were here before you left."

She said, "Yeah, I know. I figured since I've been gone for a month that it would just be you and me when I came home for a week."

I answered, "So what am I suppose to do? Just kick my money out the house for a week? They have been working just as hard as you if not harder. Those are your wife in laws and all of us are one big happy family. We are down for each other. Don't break that up just because you've been getting money in Nashville."

By the look in those hoes eyes, I knew that I was going to have to keep them separated. Pimping is 24/7 and it doesn't stop. One hoe won't stop my show. Immediately I called a meeting in the living room.

I told them, "We are on the same team trying to get ahead in life. We can't accomplish our goals if we don't stick together. Now everyone needs to re-evaluate themselves and quit tripping, before I start tripping."

Everyone nodded their head and said, "Uh uh."

I could tell that my little meeting went in one ear and out the other.

Baby said, "SS Boy, I promised Mom that I would spend a little time with her tonight. Is that okay with you?"

Yes, "That's cool, handle your business baby. You are on vacation."

She left out the door with a hurt look on her face like someone ran over her puppy or something. As soon as she left, I explained her situation to Little Momma and the stable.

"She's just use to being here with me full time. We've been through a lot together, but the script has been flipped to Y2K mode. It's taking her a little while to adjust, so be patient with her. She's been working in a whore house for a month straight. Just be understanding ladies that's all I'm asking. I'll tell her the same thing towards you all."

They said, "Daddy, we understand and we don't have any problems with her. She is the one tripping."

I replied, "Yeah, I know."

At seven o'clock, Little Momma, Special K, and Sunshine were out the door and on their way to the track where they were famous at. Baby paged me about ten o'clock that night. She wanted to see me and talk to me without any one around.

I told her, "Baby, I'm the only one home. The girls are at work. They work every night, seven days a week."

"Well can I come over?"

In answer, "Now you're talking crazy. Why would you ask a silly question like that?"

I could tell this bitch needed some pimping and direction.

I told her, "Be here in twenty minutes."

Hanging up the phone in her face.

That's exactly what she was looking for. She wanted me to give her an order. Baby was ringing the doorbell in fifteen minutes. I snatched her in the house, closed and locked the door, & pushed her on to the couch. And posted up right in front of her and never said a word. I pulled this dick out and tapped her on the jaw with it. She sat there and held this dick for thirty or fourty seconds not knowing whether to suck it or jack it off.

Baby girl just started kissing and sucking on this monster while still sitting on the couch. I stood in front of her with my hands to the side of me, talking to her. By now, she was off into sucking this dick. Baby girl just moaned and nodded her head when I asked her questions. Then I stopped everything, put my dick back in my pants, and zipped them up.

Baby wanted this night stick so bad. She looked like she was about to cry. Baby started licking her lips and trying to unzip a pimp's pants. I had her now. I was still standing in front of her with this dick on super hard just bulging through my pants. She was trying to unzip them like she was in another zone. I pulled her hair causing her to look up at me, eye to eye.

I said, "Baby, you know that you're my girl. I flipped you and I want you to continue to get my money and keep us happy. You feel me?"

While pulling her hair and snatching her head.

I asked her, "You want this dick don't you?"

"Yes SS Boy."

While breathing heavy. It seemed like the more shit I talked to her, the hotter she became.

Baby was begging, "Please let me suck your dick."

She said, "SS Boy, I'll pay you one hundred dollars if you just let me. Will you just please let me taste it again?"

I said, "Bitch, where is the hundred dollars?"

She quickly reached in her purse while I pulled her hair. Managing to put the hundred dollar bill on the coffee table. That shit there was freaky and made my Johnson even harder. I grabbed the hundred dollar bill and let her unzip my pants.

She proceeded to make love to this Johnson with her mouth. I had dick all in her jaw while steady pulling her hair. She loved it. I started fucking her face causing her to gag from too much dick in her throat. It was awesome. Shortly after, my motor started to lock up and I pulled out of her mouth. I began shooting cum all over her eyes, nose, and lips. Baby got upset about that because I didn't cum in her mouth. She loves to swallow like all the other girls.

She was satisfied for a minute and so was I. That whore house had flipped Baby into a diabolical freak. I wasn't helping the situation with this pimping. After she cleaned and wiped the cum off her face, I sat her down to lay my pimping on real thick. We must have sat on the couch for hours talking money and business.

Baby asked, "Will you pay my car note on the Honda Accord?"

I asked her, "How much do you owe on it?"

"I still owe about five thousand dollars on it."

Baby, "We'll pay the car payment this week before you fly back to Nashville. Next month, we'll just pay off the whole amount."

Little Momma and the stable made it home about five thirty am with another twenty five hundred for a pimp. I ended up going to sleep with my bottom bitch. Little Momma and Baby laid right next to me. I was surprised we all made it through the night and the next day without a cat fight (lol).

That Sunday, Baby caught a flight back to Nashville. She had a smile on her face and getting money on her mind. I had pimped up a storm that week through Little Momma, Sunshine, and Special K. I pulled over $12,500.00 out of the womb.

I scheduled a trip to work Dallas with Timer and his hoes that following weekend.

Timer already told me, "You can chill at the mansion. I have plenty of room for you, and your stable. So come on down and get some of this Texas money."

I replied, "I heard everything in Texas was big. Does that include money too?"

Timer said, "I'm going to take you to Houston's Galleria Mall and get you a pimp wardrobe."

I said, "That's right."

He said, "I should be back from out of town by next weekend. If I'm not back, I'll leave you a key and give my hoes instructions to roll out the red carpet for a pimp. They will make you and your stable feel right at home."

I answered, "That's cool Timer. I appreciate that OG. I'll get at you next weekend then."

My girls couldn't wait to work Dallas and neither could I. I knew what kind of money was in Dallas, especially on Harry Hines Blvd.

I worked my hoes real tough for another week in OKC on Robinson and at the truck stop in Guthrie. I had a pimp tight week again and clocked over $14,000.00. That Friday evening, I filled up the Escalade and my stable's Corsica. They followed me to Dallas all the way to Timer's mansion. In a way, I wanted my bitches to see Timer's mansion and how he and his stable were living. I was hoping that would put my bitches on super charge to get this money in a major way.

As soon as we hit Dallas Texas. I hit Timer's crib on my mobile phone and no one was there. I paged him on his 1-800 nationwide pager.

He returned my call immediately. Timer was on the highway with one of his crews getting money. Timer was riding with Gator from Chi-Town in the new big body Lexus 400. Timer helped Gator buy it with the million dollar hustle he turned him on to.

I heard the old man Gator, who was about 50 years old or so, banging on some C-Bo (Ride till we die) in the back ground. Gator and Timer were on super charge and on their way back to Dallas. They would be there by midnight. These niggas had that Lexus wide open with C-Bo in the background steady banging now on some, Friendly game of baseball.

Chapter 35

Timer said, "Young SS Boy, when you get to the castle, you'll see an old car parked in the driveway. Look under the front driver's side floor mat and you'll see a key to the front door. Once you get in, spell the word pimping on the burglar alarm system and it's on."

I said, "Feel that, it's on."

He said, "Show your bitches around. Have them follow you to the track in the Rolls. They keys are hanging over the stove in the kitchen."

Timer had to be drunk and feeling good from a major lick again. He started singing, which was some gangster shit, and then hung up. We were both laughing and feeling good. My stable and I pulled up at Timer's mansion about forty five minutes later. My girls couldn't believe how large Timer was.

They said, "This is movie star shit."

They were looking at the height of Timer's two and half story mansion and checking out the length of it. Now it was time for me to give my pep rally and really put these hoes on supercharge. They almost ran over each other when we stepped into the house. The big twelve foot Polar Bear rug had his mouth wide open showing those long fangs.

I laughed like a mother fucker. That shit was funny. They finally realized that the animal was dead. It was just lying by Timer's black shiny grand piano. He had an expensive marble chess board and pieces with only two chairs. There were two king's throne chairs in his formal living room.

Little Momma said, "Daddy, I couldn't live in this big ass house because I would be terrified if I was here all alone."

I said, "You would get use to the house if we had one like it. This is what we will have if we play this game with respect. You feel me? This is what a pimp wants. Don't you see how Timer and his hoes are living?"

I took them on a grand tour of the mansion. There were several bedrooms, five or six bathrooms, three living rooms, game room, weight room, wet bar, two fire places, two Jacuzzi, and a swimming pool. I took them in Timer's huge ass garage with his Double R, 600 Benz, Suburban, and racing bikes in it.

I said, "This is the life. This is the grand prize that we're after. This is our goal in life. Now who don't want to live like this?"

None of them said anything, so I assumed that I had my stable on high voltage now.

I told them, "Get ready for work, because it's on. Timer's hoes are already out there making money."

I headed to the wet bar to make a drink and twist up two blunts. Thirty minutes later, my girls were dressed and looking good. I sat them down and explained to them how to work Harry Hines Blvd track.

"You have to drive down the hoe stroll. You can't walk down the track or you most definitely will catch a case. So just drive up and down the track. The tricks will pull up on the side of you and start flirting with you. It's all up to you after that. It's as simple as one, two, three, you feel me?"

They all said, "Yes."

I said, "Let's roll then. Special K, you and Sunshine follow me and Little Momma in Timer's Double R to the track."

They headed to the bucket and Little Momma and I got in Timer's white on white Rolls Royce with the gold grill, with the bitch on the hood, and all gold twenty inch Lexani rims with the rubber band low profile tires. Soon as I started up the Rolls, Timer's system came on. It was already jamming on Bucket-Loc and Nitro, the homies out of OKC and Tulsa OK.

We headed to the track with my other two hookers following us through the mix master; Dallas's twisted and confusing highways and under passes.

I asked Little Momma, "Bitch, I bet you feel like a queen riding in this six digit mother fucker? Have you ever rode in a Double R?"

She answered, "No."

I asked her, "Bitch, have you ever seen one besides this one?"

She answered, "I've only seen one other Rolls Royce before in my whole life."

Cars were passing by and people stared at us. We were almost about to cause an accident on highway 635 W. We exited off on Harry Hines Blvd. It was now almost nine thirty in the evening. As soon as I hit the stroll, one of Timer's girls pulled up on the side of the Rolls, thinking it was Timer.

She said, "SS Boy, we've been expecting you and your girls."

I said, "Is that right?"

Yes, "I'll show them how it works out here."

I said, "Cool."

Immediately pulling over to let Little Momma out.

I told Sunshine and Special K, "Peep game. Follow Timer's bottom bitch's lead."

I headed over behind Momma's Café where all the pimps hung out. No one was there yet. I guess it was still early in the evening. These pimps don't normally come out until late night. I headed to the Valley Ranch Cowboy's Café, where the Dallas Cowboys chill. I didn't stay long; I just went in there to check it out. It was cool if you're a football fan. I couldn't stay too long with those squares. I left as soon as I finished my beer. The atmosphere was a little too square for a pimp you dig?

I headed to the mansion to wait for Timer and his crew to arrive. I was back at Timer's crib before eleven o'clock, & was sitting in the Jacuzzi with the underwater lights on. The lights were also on in the swimming pool. I was puffing on a phat blunt, sipping on an evening chaser (Remy Martin), and listening to Dallas radio station 105.7, old school, on the outside surround sound stereo system.

I must admit that my mind was out there on one. I was fantasizing about owning one of these mansions one day in the near future. I was getting higher than the US space shuttle. While I was in wonder land and feeling good, Timer and his crew came home. They came directly to the backyard where I was still chilling in the Jacuzzi and still sipping on the Remy.

Timer said, "SS Boy, come on in and celebrate with us. We have ten bottles of Don P, plenty of doddie (Indo weed), and some of the best yola that Miami has to offer. So come on in my nigga. Meet us in the game room."

I got out of the Jacuzzi and dried off before heading up to the game room with a champagne glass. Gator was in the kitchen cooking up dope (cocaine) in the microwave and popping big pimping. Timer and his YGs were up stairs rolling Indo blunts on the pool table and playing Play

Station on the big screen with about an ounce of Peruvian Blue flake powder on the wet bar. Timer was talking figures on two mobile phones at the same time. The little homies were over thrilled and talking about what they were getting ready to buy and do in life.

Timer finally got off the phone and formally introduced us. I already knew a couple of the homies and they knew me from the Cadillac Escalade in the city (OKC). They also had seen it several times in front of Timer's crib.

Timer told them, "This is Pimping SS Boy. He took the pimp game and ran with it just like ya'll took this jewelry game and ran with it."

We all shook hands and began to chop it up together like players, pimps, and hustlers do. I had to take my hat off to these young gangsters. They had much heart and big nuts. They would go in, lay those peckerwoods down, and come out with hundreds of thousands maybe millions worth of their jewelry. Really, I liked that shit and the more and more I thought about it; the more I wanted Timer to put me down.

I admired their work because they weren't robbing their own kind. They robbed the white man who had plenty. Those white folks owed blacks and Indians anyway. This was just a small way of getting some of that money that was owed to our forefathers, you feel me? Plus it wasn't hurting those peckerwoods, because I'm sure they had millions of dollars worth of insurance. After Timer and his crew left the store, I'm sure that would be the biggest sale of the year for them.

Gator came up the stairs with about seven grams hard in a paper towel. He was drying off that fat ass rock he had just cooked up, & had a Coors Light beer can in the other hand. Gator went straight to the wet bar with Timer and started poking holes in his beer can. The YGs didn't pay it any attention. I guess they were used to being around Gator and Timer. They were to busy tooting much powder.

Gator started blasting (smoking cocaine) off of the beer can. He sat a half a gram on that mother fucker. Timer was crunching up fifty pieces and rolling up primos with that Indo weed. These ballers were getting ripped. You know I had to step over to the wet bar with the big boys to get in on the moe smoking and tooting the A-1 yola (cocaine). One thing for sure, neither me nor Timer fucked with that can in any shape form or fashion.

Timer said, "I can't handle smoking that pipe or can. I've been through that before, Gator is the only brother I know who can smoke cocaine without tripping, tweaking, or fiending and shit."

Timer was right. Gator was steady blasting socially and coherent. He was playing pool laughing and joking with the YGs!

Timer said, "As long as a person can handle his shit without tripping, I can't knock him in any kind of way, you feel me?"

I said, "Yeah OG, I feel you. It doesn't look like Gator's tripping to me. It just look like he's having a good time like the rest of us."

We smoked a laced Indo joint, sipped on the bubbly, and chopped big pimping in the castle. After me and Timer smoked a couple of primos and finished a couple of bottles of Don P, Timer went down stairs and came back with two XL Crown Royal pouches. Now the little homies and everyone gathered around and I couldn't wait to see what kind of ice he had in the pouch.

Timer said, "SS Boy, we got down this time baby boy on the real. We got big skrilla."

He gently poured out the first pouch full of Rolex watches, men and ladies. It was about sixty of them. Some of them were full of ice. Some were Presidential Rolexes. There was every kind of Rolex they made, even wood grain face & some Tiger Woods models. My eyes bugged like I had taken a major blast off of Gator's beer can. Timer then placed them back in the pouch very carefully without scratching them.

Big Timer gently poured out the other XL Crown Royal pouch full of jewelry. It consisted of about forty five more Rolexes, some giant two and three karat diamond rings, and five four karat (solid) diamond rings with $40,000.00 and above price tags on them. I see why they were celebrating now and feeling good. These hustlers and gangsters hit the mother load.

Timer stated, "This was one of the biggest licks in my whole career. We got 105 Rolex watches and over 150 huge diamond rings. Ya'll sit back, relax, and make your selves at home. Tomorrow will be pay day. Fellas, I'm going to try my best to get $250,000.00 for this, but most definitely nothing under two hundred thousand. Either way it goes, it will be a lot of skrilla for all five of us."

Now the little YGs and Gator wanted to go out and find some pussy for the evening, but they didn't have any money. So Timer gave each one of them two thousand dollars each until the next day. He put all the jewelry in his secret safe in the mansion.

Soon as he returned, I corned Timer and told him, "I could call my girls from the track to come and service these niggas."

Timer said, "That's exactly what I was going to do. That's why I gave them some money. Damn SS Boy, slow down big pimping. I'll tell you what; it's four of them (crew members). I'll call two of my girls, the

Mexican girl and a snow bunny. I'll let you work two of your crows. That way we can't miss them."

Timer then told his crew, "We can provide some girls, but they aren't free. I can call my girls from the track, where they are making a thousand dollars a night."

They said, "Timer call them. It ain't no thang OG. We understand that pussy is not for free."

Timer said, "That's right. I can't let you long dick mother fuckers tear my bitch's pussy out the frame for free {lol}."

Gator and the YGs started smiling and laughing saying, "We feel you OG."

We walked down stairs and Timer called his bottom bitch on her mobile phone.

He told her, "Send home one of the white girls and the Mexican broad. Tell them to pick up two of SS Boy's girls, Sunshine and Special K."

We both left our bottom bitches at the track knowing that they will handle business and make our bread. It was now about two in the morning and everyone was fucked up and waiting on the freaks to arrive. Forty five minutes later, it was on and everyone was happy and satisfied. The girls started out dancing for everyone, giving the guys major erections. They were throwing one hundred dollar tips for the girls to continue to dance for them.

Next thing I know, no one was in the game room. They all chose a girl and was in a pimped out bedroom of Timer's. They were freaking and doing whatever they love to do . Timer and I chilled in the game room, sipping snorting yay (coke) and spitting pimping to each other.

Timer said, "I'm going to go ahead and peel them off tomorrow. I just didn't want them to know that I was the one buying all that jewelry."

I said, "That's game right there Timer. You get paid twice for one lick."

Timer said, "That's right, I get paid again when I sell it to the SA (Mexican Mafia) homies. I should come out with a hundred or better."

I couldn't do anything but give the OG dap. He not only had heart, he was also smart as hell. I just sucked up the game in a major way from Timer. We kept playing pool and popping it to one another.

An hour later, everyone was back in the game room with big smiles on their faces. They started up again after a chronic break. Everyone traded hoes and headed back into the bedrooms. Our hoes drained them niggas for major grip (money).

Chapter 36

My girls were already doing good that night. They clocked grip at the track where they were famous at. Soon as they walked through Timer's castle doors, I broke Sunshine and Special K for eleven hundred dollars. I might end up having a pretty good night after all.

Timer and I ended up in the Rolls headed to Super Sack-n-Save grocery store while those niggas was tricking. He purchased a bag of hickory charcoal, hickory wood chips, and lighter fluid. Then picked out ten fresh whole lobsters, ten pounds of jumbo shrimp, a bag of twenty short corn on the cobs, and a bag of potatoes. I already knew what time it was. We jumped into the Rolls after Timer spent about three hundred dollars. Only about five minutes away from the castle.

Timer said, "Pimping SS Boy, this is how pimps eat on a regular basis."

I heard the live lobsters trying to climb out the large box inside the grocery bag. We stepped in the crib and the homies was still tricking. They hadn't even noticed we had left the mansion and returned. Timer grabbed a large pot from under the island stove. Then filled it with water, lobster seasonings, and boiled the water until it was boiling hot. I was poolside in the backyard soaking the hickory wood chips and loading up Timer's large barrel barbeque grill with charcoal. While letting the charcoal soak with a little lighter fluid, Timer had the jumbo shrimp marinating. The shiscobab sticks (skewers) ran through the shrimp ready to get thrown on the grill with the buttered corn on the cob.

My mouth was starting to water all ready and shit hadn't even started to cook, yet. After the water was boiling, Timer poured all ten of those live lobsters into that huge steamy pot five @ a time. We went outside by the pool and Timer started the barbeque grill. He scattered the wood chips over the charcoal.

Stating, "The wood gives our meal that hickory taste that will melt in your mouth."

Once the grill heated up, Timer placed the corn on the cob soaked in butter and wrapped with aluminum foil on to the grill. There were about thirty jumbo shrimp filled with shiscobab sticks. It didn't take any time for the shrimp to grill.

Timer said, "These are appetizers until our meals get ready."

By now, everyone was in the kitchen and standing by the pool close to the barbeque grill. You could smell it all over the neighborhood at five o'clock in the morning. Timer's girls bragged on how good Timer could cook and by the looks of things, I quickly believed them. Timer's girls prepared the baked potatoes. Timer removed the lobsters from the pot after they were bright red. He placed them straight on the big barrel barbeque grill, next to the corn on the cob.

Everyone was really fiending now. Most of the crew had never tasted lobster before. My girls hadn't either. My girls think that Taco Bell and Wendy's are top flight, but I turned the bitches on to how champions eat.

We ended up eating like rich folks. That shit was A1, especially after we dipped the lobster tails into hot spicy melted garlic butter sauce.

We were sipping on Don P after we finished eating. I pulled my girls to the side to see what they were working with. I broke the bitches for over a thousand dollars each. That made a pimp smile.

Gator and the little YGs (young gangsters) said, "Yeah, we took care of ya'll hoes real proper. It ain't shit for ballers like us. We get money any day at any time and peel our homies hoes off a thousand or two."

Gator said, "They print money every day and we have unlimited spending."

Gator picked up his beer can and took a major blast from the past again.

I said, "Timer, this is big baller shit man. These are some real Gs you're fucking with."

Timer said, "I know it SS Boy, we don't squeeze this little money. We all stay sucker free."

We had to say something to uplift the homies after tricking real proper with our hoes.

About six thirty am that morning, Little Momma and Timer's girls came home from the track. I broke Little Momma for twelve hundred dollars, which gave me the record breaking high for one night's pimping of forty three hundred dollars. That was love to a new pimp on the block.

Before long, we were all passed out asleep and feeling good from living lavish. I didn't wake up until one o'clock that afternoon. Timer was already up and handling business.

He told the homies, "I ended up selling all the jewelry for $215,000.00."

He gave Gator and the homies $40,000.00 each and ended up with $55,000.00.

Timer said, "I'm getting on the highway Monday morning along with Gator and my other crew."

I asked Timer again, "When is enough enough?"

He answered, "SS Boy, I'm just getting my hustle on in the summer months. I'm taking off this winter."

Even though Gator's pockets were fat, he still had a jealous look in his eyes. The same look he had when Timer first introduced me to him. I still felt a little peculiar about Gator. It was something about him that I didn't like or trust.

I told Timer how I felt, but Timer refused to agree with me on Gator.

He said, "Gator was solid and cool."

I had to agree with Timer.

After a whole day of chopping it up with Timer and Gator, the homies went back to OKC. I had Gator figured out. He wanted to take Timer's place in the game. Gator wanted to be king of the hill, especially since he was the oldest out the crews. He hated deep down inside that Timer was the shot caller and CEO of this million dollar game. I'm sure he hated that Timer got a bigger cut of the money than everyone else too.

The way I looked at it, and the YGs look at it, Timer deserves more, because he is the OG and the play maker. If it wasn't for him, no one would be playing with six or seven figures. The first chance I got with Timer alone I told him what conclusions I had come up with and it made sense.

I said, "Timer, Gator wants to take your place in the game."

He replied, "I know it. Everyone wants to be king. 90% of haters want to be king, but wouldn't know what to do with all the power or how to run the business. They wouldn't know how to keep everyone happy and loyal to your calls and decisions. Little brother, I know you have good reading ability. You have to be able to read a person. That's why I've lasted so long in the game without a bullet in my back. Little brother, I'm two steps ahead of you. Gator has been talking behind my back to my little YGs. He has been trying to turn them against me. That's why we have a nice little plan for Mr. Gator. That's also why I'm keeping him close and working the shit out of him. The first time you told me that it was something about him; I've been paying close attention to Mr. Chi-Town Gator. I've been skinning and grinning right along with him. SS Boy, I appreciate you little brother. That's why I gave you the game. I know all about Gator. The homies and I know his only daughter and a few of his grandkids, mother, and father. We know where they all live just in case. You know that when you play the game with me, you're not the only one in the game. Your whole family is in the game with me."

I said, "I feel you."

We went in the game room with Gator and watched him hit the can. He was sitting fifty dollar pieces on the can. & was on one. Gator didn't have time to put the can down. He wasn't even concerned about spending money or turning a few corners in his new Lexus 400 sitting on twenties.

Timer looked at me and said, "That's why I don't fuck with that pipe or can, because I'll be on one much worse than Gator."

Later that evening, we put our hoes on automatic with instructions and Gator finally put the can down. He decided to go to a friend's house in Dallas to smoke. We were fucking with him really bad about that shit. Soon as Gator left, we jumped in the 600 v-12 Benz with all that jewelry.

Timer took me somewhere out in South Dallas (the hood) where he sold all of that jewelry to his Mexican posse for well over $300,000.00. We made a nonstop flight back to the mansion.

Timer said, "Today is your lucky day again. I had a pretty good day, so my pimp partner will also have a good day."

Timer made a total of $140.000.00 off the lick. We pulled up at the mansion and went inside.

Soon as we stepped in, Timer said, "Hook us up some drinks while I put my money up."

I went to the game room and hooked up two double Remy Martins on the rocks. Five minutes later, Timer came into the game room with something in his hand.

He said, "Is that the Rolex I gave you?"

I said, "Yeah."

He said, "Let me see it. I bet it's all scratched up."

I took it off and handed it to him. He was checking out how well I had taken care of it.

Timer said, "Shit, it still looks good, you must not wear it that often."

I answered, "No, only on special occasions."

Timer handed me an all gold Presidential Rolex full of ice with the diamond bezel.

And asked, "How often would you wear this?"

In answer, "Big bro., I would probably only wear this when me and you parlayed and popped major pimping on these hoes."

Timer said, "Give me two thousand dollars and your old Rolex."

I quickly said, "Bet."

Now I had the whole hook up on my jewelry once Rocky finished making my jewelry. This iced out Presidential was all a pimp needed to be complete. I peeled Timer off two thousand dollars and gave him my blue face Oyster Rolex with the quickness.

He said, "I figured that you would want this, besides, you deserve it SS Boy."

I gave Timer dap and said, "Thanks big bro."

Timer said, "I charged this to Gator's tab. I'm going to hit him where it hurts. Right in his pocket, you feel me? Tomorrow morning, we are going to Houston, Texas to the Galleria Mall to get the top flight shit."

I said, "Hell yeah, I need a new wardrobe. I'm tired of only wearing Nautica and Polo."

Timer replied, "I have a friend who works at the top flight store in the mall. For five or six thousand dollars, you can get it all. You can get Versace, snake skin, crocodile pants, shoes, hats, Armani suits, mink jackets, and full length minks. The more you spend, the more you win. I usually spend about eight or ten thousand dollars with my boy every time I visit him. All the ballers shop with him. Scarface, Pimp C, {U.G.K.} the H-Town boys, Slim Thug and all the pimps I fuck with shop at the Galleria Mall in Houston."

I ask, "What time are we leaving?"

"Before noon, we'll put the Double R on the highway."

I said, "Cool."

Timer said, "As soon as we get back, I'm outta here. Feel free to chill at the castle as long as you wish. Make yourself at home [Mi Casa, Su Casa]. Just take care of my shit like it's yours."

I said, "Timer, what's understood don't have to be explained."

I rolled up some of Timer's Indo into a phat Optimo green leaf blunt and that mother fucker tasted so good. I was staring at my new big face iced out Presidential Rolex.

Timer asked me, "SS Boy, do you ride bikes?"

"Yeah, but I haven't rode in a while."

He said, "Well you need to invest in a race bike or just a street bike so we can flex and floss."

I thought to myself, "Timer loves living dangerously. He also lives life to the fullest. That was cool because you only live once. Timer treated every day like there was no tomorrow. I also could understand where he was coming from too."

We chopped up game until about midnight or so. Then we hit the track in my Cadillac Escalade. It was plenty of action, & that's what you call Saturday night live on Harry Hines. I broke all three of my bitches for a total of fourteen hundred dollars. Timer broke his bitches for a bankroll.

He said, "Let's go to Momma's Café and chop it up with my pimp partners."

I said, "Cool."

Chapter 37

We rode down Harry Hines until we got to Momma's Café. The parking lot was full of pimps.

I said, "Damn Timer, last time I came through here, the parking lot was empty."

Timer said, "You have to learn the pimp schedule."

All the pimps were peeping out my pimp tight Escalade.

They were saying, "Damn SS Boy, that mother fucker looks better and better every time I see it."

"Thank you Pimping Beale, it's most definitely a hoe catcher and the ladies love it."

Beale said, "Damn Pimping SS Boy, the track has been doing you swell. What is that glittering on your arm?"

I held my wrist out and said, "An iced out gold Lexo Presidential."

Damn, "SS Boy, your Lexo is almost cleaner than mine. The bitches love this kind of shit don't they?"

I replied, "Hell yeah, Beale. I pulled this straight out a bitch's pussy and it won't stop."

Beale laughed and gave me dap. All the pimps out there were wearing serious ice, Rolexes, and top flight gear. The shit you won't find in Dillard's, Foley's, or Goldsmith's. Their shit was tailored made.

Timer said, "That's the shit I'm talking about pimping!"

A few pimps asked, "SS Boy, where is that sticky green?"

Well, "I've been slowing down on that tip. The pimping has been treating a hustler right. I've been holding up on the sack and hanging out more on the track."

They couldn't do anything but laugh.

& replied, "Keep it pimping. You won't last long with that sack. Just keep breaking a bitch's back on the track."

I gave Long Perm dap when he said that shit. Pimps always rhyme whenever they say shit, especially when they talk to their hoes. Hoes love that pimp shit.

Timer said, "SS Boy, twist up a couple of those doddie blunts."

I twisted four Indo blunts with the quickness and we started blazing up. A brand new Y2K Bently pulled up on the scene sittng on twenty inches.

I thought to myself, "Who could this be?"

The Bentley pulled up and parked. My boy Pimping Cobra got out of that mother fucker with a full length mink on. His jewelry was so monster that it was unbelievable. The rappers on television didn't have shit on Cobra's jewelry.

Cobra came straight to the Escalade and said, "What up Timer? What up SS Boy?"

I quickly said, "You pimping."

"Yeah SS Boy, this shit ain't hard to do. Just keep sending them hoes out the door with instructions. You see what pimping can buy you. I take that back. You see what a bitch will buy a pimp for guidance and instructions?"

I said, "Hell yeah."

I had to walk over and peep this fucking Bentley out in close caption, you feel me? I opened the driver's side door and the new smell of that Conley leather took my breath away. I knew that I really had to step my game up now. This was the life I wanted to live; no matter the cost, hours, or price of the game. Timer and the other pimps had to go over and peep Cobra's Bentley out as well. Everyone took hats off to Cobra on his pimping. His Bentley was no punk.

This young pimp was wearing a full length mink in the middle of summer. Also driving a Y2K Bentley with the AC blowing on high while sipping on a two hundred and fifty dollar bottle of Cristal. Cobra was drinking straight from the bottle.

I thought to myself, "Pimpin Cobra is doing way too much in a major way."

We all smoked until we were higher than the price tag on Cobra's Y2K Bentley. We chopped it up until about four o'clock in the morning. We must have smoked about ten or twelve Indo blunts that night and popped pimping in a major way.

Cobra didn't stay as long as we did at the track. He had major traps to go check. We pulled out a little after four am and headed back to the mansion.

Timer said, "SS Boy, that Bentley was cleaner than a white dove. Cobra is doing it. He is handling his business. That's why I kick it with those players. We all help each other out by putting the other on super charge. That will make you boost your game up just a little bit more and more everyday. Cobra just put me on super high voltage & got me turned up in a worldwide way. He was talking about buying a yacht and keeping it docked at Galveston Beach in Houston. I've got to have it. I told you that I wasn't shit compared to my homies. If you think Cobra is balling outta control, you ought to peep my SA, Mexican partners out."

I believed Timer about his Mexican friends.

I said, "Shit, Cobra put me on super high voltage too. I've got to turn my game up full speed, you dig?"

Timer said, "I feel you lil bro. That's why I'm pulling out as soon as we get back from H-Town tomorrow evening. I'm getting ready to bash on these peckerwoods real good this time. I've been thinking about making a triple play on their ass. That's three stores back to back."

I said, "Oh that would be major OG."

We pulled up in Timer's circular driveway. Popping pimping until the girls came home, & the sun was coming up.

Pimping Cobra left both of us with some major shit on our minds. I was thinking so hard about money that it took me well over an hour to fall asleep. I broke my stable for another two thousand dollars. That gave me a grand total of thirty four hundred dollars for the night. That was good, but now I needed more.

That day, Timer woke me up about ten o'clock that morning saying, "Let's ride."

I was up and dressed within thirty minutes. We smoked our morning blunt and jumped in the white on white 600 V-12 Benz. We only had two blunts to smoke; one on the way to H-Town and one for the way back. Timer kept foot in that 600 and the mother fucker ran too. He kept the cruise control on 100 mph and sometime he would mash it up to120 or more.

I said Timer, "Now I know why they charge so much for the V-12. It's all motor."

He said, "Hell yeah. I will out run almost any car in the distance. I've been thinking about that Bentley. I might have to buy me one of those $275,000.00 drop top Bentley coupes like the one Puff Daddy has. His shit is A-1. I could get one any time I want to, but it's just a matter of timing. It have to be the proper time for me to buy one. I'm going to put some serious thought into it by the time I return from this fantastic voyage. I'll know whether or not, if now is the time. Feel me?"

"Well I'm going to pay this last twenty thousand dollars on my truck. I'm probably going to get me one of these 600 V-12s, except it's going to be a two door drop top."

Timer said, "I can dig that."

We arrived in Houston's Galleria Mall within three hours. I had about eight thousand dollars with me. Timer introduced me to his salesman Bryan, who makes him monster deals on top flight shit. This store had everything a baller and pimp would and could want. They had Versace suits and clothes of all exotic skins.

I asked the salesman, "What can I get for five thousand dollars?"

He said, "I'll do you right. If you spend eight thousand, I'll set you straight in tailor made shit."

I asked, "What will I get for the eight?"

He said, "I'll give you three Versace suits, three Armani suits with matching shirts, socks, ties, handkerchiefs, and shoes. So that's six suits, six pair shoes, and six shirts. I'll give you a full length Beaver coat, Beaver hat, mink jacket, two mink hats, three silk Versace shirts, three Versace slacks, Anaconda big scale pants and shirt, two outfits, two crocodile outfits, crocodile hat, and shoes. So this is what you'll be leaving with for eight thousand dollars."

1. 6 suits, Versace and Armani'
2. 4 exotic skin outfits
3. 2 coats, one full length Beaver coat, & mink jacket
4. 9 shirts, silk, linen & Versace
5. 8 hats
6. 10 pair of shoes, all kind
7. Plus silk shirts and handkerchiefs and socks
8. 3 pair of Versace slacks

That's a good deal, because one Versace suit could cost you two thousand dollars easy, but I acted like the deal could be better.

Bryan said, "Alright SS Boy, since you're Timer's pimp partner, I'll throw in another Armani suit, shirt, and tie."

I said, "I need an Ostrich outfit since you're selling me some Ostrich shoes."

"Damn SS Boy, you are getting over $15,000.00 worth of top flight gear. I'm not making any money."

That was a lie. If he wasn't making any money, he wouldn't do it.

Bryan finally said, "Alright."

Timer said, "Plus you know I'll be back."

Timer bought a couple of new outfits he had just got in from overseas. We spent well over ten thousand dollars with Bryan. He drained me for all my little eight thousand dollars. Bryan had me measured up and suits fitting to a T. We walked around the mall for a couple of hours checking out the thick H-Town girls. Bryan broke me for the time being, but I was happy and satisfied with this wardrobe. Soon afterwards, we were back in the 600 V-12 and doing a hundred down the highway, jamming to Biggie.

I rode back to Dallas broker than a mother fucker. Now I knew I had to put some big pimping down on my stable. This means overtime baby. It was also time for me to fly to Nashville and break Baby again for a knot (money). We were back in Dallas in no time after we smoked the last blunt.

Soon as we stepped in the house, Timer put his hoes on automatic. He started packing his clothes and getting ready to hit the highway to get paid again.

Timer paged Gator and told him, "Get your ass over here because I will be out of here in thirty minutes with or without you."

Gator pulled up right on time. I'm surprised he wasn't high or should I say not that high.

Timer again told me, "Make yourself at home. You can stay for as long as you like."

"Thank you Big Bro. I'm flying out tomorrow. I should be back by Thursday."

Timer said, "Handle your business because it's time to grind baby."

"I feel you."

Timer loaded up the Suburban and I rolled him a couple of fat joints in Zig Zag papers, & He headed to OKC to pick up his other crew. Gator was right behind him in the big body 400 Lexus.

I invited my girls to relax in the poolside Jacuzzi. They had an evening martini and I had a joint for each of them. Laying my pimping on real thick like molasses.

I told my stable, "We deserve big things in life like this kind of shit."

My girls were talking about, "When can we ride like that?"

I told them, "If you all get down real hard for forty five days straight, it's on."

Now these hoes didn't know if they wanted Volkswagen Beetles. They were paying attention to what Timer's girls were driving, which was cool with me because I wasn't spending over twenty thousand dollars each. They didn't know that, but they did need the motivation. Special K hadn't earned enough seniority to get a car yet. She didn't know it, but I played this bitch like a Las Vegas slot machine. I kept a steering wheel in the bitch's back driving the shit out of her.

An hour later, it was time for the girls to get dressed and go to work. I really appreciated Timer for telling his hoes to give my hoes the game on the track in Dallas. I sent my bitches out the door with instructions on bringing a pimp his money in a major way if they wanted new cars. As soon as they left, I called Love Field Airport. Then made reservations from Dallas to Nashville for tomorrow through Southwest Airlines. I scheduled a flight leaving from Love Field for twelve thirty, noon. Also getting hooked up on a rental car for when I touched down (landed) in Nashville.

Chapter 38

My pager was blowing up from OKC. It was my boy Big Seamore.

He was like, "What up pimping? I haven't heard from or seen you flexing and flossing around the city. I called to see what was cracking with you."

I said, "Big Seamore, a pimp been pimping in a major way out in Dallas. I've been here for three or four days pimping up a storm trying to get ahead. I saw your cousin Cobra and he just bought a brand new Y2K Bentley sitting on twenty inches. It's clean too."

Big Seamore said, "Yeah, he called and told me that he was coming to the city."

"Seamore, I believe that I'm moving to Dallas. Man, these pimps are doing it and it's plenty of everything here. I've been getting over three thousand dollars each and every night since I've been here. It's like that every night."

Big Seamore said, "Is that right? I need to bring my snow bitches."

I said, "Dig that. I'll be there Thursday. I might need you to pick me up from Will Rogers Airport in OKC. Then you and your stable can bring me back to Dallas. In the mean time, you can put your hoes down in Dallas on Harry Hines. It's plenty money for everybody, but only if your hoes know how to work their jelly."

Big Seamore said, "I'm ready to work these hoes. We've been working the truck stop in Guthrie with Pimping Beanie and Slim. It's been cool, but Big Seamore needs more. I need to buy that new big body Fleetwood with the touch of gold all the way around it."

I replied, "Dig that. Well, I'll call and let you know what time my flight will be arriving in OKC. Keep it pimping bro."

I ended up resting and chilling at the mansion that evening. Looking at my new furs, Versace suits, shoes, and other shit, & was getting my game plan together. I fell fast asleep in Timer's game room watching his sixty inch big screen. I woke up about four thirty in the morning and rolled a joint.

Immediately turned on the radio to K-104 Jamz FM! They were jamming on some good shit, Computer Love, Love Train, Midnight Star, SOS Band, Atlantic Star, Star Point and etc…. the list goes on.

Next thing I knew, the girls were coming through the door. I broke Little Momma for eleven hundred dollars. Then I broke Sunshine for nine hundred and fifty dollars. Shortly after, I relieved Special K of twelve hundred dollars. That gave me a grand total of three thousand two hundred and fifty dollars.

That was all I had at the time. I spent all my money on the Lexo and clothes. I had to start all over again. No more spending. It was time to stack now.

I sat my girls down and told them, "Daddy have to go out of town for a few days. Keep working hard. No shorts. Everyone has been getting over or very close to a thousand dollars each and every night. So remember our goals and what we're trying to achieve in life. Everyone needs to work hard, like you've been bringing in every night here in Dallas."

They all said, "Okay Daddy, it's on."

The girls hit the showers, cleaned up, and came back into the den with me. We all camped out on the game room floor together. Little Momma made a pallet on the floor as well. They were telling me about their encounters with the tricks on the tracks out there. They had me laughing so hard that tears started falling from my eyes. Especially when they told me about those drunk Mexicans who speak very little English, or no English at all, and you can't understand what they were saying.

They all wanted to ride with Little Momma tomorrow when she dropped me off at the airport.

I said, "Cool, ya'll just want to see a pimp off because when a pimp is away, the hoes will play."

They all laughed & said, "No Daddy, all hoes don't play. We are going to handle business and drain these tricks for every dime. Believe us."

I replied, "By the way you said that, I most definitely believe you."

The next day, we all woke up about ten thirty am or so. I quickly packed some of my new outfits and shoes, & put on my new Ostrich pants, jacket, Ostrich shoes, and hat. My hoes loved to see a pimp dressed nice, especially in some brand new pimp tight shit they had never seen before.

We arrived at Love Field International Airport at 12:07. All of my girls came in with me and hung on my arm. They were hugging me and shit. The squares couldn't understand seeing a pimp cleaner than a white fish with three bad black women hanging all over him. I had on a twenty seven thousand dollar Lexo. I'm sure by the way everything appeared to them that it was quite clear that I was a pimp and these were my hoes.

I didn't care. My pimping was no secret, you feel me? I'm accepting all applications from these hoes I encountered. A young pimp knew that he needed a stable of ten girls or better to get the kind of money I was after. I was after eight to ten thousand dollars a night like Pimping Cobra and Kansas City Benzo, and Don Juan in Chi-Town.

This game isn't for everybody. You have to have style and finesse. You might hang around a true pimp who is sending bitches out the door with instructions. That doesn't mean this pimp shit will just rub off on you. You can learn good habits like don't pay, get paid.

I know a lot of females will hate me because they know this is real talk. They want to keep that steering wheel in a trick's back. I refuse to take a bitch out to eat, to the movies, and ride out all my gas. I flipped the script and started charging these hoes. Take me out. Drive your gas out on your expense. Pay me for this good dick. They didn't have a problem with it and neither did I. That's what pimps taught me. Women think you're supposed to pay for pussy. That's the old usual tradition.

I'll tell a bitch in a New York second, "I can jack off better than fuck. So take your pussy and run with it. You can sell the portion of pussy you was going to give me, and pay me for my portion."

Women love it when you don't sugar coat what you want to get across to them. You might go home alone sometimes, but you'll still have money. Sooner or later, you will run into a true broad who understands and feels where you're coming from. See, how it starts, is how it will ends. If you start tricking and paying for everything, that is what a woman will expect each and everyday. If you train her into paying, she will take care of a pimp real proper, you dig.

I stepped on my flight clean from head to toe. I looked out the airplane window. I could see my stable standing inside the airport waving at a player. I saw that they really cared about me and we were becoming closer and closer with a tight bond. When the flight attendant came around, she thought I was Puff Daddy. That was not the first time I've been mistaken for Sean Puffy Combs. That right there let me know that I was glistening like a million dollars and headed in the right direction.

I ordered a double shot of Hennessy on the rocks, just to get me started. It took almost two hours to arrive in Nashville International Airport. Within two hours, I knocked down three or four doubles on the rocks. I was ripped, feeling good, and couldn't wait to smoke one of the fat blunts I had in my pocket.

I rented a Ford Excursion just to see what was up with it. Believe it or not, it was cool and roomy. I returned to that same Mall where I saw all those renegade bitches, who were out of bounds by speaking and staring at a pimp. The last time I was in there, the Mall was jammed packed with women. I was passing out my business cards and accepting applications from these squares. They thought they were getting a free ride. Little did they know, the only ride they were getting free was to the track.

Broads just stared at OKC SS Boy. They admired my style and taste.

They were asking, "Where are you from?"

People can tell that you're not from their state.

I told them, "I'm from OKC, & was just passing through admiring the beautiful women of Nashville. I'm looking for a winner who is not afraid of life or big money."

I saw dollar signs light up in their eyes. Now they wanted to know what a pimp was talking about. I never told them anymore. I let them wonder and guess what I could be talking about.

Some asked, "Are you an entertainer or in the music business?"

I answered, "No, but I am a manager and I assist in the entertainment world."

Now they were paying close attention with their ears standing up like a German shepherd's. Two country fine ass white girls were interested. They kept reading my business card I gave to them. I got tired of shooting the shit with these squares.

I told them, "You can give me a page later. I'm staying in Nashville for the night."

The two white girls, which were sisters, said, "We will be sure to call you tonight between six or seven o'clock this evening."

I shook their hands like the gentlemen I am and told them, "It was my pleasure to meet you, & will be looking forward to your call this evening."

I pimped off and explored the rest of my prospects, & left the mall and checked into a nice elegant hotel. It was more like an apartment with two bedrooms, kitchen, one and half baths, dining room, and the whole works.

I called Baby and let her know, "Your man is in town. But, first I'm going to handle some business and I will see you first thing in the morning. Just wake a pimp whenever you wake up."

Baby said, "Well, I'm going to call you tonight on my first break."

I said okay, "Cool. I can't wait to see you tomorrow."

"I can't wait to see you either because you're going to be real happy to see me Daddy."

At six thirty sharp, my 1800 pager blew up with a Nashville area code. I knew a pimp had a bite on some new prospects, which meant more skrilla to a pimp's table. I returned the page and it was the two snow bunnies who were actually biological sisters. I spit pimping at them in a square way before inviting them to my hotel room for drinks and conversation. The little broads quickly bit the bait and accepted a pimp's invitations. By eight o'clock sharp, they were knocking at my hotel room door.

I invited them in and told them, "Relax and make yourselves comfortable. Would you like a drink or a beer?"

They both preferred the same drink that a pimp was drinking, so I prepared three double Remy Martin drinks on the rocks. I served them with style and class, & they loved that shit. The girls were commenting on my manorizm. They also noticed my fresh manicure.

They said, "Your finger nails are prettier than ours. Your cologne smells really nice."

I also found a few complimenting qualities on them. Everything was going smooth so far. I could tell that I wasn't the first brother they had been with. They tried to talk black and shit, which was really funny. I managed to hold in my laughter. These broads were pretty cool.

I had to ask them, "Do you smoke weed?"

They looked at each other and giggled.

"Hell yeah," while giving each other dap.

I rolled a fat blunt while Shelly prepared more drinks. Kelly just sat there talking and staring at a player. By now, these girls had obviously forgotten why they came over. It was all business, you feel me.

I was first going to get these squares fucked up, then spit my pimping at them on the real. Two white bitches were exactly what a pimp needed to add to my stable. Shelly returned with our drinks as I blazed up.

We watched BET videos and those broads knew every video. I knew they dug brothers. They had been through the ringer, but not on a pimp and hoe scale. I was pretty sure that they were just use to a lot of free fucking. They let them long dick niggas lay pipe in them for free.

We were starting to feel the Remy and the bomb ass sticky green. Everyone was getting a little loose. Shelly and Kelly started dancing with each other. They were laughing, giggling, and getting freaky. I sat in the chair clean as a mother fucker looking at these square girls act a fool.

I asked them, "How old are you?"

Shelly answered, "I'm twenty three and Kelly is twenty one."

That was legal and it was time for my game to elevate and begin.

I asked, "Do you have a man?"

They both said, "No."

I was sure that was a lie; because they thought they had a little game about themselves.

So the next question I asked them was, "What do you do for a living?"

They both answered, "We have jobs, but the jobs aren't shit. We are looking for something better. That's the reason we came to the hotel room to kick it with you."

Then I asked them, "Do you like to travel from state to state?"

They both answered, "Yes."

"I see that you both like to dance. Are you two dancers?"

They both looked at each other and laughed.

"No, but we were thinking about it, because they make good money."

Shelly just came out with it, "We make around three hundred dollars a night."

I said, "Yeah, I guess that's pretty good money."

The girls said, "Good money, shit, that's a lot of money for one night's work."

"Maybe they were'nt so square after all," I thought to myself.

I said, "Well, in that business, the real money is when you do private dancing for the clients. It deals with a little bit more than dancing."

They both quickly said, "Long as we're getting paid, we don't have a problem with it."

Chapter 39

They both gave each other five, again. These two squares were saying everything a pimp wanted to hear. So far, so good.

I told them, "You make the real money when you service the tricks. Every time I go to the strip club, I see women working hard performing on stage. All the customers would tip her a dollar. A dollar ain't shit for all that work. When they go behind the red door, in the freak room, that's when they rake in the money, you feel me?"

They said, "SS Boy, how do you know about all of that?"

"Like I told you, I've been around the track a few times myself."

Kelly asked, "Well, what exactly do you do?"

I just came on out with it.

"I'm a manager of females that I set up with dates and good places to work all over the US."

They both said, "Oh, so you're a pimp in other words?"

I said, "You can say that, but I prefer manager. My girls and I are a team. They used to do the same thing you two are doing, until I took them under my wing. Now they are living lavish. Drinking, smoking, hair done, finger and toe nails done, wearing the phat gear, and driving new cars are a part of everyday life for them."

They were like, "Damn, so you hooked them up like that?"

I answered, "Yeah. They also hook me up and take care of me real good. Can't you tell?"

By then, the telephone rang and it was Baby.

She said, "I was just calling to speak to you for a minute while I'm on my break. I will call you again later on tonight."

The little white girls were fucked up in the head by now. I didn't want to put too much on them at one time, or I might scare the little squares off.

I asked them, "Are you hungry?"

"Kind of."

That meant, "Hell yeah."

Okay ladies, "Let's ride and find something to eat. You two can show me around Nashville a little bit."

We rode around Nashville for a little while. They showed me the hang outs and what was happening in their city. We ended up in a Taco Bell drive thru. These squares were Taco Bell fans and thought it was the greatest thing that Nashville had to offer. I bought them some tacos while steady putting selling pussy on their minds.

I went down the street to Chilli's and ordered me some baby back ribs, fries, and some mozzarella sticks for an appetizer. We headed back to the hotel where I ate my dinner. Those hoes loved that big Ford Excursion that a pimp was temporarily rolling. They thought that it was mine at first.

I quickly told them, "I ride way better than this, on gold ones."

Soon as I finished eating, I rolled another blunt.

& told Kelly, "Make us some drinks."

These square white broads loved kicking it like this.

I told them, "Me and my girls kick it like this all day, every day, 24/7."

Shortly after smoking that blunt, the snow bunnies were dancing again with each other directly in front of me. They were pussy popping and percolating.

I said, "Since you lovely ladies are doing all of that, let me see what you're working with."

"What are you talking about?"

I answered, "Dance for me. Strip and let me see what you two are working with."

They slowly started undressing and giggling while dancing. I was quite stunned because the white girls had a little ass on them and nice tits as well. It looked like they also knew how to work their jelly. Next thing you know, I had the two bunnies freaking with each other while I sat at the table and rolled blunts. They were doing some big power freaking. There was a lot of ass licking and pussy sucking going on. The bunnies must have freaked for an hour or so. They were really enjoying themselves while a pimp just sat there and watched.

I was thinking to myself, "A pimp might have two new turnouts. They fit the qualifications and descriptions of a hooker."

These snow bunnies loved sex and wanted me to come join them.

"I don't fuck for free. Do you know that a trick would pay us good money just so he could sit in on one of your sessions? He would love to watch and jack off while fantasizing about you two."

They both replied, "SS Boy, are you serious?"

"Hell yeah. I know you two have been giving away plenty of pussy, haven't you?"

They just kind of laid there with a slight grin on their faces.

I said, "Ya'll are getting your pussies wore out for free even though you enjoy it. I've got the hook up. You can enjoy yourselves and get paid for your services. You feel me?"

The freaks started to feel a little stupid and started to put on their clothes.

I said, "Don't get embarrassed for something you didn't know anything about. See, I have to get paid for my services. No free dick; it costs to ride this boss."

It was now about two thirty in the morning. The ladies had to move around and go home or find some free dick somewhere else.

S.S, "We enjoyed ourselves, & will call you tomorrow evening as soon as we get off work, okay."

I told them, "That would be cool. I might stay in Nashville for a couple of days, since I found two beautiful snow bunnies, who love having fun."

They smiled, gave me a big hug, and said, "We will surely call you tomorrow evening around seven or so."

The snow bunnies finally left the hotel room and I undressed and fell fast asleep. I wanted tomorrow to come so fast, so I could check my Nashville trap from Baby.

Baby called me the next morning about ten thirty am.

"Wake up and get dressed so you can pick me up before twelve noon."

"Okay Cool, I'll be there."

Instantly getting out of bed to hit the showers. I put on my new crocodile outfit with the crocodile shoes, hat, and Versace shades. I was looking like a million bucks. Immediately pulling in front of Meeko's by eleven forty five am to pick up my money and Baby.

I walked in with my safe deposit key in my hand. Baby was sitting in the lobby area waiting on me with a big smile on her face. Baby gave me a big hug and took a step back to check out how sharp a pimp was dressed.

Baby gave me my props where they were due. After all the greeting and compliments, we headed straight to the safe deposit box. I opened it and that mother fucker was full of big faces. There were twenties and fifty dollar bills. I had to stuff it all in Baby's Dooney purse. I pimped on out the door with Baby in front of me with a tight grip on a pimp's money.

Again asking Baby, "How much skrilla is this?"

Baby answered, "It's about twelve thousand dollars."

"Damn, is your pussy okay Baby? Is it sore?"

She was like, "Oh, so you got jokes today? Ha ha ha."

I said, "Fuck it, if you can't take a joke, in a nice way."

We stopped at three different banks to purchase cashier travelers checks for four thousand dollars each. Then stopped at IHOP to grab a bite to eat, which was some good shit. I took her to the mall and purchased her a couple of Gucci outfits and a Gucci purse. That made her very happy, but not as happy as I was to get that twelve thousand dollars I broke her for.

After all the eating and shopping, Baby grew horny for sex and so did I since I hadn't fucked in a week or so. I knew that she was going to ask for some of this joy stick. So you can say that a pimp saved his self for his hoe. We headed over to my hotel room and got butt naked.

I took a couple of puffs off my blunt. Baby immediately started puffing on this black Cuban cigar (dick) and damn could she suck some dick now. She had gotten even better and I loved it. Before long, I was cumming all down her throat. Baby refused to let this night stick go down, she constantly sucked and jacked it off until this mule was standing up tall at attention again.

I fucked the shit out of her until she had multiple orgasms back to back. It took me almost forty five minutes to cum again. Her pussy was sore for real this time. She went into the restroom to get a cold face towel. Baby placed it on her sore and tender pussy while lying back on the bed.

I fucked her so hard that I fucked my dick up. It was all scraped up and sore as hell. Now that shit was uncalled for and outta line but, it had to be done. I had to fuck the bitch real proper like.

We laid up butt naked for a few hours getting high and enjoying ourselves while watching movies on cable. Around six o'clock that evening, we crawled out of bed and climbed in the shower together. We washed each other's backs and so on. My shit was all fucked up (my penis). My fucking days were over for a week or two until my shit was healed up.

I had Baby back at the whore house by seven o'clock that evening. A young pimp sent her right back out the door with instructions and a sore pussy, just like she liked it.

I headed to the hotel room with a jar of Vaseline to put on my night stick. I was hoping that would help the healing process a little quicker. Even if it didn't help the healing process, it helped put out that burning sensation around my dick. That shit felt like a second degree burn. I fucked the bitch until her pussy went dry and that's what fucked up my shit. I'll never do that again and neither will Baby.

Next thing I knew, the hotel phone was ringing.

I said to myself, "Damn, what does Baby want now?"

It wasn't Baby. It was those freaky white hoes Shelly and Kelly. They wanted to come over and talk to me for a second. I invited them on over. I was ready to set those square hoes off or put them down. My first impression was that they wanted another free ride tonight at a pimp's expense. I was ready to dismiss the square hoes.

I was going to tell them, "Go and find somewhere else to play. As far as I am concerned, you already owe me. Time is money and money is time, you dig?"

Kelly & Shelly were knocking on my hotel room door about thirty or forty minutes after talking to them. They came in and sat down. Shelly reached in her little purse and pulled out a nice quarter sack of trees (weed).

She threw it to me and asked, "Would you please, roll up a couple of blunts?"

I rolled a blunt with a little amazement. A player was a little surprised that these hoes bought something to the table for a pimp. We smoked two blunts and the trees were pretty good I must say. I started back talking about the same subject we had talked about last night.

They said, "Yeah SS Boy, we've been thinking about your proposition."

Yeah, "I haven't made any propositions to you, yet."

That fucked them up.

They were like, "Oh, we aren't good enough for you?"

"No ladies, it's not like that. Before I put you down completely, I have to see if you are qualified. Not everyone can get this kind of money. You have to be a special kind of lady. First I would have to give you a little initiation. A manager can't send you out there with my girls yet. I can't have you two standing around looking silly, expecting the same benefits as the rest of the stable. I know for sure that you two could make plenty of money because I don't have any snow bunnies in my stable."

They asked, "SS Boy, will you put us down on some money? We can do it right."

"First thing you have to get right is that I tolerate no stuffing (stealing). Every dime you make out there on that job you bring it to me. I'll take care of you. Besides, it's not good to be working with a lot of money in your possession. You could lose it or get robbed. We work too hard to let any of that happen, you feel me? So ladies answer this: Are you still ready for your manager to put you down?"

They looked at each other and answered, "Yes, we want to get paid. We are tired of being broke and fucking for free."

I said, "Dig that."

I proceeded to put them down and explain the rules and regulations of the game and how the track and truck stops work.

"There will be no snitching or running your mouth. If for some ridiculous reason you go to jail, keep your mouth shut. I'll be there to bond you out before the ink dries. If you snitch, I won't get you out. If someone else makes your bond, that's your body. You can kiss everything good bye. Do you understand?"

They both said, "SS Boy, we are down. We hate snitches."

Kelly said, "I used to sell dope with my boyfriend. We got busted and I didn't tell shit. My punk ass boyfriend told on his friends. I bonded out of jail and never called him again. Plus I told him to never call me again because he was weak and sorry. You don't have to worry about us snitching on you SS Boy. We could never snitch on you or anyone else."

I said, "Shit, it sounds like you two are down like four flat tires and true to the game. I'm really starting to like you two fine mother fuckers. It's nothing left to talk about. Let's work the big truck stop in Nashville and get paid. All you have to do is walk sexy in front of the truckers sitting in the 18 wheelers. They will call you over to talk with them. You tell them your price. It's usually twenty dollars for a shot of head and twenty dollars for a shot of pussy, but you can put your own price on it."

They both said, "Hell yeah, my pussy is the bomb and I want more than twenty dollars for it."

Chapter 40

I replied, "I feel you. You two are already dressed sexy. All we need is a box of condoms. Don't lose the condoms or I'll think that you're stuffing on me. Condoms are money to me. Shit, let's see what's popping then. Let's ride."

Both of the girls said, "Let's ride then. You haven't said a thang."

I put those bitches in the Y2K Ford Excursion and headed to the same big truck stop me and Seamore worked a couple of weeks ago. I checked into the same motel across the street from the truck stop. Plus I could watch them to make sure they were cool and could follow instructions. A young new pimp put the girls down with the quickness.

I looked out the motel window and saw them getting busy. The snow bunnies were hopping from truck to truck getting money. Now I just had to see if the bitches would bring my money to me without running off. I watched them closely. It's kind of like making a dog fetch a bone. You know the dog will go & get the bone, but you usually have trouble getting him to bring the bone back to you {lol}.

I refused to give them the game for free. Two hours later, I was driving through the parking lot of the truck stop. My new turnouts spotted a pimp and ran over to the Ford Excursion to get in. These white hoes were amped up on super charge. I broke the little bitches for about two hundred dollars each and gave them more pimping and instructions. I sent them right back out the door for two more hours.

I told them, "Go across the street in two hours and meet me. The room number is 405. Don't be late and don't be early. Do exactly as I say. You are under my command."

I punched out in the big Ford heading to the motel room across the street. Two hours later, the little broads were knocking on my door with a pimp's money. It was another two hundred dollars each.

I quickly told them, "Girls, let's ride."

We left and headed back to the hotel.

I sat the girls down and asked them, "So what do you think about this game?"

They said, "That was easy money. Now SS Boy, how much do we get?"

I said, "That was initiation. We have another night of that tomorrow for me to decide whether or not if I'm going to take you two with me. Have you ever been to Oklahoma City or Dallas, Texas before?"

They both answered, "No, but we would love to go with you SS Boy."

"I would love for you two to go back with me as well, but let's see if you two can handle business again tomorrow night."

A young pimp reached in his pocket and peeled them off one hundred dollars each.

& told them, "Get at me tomorrow."

Since they had to work early in the morning, I gave both of them a hug and sent them out the door, imagine that.

The next morning at ten o'clock sharp, Baby was calling to wake me up. She was ready for a pimp to come pick her up again before noon. I finally got out of bed and hit the showers, & got clean as a white dove with my Versace outfit on from head to toe.

I was at Meeko's to pick baby up by eleven thirty Wednesday morning. We did the usual shit of going for a bite to eat, spending a little time together, but no sex. My shit was still fucked up. We just chilled all day; reminiscing and laughing. We parlayed until it was time for her to go back to work.

I told Baby, "I will be flying out of here tomorrow morning sometime."

I dropped Baby back off at Meeko's and headed back to the hotel. At seven thirty sharp, my new turnouts blew a pimp up on my 1800 pager. I called them right back at their Mother's house where they lived, & quickly invited them over to spend a little time with me before we left town. They were knocking on my hotel door forty minutes later with some sexy outfits and high heel open toe shoes on.

I immediately put those snow bunnies in the Excursion and dropped them off at the track with instructions on getting a pimp his money. I worked those hoes until three o'clock in the morning. I broke them for a total of twelve hundred dollars. We went back to my hotel room after they cleaned up.

I told them, "I am leaving tomorrow. So what's up? Are ya'll going with me to the land of plenty?"

Shelly answered, "I can't leave tomorrow. I'll be ready to leave by the weekend."

Kelly said, "I don't like my job. I'm ready to quit anyway. I'm going with you SS Boy."

I said, "Cool."

Kelly chose to leave Nashville with a pimp.

Shelly said, "I will most definitely be in Dallas by this weekend."

Okay, "Cool, but whatever you do, don't go back out and work alone. It's some crazy people out there. If a pimp sees you out there without a pimp, that's your ass. We probably won't ever see you again, so don't out slick yourself. Shelly, take Kelly home to pack her shit. Kelly, if you don't like kicking it with me, you can always come back home anytime you wish. If a person no longer wants to be with me, I no longer want her there. It's a privilege to be with me, live lavish, and have the finer things in life."

Kelly hurried up and told Shelly, "Let's go."

She then told me, "I will be back in a little while."

Okay, "Cool. I'll be right here waiting on your fine ass."

Kelly called me about an hour later from her Mom's house telling me, "I will be at your room before nine o'clock am. My Mom was tripping and didn't want me leaving with a stranger. I told her that I was only going on a short vacation, & will be back in a week or so. She wasn't trying to hear that. So I told her that I was going anyway, & will have Shelly drop me off at the room in the morning on her way to work."

I said, "Cool, if you're not here by eleven o'clock am, I'm out of here."

She said, "SS Boy, you're not leaving me. I will be there by nine o'clock, okay?"

I said, "Imagine that."

Kelly knocked on my hotel door at eight thirty with two large suit cases. She was ready to leave Nashville and see the world for the first time in her young life. I called Southwest Airlines and made reservations for two to Oklahoma City. We would be departing at twelve thirty five pm.

Baby called at ten thirty and I was ready, dressed, and waiting on her call. I needed to see her, tell her goodbye, and check my trap again. I pulled up by eleven o'clock that morning with my safe deposit box key in hand again.

Baby was doing well. She had already clocked thirty two hundred dollars in three nights of work. I talked to her for ten or fifteen minutes.

Then told her, "I have to go because my flight departs at twelve thirty. I'll see you in OKC when you come home, & I love you."

I hugged baby before I punched out in the big Ford Excursion to the hotel to pick up my new turnout. I picked her up and we loaded up the Ford. We then headed to Nashville International Airport to turn in the truck and pick up our flight tickets. We caught our flight at twelve thirty five and headed to OKC.

I called Big Seamore to tell him, "Pick us up at two forty five. We're riding Southwest Airlines Bro."

Me & my new turnout walked on board and buckled up with the quickness. I couldn't do nothing but think about adding more money to my payroll. Pimping had a pretty good trip to Nashville. I left there with over seventeen thousand dollars, & broke Baby for fifteen thousand. Shelly and Kelly kicked in two thousand dollars, which was cool. Before long, I planned to have ten hookers or more in my stable.

A young pimp had to snap out of counting heads and continue counting bread. I needed to start thinking about my money and concentrate on putting this bitch down to the fullest. A manager started laying on his pimping rather thick to Kelly. I had to enforce the rules.

I explained to her, "Never get out of bounds with another pimp, or you could be held accountable. That would be out of my hands, because you shouldn't have been flirting with him in the first place. In this game, if you got eyes, you got action. You must want to choose up, if you keep staring at a pimp, you dig?"

I put some serious shit on Kelly's mind that made her put some consuming thought into our conversation. This was a new game of no return that she had just signed a life time contract for. Once a hoe, always a hoe in my book.

Two hours later, we were walking through the lobby of Will Roger's International Airport looking for Big Seamore. We stood outside waiting on him. Five minutes later, Seamore pulled up in a black on black Y2K big body Fleetwood Cadillac Brougham, with the gold grill, gold Cadillac tru spokes, Vogue tires, bumper kit, and a touch of gold all the way around it. His shit was pimp tight and he was clean as ever.

Kelly was straight tripping on all this high powered shit. I put the bitch in the back seat and the manager sat up front where pimp's sit, you dig? Pimping Seamore pulled off real slow and the Y2K Lac rode smooth like a dream. We were listening to the Isley Brothers.

Big Seamore said, "Let's stop by my house first. I've got something for you."

"Cool, I need it. Do you still have the 98 Olds Seamore?"

"Hell yeah, that's my baby. She isn't going anywhere."

We pulled up on the set. My Boy ran in the house, & left us in the Lac with the motor running and the ac blowing.

I asked Kelly, "Do you like this kind of shit?"

She replied, "Hell Yeah. I love this car. It's cute."

Well that's how it is in OKC. We ride in nothing but the best of the best from state to state."

Big Seamore came out the house with a brown paper sack jogging to the car at a slow pace. Real cool we rode out to my house so we could chop up more game and pop pimping in a major way.

I told Kelly, "Have a seat and make yourself at home."

Then turned on the big screen television for her.

"Feel free to go in the kitchen and get whatever you want and relax."

Me and Big Seamore went into the bedroom and started counting money. He had the thirty thousand dollars that he owed me.

"Damn Big Seamore, you've been getting down."

"Hell yeah, I've been selling plenty of pounds like cake."

"I feel you bro."

Big Seamore replied, "On top of that, a hustler still have thirty pounds left. As soon as I finish, I will be ready to re-up."

I quickly answered, "Cool, I'm ready for you big baby."

As Seamore was leaving, he asked, "I know you heard about Pimping X?"

"Pimping X? What about him?"

"He's been kidnapped. They found his car in the parking lot at Crossroads Mall, & he was nowhere to be found. His photo has been all over the news. Channel 5 news asking has anyone seen this man? If so, please call crime stoppers or the Oklahoma City Police Department."

I said, "Damn, someone kidnapped Pimping X? That's fucked up. But that's how the game goes when you go A. wall."

I put my money in the safe along with my $52,835.00 I already had. Then added the thirty thousand that Big Seamore just gave me and the fifteen thousand from Nashville. Now I had a grand total of $97,835.00, 265 pounds, and five hoes in my stable.

I was doing ghetto fabulous. Having twenty three thousand dollars out on credit, fifteen thousand to the Prospect Posse, and eight thousand to OG from California. Kelly and I jumped in my drop top Monte Carlo SS and headed to the East Side so a hustler could check his traps.

I caught up with OG, & OG paid me my eight thousand dollars that was owed to me.

OG mentioned, "My spot is hot. The police have been riding up and down the block. That makes business very hard for me. I was thinking about moving to another spot."

I answered, "That's your best bet OG. Well, I'm out of here. Page me whenever you get ready to re-up."

OG answered, "Okay."

We gave each other dap and I punched out with my snow bunny, Kelly. Then headed over to the set, where Seamore and the Prospect Posse were. Everyone was on the block chilling and handling business. Plus the posse had a little money for me. They gave me seventy five hundred dollars. That left a balance of seventy five hundred dollars.

I asked, "Big Seamore, what time are we leaving today?"

Seamore answered, "Let's roll out by seven o'clock this evening."

"Okay cool, I'm going to drop my new turnout off at the track in Dallas before ten o'clock tonight. I'll be at home and waiting on you to pick us up by seven."

"Okay S.S. Boy. My stable and I will be there."

Kelly and I grabbed a bite to eat then headed to Redrum's house. I needed to get some of that good powder for our little road trip to Dallas. When I pulled up at his house, he had about four of his Blood homies standing in the front yard on guard duty. Redrum had it going on now and was ready for war. Redrum also had a couple of new faces on the set. There were some brothers whom I had never seen before.

He invited me in and we talked for a minute while he weighed me out another quarter ounce for free.

I asked him, "Who are those new dawgs out there?"

"I flew those killers in from California because these niggas been tripping around here. Niggas are kidnapping one another. Did you hear about Pimping X?"

"Yes I did hear about that."

Well S.S. Boy, "I'm not going for that shit. Fuck that."

"I feel you Redrum."

We walked outside and he introduced me to his new dogs (Bloods) from Cali. His name was J Crack. This nigga was a dark skinned black man with Chinese eyes. I could tell by the look in his eyes that he was a killer and true to the game. Before long, I started calling J Crack Black China Man.

Black China man said, "SS Boy, I've heard alot about you. How you handle business and came from rags to riches."

While giving a pimp dap.

J Crack said, "I'm trying to do the same thing with my homie Redrum. We are going to peel some caps if these haters get in our way."

I said, "I don't blame you. I feel the same way dawg."

Chapter 41

I fired up a blunt with these young brothers. They were about their paper and they were down for anything: killing, robbing, and moving weight. I like that. In order to get rich from the streets, you have to be a jack of all trades.

Me and Kelly left Redrum's house and headed to my house so I could put up my new money I just collected. That was a total of fifteen thousand and five hundred dollars. My stash was stacking up. I was in the six figure zone again with a total of $113,335.00, & still had $7,500.00 owed to me.

A hustler couldn't wait to get to Dallas so I could check my hoe trap. Kelly had jet lag and needed a short nap from all the action. We both took a short nap after she quit complimenting me on my blue SS drop top M.C. with the white guts, (interior) blue stitching, sitting on 17 inch gold Daytons, and the Alpine system in it that was shoving up a storm.

Kelly also loved a player's house; how everything was laid out, clean, and fresh. I could tell this girl was squarer than a pool table and twice as green. She wasn't use to this kind of shit at all.

Kelly said, "OKC is a small LA isn't it?"

I asked, "What would make you think that?"

She answered, "Because the city is full of nothing but Crips and Bloods. Everyone is riding Daytons and low riders. Everyone talks proper like the people from California. I never knew that OKC was doing it like this. This city is much faster than Nashville. It's a lot of pimps here."

I said, "That's right, OKC is known for pimps and hoes. That is the best thing going. This city is if full of bandits who will kill you in a New York heartbeat if you're out of bounds. That's why I call OKC the OK corral."

Just as I said that, the news came on. The first topic the reporter talked about was my boy Pimping X. They showed his face and then his car in the parking lot of Crossroads Mall.

"There were no finger prints or witnesses. The last time someone saw him was Sunday evening around four thirty or so. If anyone has any information on the whereabouts of this man, please call this number. His family is worried about him."

The first thought that came to my head was Timer and one of his crew got him. Timer left Dallas Sunday and I knew that Timer hadn't forgotten what Pimping X tried to do to him. Timer wouldn't let the matter go for a long shot.

Then the news showed where two or more people had been getting killed every day. They believed it was a gang war between the Crips and Bloods over money and power. Now I could see why Redrum was ready for war.

He said, "Those niggas was tripping and he wasn't going for it by a long shot."

Redrum and J Crack said, "No one was allowed to serve on our block or it's on. It's war time baby."

J Crack, Redrum, and three other dawgs ran up in this brother's house with ski masks on. They got him for three birds (kilos), thousands, took his car, a couple sets of Daytons and Vogue tires, plus jewelry. These young gangsters were serious about their scratch and were taking no shorts from anyone. Not even relatives.

They told me, "If you run into any problems, call us ASAP. We will be there in less than ten minutes; ready to rock and roll, baby."

I honestly believed Redrum. He was the OG of his click, the shot caller, and the big dawg with the big nuts. Every one can't be a chief. Who would be the Indians?

I called Big Seamore and told him, "Bring me a zipper (ounce) of that sticky, because I can't go to the country with anyone or leave this new turnout in a pimp's crib all alone. I didn't know this bitch from a man on the moon."

Seamore said, "I got cha baby, say no more."

At seven o'clock sharp, Seamore pulled in my drive way with three white hoes in his black on black Y2K hog, on factory gold ones and vogues, with the booty (bumper kit) on the back, clean as a mother fucker, pimp tight and ready to hit the highway.

Kelly and I put our luggage in the trunk.

Big Seamore told his bottom bitch, "Get in the back seat and let a pimp sit in the front."

I put my bitch in the back seat with his hoes. We punched out getting on the highway I-35 south headed to Dallas, Texas which was a three hour ride. We were jamming all the way to the latest hits puffing on powder laced blunts. We even gave the hoes a cocaine blunt and watched them trip. The girls didn't even know what they were smoking. The bitches got cotton mouth all of sudden.

They started sweating and saying, "This is some bomb ass weed."

We knew the coke would keep the bitches hot. Their pussies would be soaking wet and they would be ready to hit the track and make our money in a major way.

All of us was riding that big hog with the black leather seats wrapped around us. Big Seamore was riding so deep that he could barely see over the dash board. He was leaning harder than the Iffle Tower, me and him both.

I told him, "You might have to go rent a couple of cars so your girls can work Harry Hines."

He said, "Yeah, it ain't no thang baby boy. I'm going to drive these white hoes like I'm driving this Y2K hog."

The music was turned up so they couldn't hear what two pimps were talking about. We keep hoes and squares in the dark. This shit ain't for all ears to hear.

I told Seamore, "You need to get a motel room for your girls. I can't invite everyone to stay at Timer's castle, but you can chill with me. Timer is out of town doing big thangs, handling business, and getting paid in a major way. He is on a mission."

We hit Dallas two and a half hours later.

I told Big Seamore, "Take me to Harry Hines."

We were riding up and down the track for about thirty minutes before I noticed Little Momma in her bucket (old car). We flagged her down and pulled her over. I quickly introduced Kelly to my bottom bitch Little Momma.

I told her, "Break her in for me. She is your new wife in law. So show her the ropes and take care of her. I'll be back in a couple of hours or so."

Seamore was ready to let his bitches out of the stick of wood to work, but they didn't have a car to drive yet. Plus we were on the right street to rent a car. Big Seamore rented three cars for fifty dollars each for two days and dropped the old white man three hundred dollars. Then we went back to the track with Big Seamore's hoes following us.

Big Seamore, "You owe me. This game isn't for free. The game is not to be told, but to be sold."

He said, "SS Boy, it's on."

I replied, "My cost will be cheap since you're my boy. I want two bottles of Don P. and an ounce of doddie (indo). Seamore, if your hoes don't make anywhere from eight hundred to twelve hundred dollars each, you need to beat their asses because someone is stuffing on you big pimping."

I told my bottom girl, "School all of them. If they don't listen, fuck them and let them figure it out."

Big Seamore told his three girls, "Follow Little Momma's lead."

They all rode off. We headed out to Timer's mansion that was sitting off Dal Rock rd. on lake Ray Hubbard off of highway 30 East in Rowlett, Tx.

We pulled up at Timer's mansion and Seamore said, "Damn, Timer has a monster mother fucker. That brother is rich for real."

I said, "Yeah, this is how pimps live in the real world. I've been here lounging for a couple of weeks almost, getting this big Dallas money in a fast way."

When Big Seamore stepped inside, his mouth fell wide open. He was trying to figure out how he can come up with this kind of shit in a fast way. I took Seamore straight upstairs to the game room. Prepared us some double Remy's on the rocks and made a couple lines of that good cocaine. We blew a joint and I took him to my favorite room in Timer's castle; the garage.

I loved looking at Timer's white Roll Royce, his white four door 600 V-12 Benz, and his racing motorcycles & shit.

Seamore was like, "Damn, Timer's hoe catchers are top flight and cost big paper. That white on white is gone in the game, it can't be faded."

Then I took him in the backyard to show him Timer's swimming pool and Jacuzzi. I turned the pool lights on and the water fall in the Jacuzzi. Afterward I turned on the outdoor stereo system with the Bose speakers. Big Seamore couldn't do anything but take his hat off and bow down to pimping. This is what the game brings you if you play your cards right.

We got our buzz on and our heads tight.

I said, "Let's hit the track to see how everything is going in Timer's Roll Royce."

Big Seamore answered, "What are we waiting on? Let's ride pimping."

I locked the house down and shut everything off. Gently sliding in this monster Rolls Royce to sit down, while I backed out the garage real careful and slow. I put that big mother fucker in drive, straightened it out. Slowly mashing out listening to Dr. Dre, Chronic, headed back to Harry Hines track off of highway 635 west.

We parked at the adult book store for a minute to check out the action. Everything was rolling. Immediately we started soliciting in a major way out of Timer's Double R, which was double parked in the parking lot. The security guard had to run us pimps off the premises. We rode back down the track and one of Timer's girls pulled up on the side of us hoping that I was Timer.

I asked her, "Have you heard from Timer?"

"Yes. He will be home by Tuesday evening."

Okay, "Cool, is everything alright with you?"

"Yes everything is cool S.S."

I told her, "I appreciate you helping my girls out."

"Okay you're welcome SS Boy."

Then we pulled off and went behind Momma's Café where all the pimps hung out. I was surprised this time because a few pimps were in the parking lot popping pimpin and checking hoes. Big Seamore's cousin Cobra was also there chilling in the Y2K Bentley, smoking on an Indo blunt.

Me & Seamore pulled up next to Cobra in Timer's clean ass Double R sitting on gold 20 inch Lexani rims and got out. While smoking with Cobra and chopping up some game with the other pimps. Pimping Beale was out of Memphis, TN. He was a cool brother who didn't endulge in drugs or alcohol. He kept his game pimp tight at all times.

Pimping Beale told me, "I get high off of money. The more money I get, the higher I get."

I said, "Feel that."

I wished I could do the same thing; stop getting high and drinking. Just be strictly about my paper with no weaknesses. A young pimp picked up a lot of game that night from my pimp partners. Seamore ended up turning a few corners with his cousin Cobra in the Bentley and I found my girls at a motel on Harry Hines.

When I pulled up in the Double R, Kelly couldn't believe it. The hoe almost fainted.

"You're rich aren't you, SS Boy?"

"No, this isn't my car."

For some reason, I don't think she believed me.

I asked the bitch, "Where is my money?"

She quickly reached in her bra and handed me a little over four hundred dollars. I broke Little Momma for five hundred dollars. Sunshine and Special K had about four hundred and fifty dollars each. That gave me a total of eighteen hundred and fifty dollars. It was only one thirty in the morning too.

I asked Little Momma, "Where are Big Seamore's hoes?"

She said, "Seamore saw them and told them to follow him and this other pimp in a Rolls Royce."

They thought it was a Rolls Royce, but that was a Bentley, top of the line. I quickly left the motel parking lot and let my girls proceed with their business. Me, & the Rolls headed to the club, Park Avenue off of Greenville Road not far from the West end. Park Avenue had it going on almost better than Deon Sanders club, Prime Time 21.

The ladies were classy, & were model material and strictly gold diggers. Their noses were high in the air thinking that a man owes them something. A couple of the ladies noticed a pimp pull up in the Double R. I let the valet attendant handle the parking. He parked the Double R under the night lights by the front door of the club.

Soon as I walked in, I headed straight to the VIP section. A Pimp was escorted to a table with candles and fresh roses on it. I ordered a bottle of Moet and a phat Cuban green leaf cigar, & sat back peeping the crowd.

While noticing ladies pointing and staring at me. They were calling me with their eyes. They thought that a pimp was a rich trick, because I'm sure the gold diggers knew that I was the one pushing that white on white Double R.

The ladies were looking for a free ride. I'm not knocking their game, but I'm just not that guy. I'm looking for a rich bitch to take care of me, the manager. Needless to say, I was clean. Versace down, with croc shoes matching, and a player brim with the matching feather in it. I wished that my jewelry was ready so I could really flex and be flossy floss, you feel me.

A couple of super fine sisters couldn't hold in their feelings and curiosity any longer. They had to come introduce themselves and find out a pimp's name.

"Hello, what is your name? My name is OKC Mink."

"OKC Mink?"

"Yes that's right."

The ladies ask "Are you from Oklahoma City?"

"Yes I am."

"Damn, we didn't know OKC produced such fine looking gentlemen such as yourself, who got it going on."

I asked them, "What makes you think I have it going on?"

Chapter 42

They said, "Look how you are dressed. You're sitting in VIP, drinking a hundred and fifty dollar bottle of Moet all alone. So do you play for the Cowboys or Dallas Mavericks or something like that?"

I said, "Well, you're halfway right. I do play sports, I'm a professional, & I do get paid well."

Now the ladies started looking at each other knowing that they were on the right track. They might could get some fast easy money for a shot of pussy, a dream, or just tease a brother with the pussy. They knew how squares be tricking. Buying drinks, taking them out to dinner, and other things and still won't give him any pussy, you dig? True players don't fall for that lame game.

They asked, "Well, what sport do you play Mink?"

I replied to them, "I play hoes like a sport and I'm always accepting applications. Would you two lovely ladies care to play?"

Their facial expressions changed dramatically.

"Sorry, but you got us mistaken, we are not hoes."

I answered, "I know that or you wouldn't be here."

"Then where would we be Mr. Mink?"

I said, "You would be on the track where you're famous at, where my girls are."

Those gold diggers quickly got out of a pimp's face. I guess they thought I was going to invite them to drink my $150.00 bottle of Moet and leave, but a pimp can't go for that. If you drink my Moet, you're going to buy me a bottle. Then I might let you have some or we're on our way to Harry Hines. I assume that they told all the other gold diggers that I was a manager and I talked real crazy to them.

Then two more broads came to my table and introduced themselves. These women where a lot different and had plenty of class and money. They were sharp and looking good, & had big rocks (diamonds) on. The ladies saw what a player was drinking and ordered two more bottles of the same. These broads were some big dope girls handling bricks and probably rolling something real phat. Believe it or not, we had good conversation and a good time. They also knew that I was a manager and had plenty of girls, but they didn't care. They just wanted a player's company no matter what it cost them in the process for the conversation.

The fine young ladies told me, "We knew you weren't from Dallas by the way you carried yourself and how proper you talk. We never saw you before in club Park Avenue."

We even went out on the dance floor to dance. I was doing the pimp step and freaking the ladies. We had a marvelous time together that night without neither one of us shooting game at the other.

The ladies said, "Your money is no good tonight. Everything is on us."

It's hard to resist that red carpet invitation. I let the ladies spend money on a real player with no questions asked. The club finally closed at four am. The ladies invited me to breakfast, where ever I wanted to eat.

Well ladies, "I don't know what I want to eat. Plus I don't know too much about Dallas. Wherever you want to take me is cool with me."

We walked out in front of the club and the valet went to get the ladies' car. While we were waiting, the ladies complimented the Rolls parked up under the club night lights. I'm sure they knew it was mine, but they acted like they didn't know what a player was driving. The valet pulled up in their drop top Jaguar Y2K, sitting on chrome.

I said to myself, "These bitches are handling kilos and having big money."

The valet pulled up in my so called Rolls Royce. I gave the parking attendant a hundred dollar tip just for watching and taking care of Timer's Double R with no problems. Those ladies mouths fell wide open when they saw a player falling up in that white on white Double R.

They quickly said, "Follow us."

So I followed them to club GG's, which was right around the corner from Park Avenue.

Ladies, "My name is OKC Mink, with meaning on my name this time."

They asked, "Can we ride in the Rolls with you? We never rode in one before."

I really couldn't deny them since they had spent about five hundred dollars on me already.

The ladies said, "We can park our car in the parking lot of GG's while we eat breakfast."

I replied, "Cool, let's ride."

The fine young ladies got in and those thick white leather seats wrapped around their thick asses. I played that Horace Brown and Faith Evans and saw love in their eyes. Now I could see that they had no problem in sharing a real man. We slowly cruised down Greenville

Boulevard with Faith Evans blowing in our ears. I was leaning harder than a mother fucker with my brim on. Pimping don't stop baby boy.

The ladies took me to an exclusive restaurant on the West End where we ate and had a good time. It was almost six am in the morning. I had to get back to the mansion, & relieve these hoes of my bank roll.

Ladies, "I had a lovely evening and I really enjoyed myself. It's time for me to go check my traps now."

The ladies thought I was going home with them. We exchanged numbers and I dropped them off at their drop top Jaguar.

"You can call me tomorrow evening ladies. It will be my treat on a lovely dinner."

They both answered, "Okay. This better not be a joke phone number."

"I could never do two beautiful ladies who rolled out the red carpet for a player like that. Call me and it's on."

They both said, "Okay, tomorrow evening. You better call us back when we page you. Our code is 4-2."

Okay ladies, "I feel you, & I will be sure to return your call."

Quickly a pimp punched out still listening to Horace Brown. The time was six forty am when I pulled up @ the mansion. I made it there five minutes after all the girls pulled up. Timer's girls came in and went straight up stairs to their bedrooms.

I called my girls into the kitchen for a conference. I ended up clocking over four thousand dollars that night. My new turnout did great. I knew she would because most tricks love white girls.

I asked Little Momma, "Where is my money you all made while I was out of town for four days?"

Lil Mamma quickly answered, "Upstairs."

And up the stairs we went, so I could relieve her of my money. Little mamma had that shit hid under the mattress and it was a bank roll that made a hustler very proud of his stable. It was well over twelve thousand dollars in four days. I had a brand new bank roll of sixteen thousand dollars and some change.

Kelly was down stairs tripping on all the nice artifacts inside the castle. She had never been in an environment like this before. There was no way she wanted to leave this life either. Kelly's clothes were cheap and her shoes were bent out of shape and scuffed up. This bitch needed a full make over (lol).

Since she been working and brought a couple grand to the table for her choosing fees. A pimp wanted take her shopping now. Also spend a couple hundred to get her hair and nails done, like a good pimp should. I can't have a bitch out there representing me, looking (raggedy) bad & shit.

That afternoon, we woke up & I told them, "Get dressed. We are going to the mall and after that we are going to Sweet Georgia Browns. It's a soul food restaurant in south Dallas."

I even asked Timer's girls, "Do ya'll need anything? Do you want me to bring you some food back?"

They all answered, "No, but thanks anyway SS Boy."

We all hopped into the Cadillac Escalade, which was parked next to Seamore's Brougham. Mashing Kelly to Redbird Mall in Oak Cliff (South Dallas). My girls helped her pick out seven sexy outfits and a couple pair of nice shoes. Her hair and nails were done inside the mall. I bought her makeup from a Mary Kay consultant. Kelly was happy and frisky as a little puppy who wanted to play. She gave me a hug and kissed me on the jaw.

"Thank you SS Boy. You're the first man who ever bought me a seven day wardrobe and got my hair and nails done. You have me looking so pretty."

Baby, "You deserve it. Today is your day Kelly. What else do you need?"

"Daddy all I need is something to eat, and I'm straight."

Okay, "Well, let's go to Sweet Georgia Browns. Do you like soul food?"

Kelly quickly replied, "Hell yeah, I love it."

I said, "This is real down home soul food girl."

All of us left the mall and went straight to the restaurant. We got down on macaroni and cheese, ribs, rice, beef tips, sweet potatoes, greens, fried and bake chicken, banana pudding, cakes and pies, and the whole nine yards. We were full as ticks. We grew extremely lazy and tired all of a sudden.

Kelly loved my Cadillac Escalade sitting on twenty inch gold Daytons. Me, & the girls went directly to the mansion to get in Timer's Jacuzzi. We smoked blunts, got high, relaxed, and enjoyed life.

The baller girls I met last night called.

I told them, "That I was headed out of town, & will call you Monday."

Big Seamore returned with a phat bank roll, & him and his girls went swimming.

Seamore stated, "I found a new spot to work and it's on and cracking. My bitches clocked over one thousand dollars each last night."

I told him, "So did mine."

At seven o'clock sharp, Seamore and I were out the door. We were over loaded in our vehicles with our stables ready to hit the ground running. I followed him to South Dallas to a serious hoe stroll. There was nothing but hookers walking up and down the street. Most of those hookers belonged to Cobra.

He said, "It's on and cracking out here. Not too many pimps know about this spot Bro."

We let our hoes out the car and watched them get down for a couple of hours. There were plenty of patients pulling up left and right. It was mostly Hispanics and white guys. Some tricks came two or three times a day; just to be with different girls or the same girl. Everyone has a weakness; some people are alcoholics, dope heads, thieves, liars, gamblers and tricks in a major way.

We ended up spending most of the evening with Cobra in his condo, right around the corner from the track. Cobra had several cribs: mansions in Dallas and Houston, a condo in Hawaii, and several other places. We smoked Indo and drank expensive wine with him all night. I took plenty of notes on the game. Cobra paid much props to Timer.

He said, "Timer is a millionaire many times over. He is what you call a hustler. He does it all. Timer's game is well rounded."

I clocked over four thousand that Friday night. Big Seamore made around three thousand. Cobra probably broke his hoes for ten thousand or better. I ended up getting over four thousand on the next two nights as well.

Monday afternoon, at about one thirty, we got the news that we never wanted to hear. It was a sad phone call. It was a collect call from Timer. It could have been worse. He had gotten arrested on a jewelry store robbery in Virginia, a common wealth state.

Timer said, "It is all good. I am not worried about it."

The Feds were tripping once they found out it was him who had gotten cracked. They had been investigating him on a string of similar jewelry store robberies in several other states.

Timer said, "It was a bunch of bull shit because I don't know anything about it and don't know anything about shit. SS Boy, I'm in Norfolk Virginia county jail. Visits are Thursday through Sunday."

I asked Timer, "How much is your bond?"

He said, "Five hundred thousand dollars, but they took the bond back. Now I don't have a bond. The Commonwealth is fucked up."

I asked, "What do you need me to do?"

Timer said, "Get down here and find me the best lawyer in the state of Virginia. Bring my bottom bitch with you. Some brothers in here have been giving me names of some of the coldest lawyers in the state. These lawyers can talk to the judge and maybe get me a bond of some kind. So that's why I want to hire a lawyer from the Commonwealth state. My lawyer in Dallas can't do anything for me right here. My best bet is to roll with the lawyers here who have the hook up in the buddy buddy system with the judge's."

I asked, "Find out the best three lawyer's names in Virginia? I'll be there to talk and hire the one you feel comfortable with alright?"

Timer said, "Alright, I'll call you later on tonight before nine o'clock before they shut the telephones off. Let me talk to Honey."

She was his bottom bitch. I was just sitting there all fucked up in the head because my big brother got knocked more than twelve hundred miles away from home. I was glad those crackers hadn't killed him, or he killed a couple of them. I'm also glad none of that happened because Timer feels that he will be home real soon. His plans were to fight this shit or buy the case.

Honey finally hung up the phone. She was crying and all that shit. I had to give her a little encouragement.

I told her, "Timer will be home soon. We are going to get him out. We have to hold his shit down just like he left it. What did Timer tell you to do?"

While crying her pretty little head off.

Chapter 43

"Daddy told me to stay down and everything will be alright. Timer is innocent and didn't do anything wrong. He told me to go to work and handle up around here. Daddy will be home hopefully next week, when he goes to preliminary court."

I gave Honey a hug and told her, "Everything will be alright. You and your sister in laws need to really get down and stack some chips."

Honey sniffed and said, "Okay, you're right."

I told Honey, "I'll be around until Timer come home. If I have to, I'll look after ya'll on the track if you have any trouble what so ever."

Shortly after, Shelly paged me from Nashville. I immediately returned the page. She said, "I'm sick of my job. My Mom is getting on my nerves. I am ready to get in where I fit in."

I said, "Well, it's on. We are having a ball. Here, talk to your sister and she will tell you."

Kelly got on the phone bragging, "He is rich and has a mansion and a Rolls Royce. We have been getting ripped, going swimming, and chilling in the Jacuzzi."

I could imagine Shelly on the other end of the horn jealous and wanting to come join her sister. Especially when Kelly told her that I bought her a new wardrobe and also got her hair and nails done. Kelly handed the telephone back to me because Shelly wanted to talk to me immediately.

I said, "What's up sweetness?"

Shelly asked, "Can I come to Dallas with you all?"

"Girl are you ready for this kind of shit?"

"Yes I'm ready S.S. Boy. You know I'll handle my business."

I said, "That's right. Are you still sitting there letting opportunity pass you by? Your sister seen a good thing and jumped right on it."

"SS Boy please let me come."

"Okay, come on."

Shelly asked, "Will you please buy me a plane ticket?"

"Shit girl, I don't have it like that right now. You can't hustle a ride to Dallas?"

She quickly answered, "No."

"Well, all the good hoes I know can hustle a ride to anywhere they want to go in the world."

"SS Boy please, I'll make it up to you."

"Well drive your car, baby."

"My Mom took my car from me because we fell out."

"Shelly I'll loan you money for a bus ticket, & you better be on the mother fucker."

"I'll be on it S.S. Boy."

"Okay, Kelly will call you back in ten or fifteen minutes after she call the bus station."

Okay, "Thank you SS Boy."

I told Kelly, "Find out when the next Greyhound bus leaves from Nashville to Dallas and how much it will cost. Be sure to make it non-refundable on that end."

"Okay S.S."

Kelly got on the phone to do what a pimp instructed her to do.

Kelly handled business and told me, "A bus is leaving Nashville at four thirty this evening and will be arriving in Dallas by nine o'clock am tomorrow morning. It costs eighty nine dollars Baby."

I said, "Cool. Kelly, call Shelly and tell her to catch that bus at four thirty and don't miss it."

Kelly called her sister and told her what was up.

"Okay tell S.S., I'll be there, even if I don't have a dime to my name."

"Well bitch you better pack a sack lunch or two with you. Get down here girl."

Kelly hung up & I quickly sent her and Little Momma to the bus station to pay for Shelly's ticket. Now it was really on. I'll be working with six hoes in my stable. I was going to work the shit out of these girls, & there will be no shorts.

Timer called us around six o'clock that evening.

Timer was telling me, "Get with this brother who is cold in the game. I hear he's almost as cold as Johnny Cochran. His name is Ken Jackson. Call him and get him up here."

I said, "Cool, I'll get right on it, but its past six o'clock. I doubt if his office is still open, but I'll call anyway. If no one answers, I will leave him my pager number for him to call me first thing in the morning. Are you alright? Are your books straight? Do you have money?"

"Yeah, I'm good lil Bro. I have about four thousand dollars on my books. I have enough to buy zoom zooms and wam wams (lol)."

I told Timer, "Call tomorrow at noon and I'll have some good news for you Big Bro."

"Alright lil brother. Keep it pimping. It don't stop. Keep getting your money."

We hung up.

Little Momma and Kelly made it back from the bus station and now it was time to get ready for work.

I paged Big Seamore and told him, "I'll meet you at the track by seven thirty this evening. Pick up a fifth of Remy Martin. I need a drink bad."

My stable was ready by six forty five. We went out the door and got in the Escalade heading to highway 75 south. We were headed to south Dallas with money on our mind. I was ready and prepared to break myself of every dime for my big brother Timer. If it wasn't for him, I would still be cutting hair & pushing a broom at the barber shop.

We were in south Dallas at the hoe stroll by seven forty five. As soon as I dropped my stable off, I noticed Big Seamore dropping his hoes off. We then headed over to Cobra's condo, & had a few drinks and blunts; which I really needed. I didn't tell Seamore that Timer got cracked because he didn't want anyone to know. Especially pimps, because most of them gossip like hoes. They will put a man's business in the street with the quickness, & also try to shoot at a pimp's hoes. Also a true pimp will try to make a hoe re-choose or get out of bounds, if they knew that Timer was in jail.

Soon after, my baller broads called me and wanted to take me out to dinner again.

I told them, "I am not alone. I have one of my partners with me."

Okay "We don't care. Let's just hook up."

I replied, "Okay Cool."

I held my hand over the receiver and asked Seamore, "Do you want to meet some rich bitches?"

Seamore replied, "Hell yeah, what kind of question is that for a pimp (lol)?"

Ladies, "We are in south Dallas."

"So are we, Mink."

"Okay Well meet us at the main entrance of Red Bird Mall. I'll be in my white Cadillac Escalade. Be looking for us."

Me, & Seamore was clean from head to toe, like every day.

I told him, "They aren't the finest, but neither are they the ugliest. But, their purses were real cute."

Seamore said, "I don't give a fuck. I'll accept a pig with a wig, as long as she can pay what she weighs."

I answered, "I feel you pimp."

We pulled up and this time the other broad was driving her car which was a drop top 500 Benz. That car was cleaner than a mother fucker.

I said, "See pimping, I told you they were having money, handling big dope, or whatever they do."

The ladies parked the 500 Benz at a friend's house who lived close by and jumped in the Escalade with us. Seamore was all over those girls, but wasn't getting too far. I believe he was too aggressive. I still had both of the ladies full attention.

"OKC Mink, we really like your truck. It's cute."

"Thank you, but I really like that 500 Benz much better."

They both giggled and laughed.

I asked them, "What do you have a taste for?"

They said, "Let's go to this nice restaurant on the Dallas skyline which overlooks the city."

I said, "Cool."

So we headed toward downtown Dallas, but exited on to highway 35 North as if we were headed back to Oklahoma City. When we fell in the restaurant, it was a joint strictly for rich people. We spent well over four hundred and fifty dollars. The restaurant overlooked Dallas Metro plex & was spinning at a very slow pace like the Earth spins in the heavens. By sitting in the restaurant, you would never know that the restaurant was spinning around.

We were really tripping that the ladies tried to pay for everything. I had to be a man of my word and pick up the tab. We parlayed about two or three hours before we dropped them off so we could handle our business and check our traps.

Ladies, "We had a great time and it was our pleasure to spend an evening with two beautiful and powerful women as yourselves."

The ladies wanted to hook up again tomorrow night about the same time.

I told them, "Okay, just give us a call."

"Okay S.S. Boy."

Me & Big Seamore blew them a kiss and punched out back toward our money (the track), to break our girls. I collected twelve hundred dollars and I'm sure Seamore did pretty good as well. Then we went over to Cobra's condo and popped more pimping.

Big Seamore, "I'm going back to Harry Hines tomorrow unless my girls have a super night."

My girls ended up making thirty five hundred dollars total. That was on a Monday night, which was cool. I couldn't complain. I just knew that I had to be able to put my girls on automatic while I was out of town with Timer's bottom bitch, Honey.

I made plans to call Ken Jackson, the lawyer in Virginia, in the morning by nine o'clock. Depending on what he said, we would know whether or not if we needed to make reservations to fly up there. At nine o'clock sharp, we were on the telephone talking to the lawyer. I made him aware of where Timer was and what his charges were.

I asked the lawyer, "Can you go up there and talk to Timer?"

"Well SS Boy, I charge two thousand dollars for consulting."

I said, "Be at the Western Union in thirty minutes. Here is my pager number. Give me your pager number. Can you go talk to my big brother soon as you pick up your money?"

The lawyer said, "I'll be there, believe me."

I told him, "I will call you back in twenty minutes."

Mr. Jackson said, "Okay."

I hung up in his face probably, & was at Western Union in ten minutes with two thousand dollars already wired to him.

I called and told Mr. Jackson, "It's on. Now go handle your business. Call me back ASAP after talking to my big brother."

Okay S.S. Boy, "I will do just that."

Kelly and Little Momma went to the bus station to pick up Shelly. I had my mind set to make pimping full time. Fuck the weed and kilos. You can go to jail for a long time fucking around with that shit. I'll be six hoes deep and seeing over six thousand dollars each and every night. That means that I would be making forty two thousand dollars a week. That equals $168,000.00 a month, which ain't no punk money.

Chapter 44

Fuck that weed, I need to concentrate on these hoes and money, you dig. I was already $35,700.00 strong off of new hoe money, & was trying to ride back to OKC with a stack of $100,000.00. By the way the money was coming in, it wouldn't take a hustler long to get a hundred stack.

Little Momma showed up about ten thirty am with Shelly. She was also deeply amazed at the mansion and how we were living without her. One hoe don't stop the show.

I told Shelly, "Make yourself comfortable."

Timer's girls cooked a little breakfast because Shelly was hungry.

Ken Jackson called back before noon and told me, "I talked to Timer & I need to find out more information before I can quote a fair price. I need to do some research on the case and read the police reports to see if any statements have been made. I will call you back later on today or before ten o'clock in the morning."

I said, "Okay."

Timer called right after I hung up the telephone with Mr. Jackson.

"SS Boy, guess what?"

"What is it Big Bro?"

Timer said, "I have a very bad feeling about Gator. I believe he turned weak. That's what the investigating detective told me. He said that I might as well tell the truth because my so called buddy rolled over on me. He said that I am the brains of the bunch and that I made him do it. SS Boy, I don't know why a person would want to lie on me. I don't know anything about that kind of shit. I told the detective that I don't know shit."

I said, "Timer, I know you don't mess around like that."

We both knew that the telephone conversation was being recorded and Timer's phone was probably tapped.

Timer stated, "Gator couldn't even look me in my eyes. They got him in protective custody and he's acting like he don't know why they put him in there. The little homies are following the script and down like four flat tires. They are telling the truth. They told the detective that I don't know anything about what they did, nor was I involved or had any knowledge of the robbery what so ever. Which is the truth. I believe that Gator is going to try to implicate me on that bull shit."

I told Timer, "Gator better tell the detective's the truth. He's a punk mother fucker for that shit."

Timer said, "SS Boy, I was at the hotel room still sleep. The homies must have left early in the morning to get down, if that's what happened in the first place. All I know is when they came back to the hotel room, we got in the 'Burban and headed to Virginia Beach to knock some hoes. Then the 5 0 (police) knocked us before we could get on the highway. They brought us directly to jail and charged me with 1st degree armed robbery, 6 counts, what kind of shit is that?"

I said, "Surely the people who work at the place, (jewelry store) will testify that you weren't one of the robbers."

Timer said, "Yeah that is why I'm not worried about it. I just have to sit here a minute since they refuse to give me a bond. I believe the Feds told the Commonwealth not to give me a bond."

"You're probably right big homie."

Timer said, "My lil YGs are down. They know I'll come get them out, but how can I, if I'm still in here? I'm the one with the skrilla. I'm going to find out for sure what is up with Gator."

I told Timer, "The folks (detective) are probably telling the truth about Gator. It was something I just didn't like or trust about that man and Timer knew it. We already knew that he was a compulsive liar and smoked out. I wouldn't put it past that bitch ass nigga to lie on my big brother, hoping that he might be able to get out or get a deal. Bitch ass nigga."

"Lil bro don't get upset. Just keep handling business and stay focused. I'm just on a short vacation. I need the rest any way. You feel me?"

"Yeah big bro."

Timer stated, "Let me speak with Honey?"

"Okay Timer, but first what is up with the lawyer?"

Timer said, "I like him. He's down and smart. He hates this prejudiced court system and loves sticking it to them in that court room. He is a cold and high dollar mother fucker. Mr. Jackson is going to find out why Gator is in the hole, (protective custody) or where ever he is. Also how can they charge me with 1st degree armed robbery?"

This is the meaning of first degree armed robbery:

1. To cause physical injury to anyone who is not a participant in committing the offense.
2. Or is armed with a deadly weapon.
3. Uses or threatens the immediate use of danger or a weapon or instrument upon anyone who is not a participant in committing the offense.

I told Timer, "You know your shit. You're a true OG!

He also told me about the case: Meadow v. Commonwealth.

The court cited the following Penal code commentary on the respective roles for a deadly weapon and a dangerous instrument in defining robbery in the first degree.

If a robber is armed with a deadly weapon, one having no usefulness other than as a weapon, he is a robber in the first degree.

If he is armed with a dangerous instrument, an object having legitimate use or threaten to use the instrument.

Timer said, "SS Boy, I did neither one of those things. For the simple fact, I wasn't there or had any knowledge of the crime what so ever, you dig? So how can they charge me with six counts of first degree armed robbery? That is what Ken Jackson was tripping on."

I said, "Shit you're all good. You'll be home soon. Thank you for breaking that law down to me Big Bro. Now I can sleep a lot better. Even though that's what the law stated, you know those crooked crackers will still cheat. They will do anything to nail a real one even if it's on false pretenses and false charges."

Timer said, "I know SS Boy, that's the scary part. These white folks make the laws. They hate to see a real one walk scot free and beat them at their own game. A lot of times they will ignore their own laws and bend them for themselves. The court system are some dirty mother fuckers. If they get to bull shitting and don't want to drop the charges, I'll take them all the way to the box (jury trial). I'll make them spend some money and do their homework. I'm not copping out. There will be no plea bargain for shit because I didn't do it. Would you take some time in a plea bargain for something you didn't do or know anything about?"

I answered, "Hell no, I'll take them all the way to jury trial as well. I would get a lot more time than on a plea bargain. The judge will be angry that you took your case all the way to the box (jury trail)."

Timer said, "And even if you lose in trial, you still have plenty of action on appeals, direct appeals, RCR 11, 42 motions, 60.02 motions, heabeaus corpus and etc. You can get your case over turned."

I said, "That is what a lot of these clowns don't know. How can you call yourself in the game and don't even know the law or how much time your case carries? That's why Baretta sings that song (Don't Do the Crime, If You Can't Do the Time).

I said, "Big bro, you are a down mother fucker. No way will I let my innocent brother go to prison for something he didn't do. Good bye."

I handed the phone back to Honey. I was feeling a load of relief and pressure off of my back. Timer was smart and well educated. I called a meeting with all five of my girls upstairs in the game room. Then had to go over all the rules and regulations again since I had Shelly, a brand new turnout. I didn't want any of them to think that my pimping and their work was just fun and games.

I told Shelly and Kelly, "You two joined the family at the right time. We are on a serious grind and don't need any dead weight standing in the way. I don't have any problem sending anyone of you home."

I also stated, "If anyone ever decides they want to leave, the door is wide open. There will be no hard feelings. How it start is how it ends, on good terms, you dig? Absolutely no holding back or stuffing money. That could get you in big trouble and get your ass beat real good, just ask special K. You don't have to steal from SS Boy. Just ask me and if you need something, nine out of ten we will work something out."

By Wednesday afternoon, the lawyer Ken Jackson had all the inside information that he needed to tell Timer about his case. Timer called home after the lawyer updated him on what the authorities had and what evidence they didn't have.

"Number One, we were right about Gator. He wrote a statement telling lies on me and said that I was in on the robbery, & also I was rich behind robbing jewelry stores. This bitch ass nigga was talking so much they had to tell him to slow down. He was telling so much shit the detectives told him to shut up. Gator also told on the little homies and everything he thought he knew about them. He is a lying bitch. The lawyer likes me and would love to represent me. Mr. Jackson doesn't represent any snitches or statement writers."

Jackson said, "Timer, I like the way you and your co-defendants kept your mouths shut and didn't say anything. Those statements are ninety percent of how convictions stand in the court of law. If Gator wouldn't have made up those felonious lies on you, you would be at home right now. That's why Gator is in protective custody. He is working with the state, Commonwealth. He told the detectives that he was afraid of losing his life in population (jail or prison). Gator also told them that I was very powerful and could most definitely reach him if he was out with other inmates in the county jail."

Everyone loved Timer because he is a real mother fucker. They assumed he was after some real money. Other inmates would do anything to get brownie points with Timer.

Timer said, "Mr. Jackson can beat the case even if Gator testifies in open court for $100.000.00. I didn't hesitate to hire him. I told him that

I'll start making arrangements to pay him. I also told him that I needed three more lawyers for my lil homies. Fuck Gator. Mr. Jackson said that he can help me in that area too. He owns a law firm and has a building of top flight lawyers who would love to take my lil YG's cases. He will handle their cases for five thousand dollars each. So that's a total of $115,000.00. Be at my house at eight o'clock tonight because my Mom is coming over and she is going to give you a few dollars for me. I want you and Honey to be here tomorrow and go see Jackson alright?"

I said, "Cool, I'm riding with you big bro, we have a lifetime contract until death do us part."

Timer just laughed and said, "I feel you lil bro! Gator has probably been talking to the feds."

That evening, about seven o'clock I sent my girls out the door with instructions. Timer's girls were set on automatic and out the door. Honey stayed with me until we made reservations through American Airlines. We were departing from DFW at six forty five in the morning and arriving in Norfolk Virginia at ten forty five am tomorrow. After we made the flight arrangements, Honey left out the door to go make her man's money in a fast and major way. I headed to the wet bar to mix me up a white Russian. I then went poolside to smoke a blunt before Timer's Mother arrived.

Timer's Mother rang the doorbell by seven fifty that evening. She was feeling a little sad because her millionaire son was in jail without a bond. She was a very down to earth, sweet, and a beautiful woman who was strictly business. I could see where Timer got his priorities from.

Timer's mom went straight up stairs to his safe. Mrs. Timer was the only one in the whole wide world that knew his combination numbers.

Timer trusted his mom with all his heart. It took her about twenty minutes before she called me to come up stairs. Mrs. Timer wanted me to re-count the $120,000.00 that she had scattered out all across Timer's California king size bed. We were lucky Timer had $10,000.00 stacks already in his safe. Mom had twelve stacks, with ten thousand dollars in each stack with rubber bands around them. That saved us a lot of time from counting each and every bill.

Timer's Mom said, "I'm keeping three thousand dollars. Two thousand is for you and Honey's expenses. SS Boy, please go and get my son."

I answered, "I sure will. He is coming home real soon Ms. Timer, don't worry about a thing."

I hugged her around the shoulders.

She embraced me back, and said, "I hope so son. But you know how the white man and his crooked system operate."

"I know mamma Timer, but for some reason, me and Timer both seem to think that everything will be alright. After we pay this lawyer all of this money, he better get Timer out."

Ms. Timer gave me her phone number in South Padre Island where she lived.

S.S. Boy, "Call me as soon as you return to this house."

"Okay Mom, I sure will."

Chapter 45

I chilled at the mansion that Wednesday evening with the two baller bitches, Candy and Cinnamon. They were all in after I invited them to the castle. We had a marvelous time; chilling in the Jacuzzi and eating grilled chicken breast. I had them both in the Jacuzzi with no tops on. There were big pretty titties everywhere. You know I had to play with them and kiss all over them tits. I would have fucked them or got my dick sucked if my dick wasn't on the verge of healing up. I just couldn't take the chance of fucking this mule up again, you dig (lol)?

I know Candy and Cinnamon were probably tripping because I didn't bite the bait. I put my pimping down on them.

I told them, "I wasn't used to having sex for free, but it was time for me to make some exceptions. What do you two do for a living?"

They said, "We are madams and brick layers (moving keys), imagine that."

I changed the subject trying to figure a way to tap off into their bank rolls. We slow danced together. They loved the way I danced. They were trying to get in where they fit in.

Before I knew it, it was two o'clock in the morning. It was time for me to get some rest because I knew that I had to wake up early and handle business all day. So I kissed the ladies on the cheek and dismissed them. A hustler retired for the evening, with nice thoughts on my mind about those two ballers.

Fifteen minutes after they left, Honey came home early so she could rest up for our busy schedule. At six forty five, we were on our flight to Norfolk, Virginia with thousands on us. By eleven thirty am, we were at Ken Jackson's law firm counting out $98,000.00 to Mr. Jackson for Timer's case and $15,000.00 for the three lil homies. They were staying true to the game, like real ones do.

Mr. Jackson was cool as a penguin and down in the game. He represented all the ballers of Virginia.

He said, "I see you and Timer handle business. How did he get hooked up with that weak link in his click?"

"I don't know Mr. Jackson, I always told Timer that I didn't trust or like that bitch ass dick sucking nigga."

Ken said, "I don't like him either. I have something for Mr. Gator. He sounds like an intelligent man, but he's weak and soft as pre-medicated cotton."

I answered, "You got that right. Now when are you getting my brother out? I can't afford to take anymore losses. We just dropped $113,000.00, so don't let me down Mr. Jackson, you feel me?"

He answered, "I got you. I'm going to ask for a bond next week when we go to arraignment court. I'm going to ask the court to drop all charges due to lack of evidence."

I said, "Dig that."

Honey and I left the law office and went to the county jail, so I could visit my big brother.

The lawyer said, "Tell Timer that I will be up to talk to him later on today if not tomorrow."

We finally got our turn after waiting in the long line of visitors to see their love ones. Timer came out real calm, cool, and collective with a big smile on his face. He was happy to see us. I let Honey talk to him first through the thick glass on the visitor phone. Once she was finished, I talked to my big brother.

I told him, "We handled business and everything is cool around the crib. Hopefully your lawyer can talk the judge into setting you a bond."

Timer said, "Cool, I'm missing money."

Gator sent Big Timer a kite (note) from protective custody.

The note stated, "I don't know why they have me in here. I want to come into population with ya'll until we get out of here. I am staying down. They are trying to get me to talk. I refuse to snitch. That is why they have me in protective custody. I don't have any money or cigarettes in here. I really need some help Timer."

Timer wrote him a kite back, playing the game with him.

"Gator was acting like he didn't know the real reason why he was in protective custody. Gator thinks he is so slick and far sharper than me. I'm playing like we're still cool. I'm trying to convince him to check out of protective custody so he can come into my cell. I told him we have it going on: weed, homemade Hooch, beer, cocaine, and rocks. That is the truth, because I stay high, you feel me? It don't stop. I told Gator to write out an affidavit stating my innocence. Say that I had no involvement, plus get the affidavit notarized and send it to me. All I was doing was putting Gator on the spot. There is no way he can testify against me if he wrote and signed an affidavit stating my innocence. That would be a conflict of interest."

I asked Timer, "Did he do it?"

Timer said, "I haven't heard from him anymore. That was day before yesterday. Gator was burning his candle at both ends. He was trying to stay down with me by claiming he is keeping his mouth shut. On the other end, he is helping the police build a case against me, the crew, and even himself. He is a dumb bastard. That's why you always stay down and keep your mouth shut. Never snitch, always take your medicine like a champ. Gator wasn't complaining while he was driving that new Lexus and spending hundreds of thousands. Now he wants to turn into a bitch. He is only hurting his self. It's all good. I'm not sending him one red cent. Gator also smokes like a locomotive and he needs money. I'm going to sweat him out. Protective custody is no place to be. You can't have any extras. It's already killing him. I also know that he needs some cigarettes."

Timer, "Gator needs to ask the detectives for some cigarettes and money. He's a weak mother fucker."

Then I asked Timer, "Did you hear about your boy Pimping X? He's been kidnapped and hasn't been found yet."

Timer said, "Is that right? That's how the game goes. When you disrespect the game, the game will disrespect you lil bro."

"That's right, Big Bro."

I could tell that Timer wasn't about to lose any sleep behind Pimping X or his family problems.

Timer guest what, "I knocked two white hoes and they are sisters. Now I'm six deep in my stable. I'm seeing well over fifty thousand dollars a month. I don't know how long it will last. A hoe could re-choose on me at any given moment. So I'm mashing the pedal to the medal while I still got them."

Timer said, "That is what you are supposed to do. Work those hoes 24/7 and don't let up, keep it pimping."

Our visiting time was now up.

I said, "Call the castle. We should be home by twelve noon tomorrow, we love you Big Bro. Peace."

I handed the phone to his bottom girl Honey. She talked for about five minutes. Honey was crying and shit making matters even tougher for a hustler like Timer. Her last five minutes was up. We had to exit the building and leave my big brother behind. We were back in Dallas by noon Friday and back to work that evening doing what we did best, pimping and hoe in.

I had another eight thousand in my trap. That was hella cool coming from five hoes in forty eight hours. I had my mind set to get five thousand or better this weekend and every weekend afterward.

That Friday night, I pimped the shit out of Shelly and Kelly's ass. It was time for Shelly to make her quota and get my cheese in a major way like the rest of the girls. Since Kelly was her sister, I had to make an example out of her just so her sister would know how a pimp likes his money.

I ended up with five thousand, five hundred dollars that Friday night. Saturday I pimped a record breaking high of six thousand dollars out of my stable. Sunday night wasn't that much different with a total of five thousand, two hundred dollars. Giving me a grand total of sixteen thousand, two hundred dollars. The pimp game was lovely and treating a player great. A young manager was totally spoiled knowing that pussy will sell any day of the week. I wouldn't have it any other way.

A hustler ended up leaving Dallas again Thursday evening. Then headed back to OKC to put my stable on automatic until Monday. I also talked with Timer's Mother.

I told her, "Everything will be alright. Stay strong, & he'll be home before you know it."

I rode out of Dallas and down highway I-35 north back to OKC with fifty two thousand cash and more to pick up from Baby once she got here with my money. Luckily, I left her a safe deposit key and didn't have to fly back to Nashville this weekend. Baby should be arriving at Will Rogers Airport tomorrow about one thirty or so on Southwest Airlines.

Soon as I made it home, I went directly into my bedroom and opened my safe. I dropped all fifty two thousand dollars in my safe, giving me an overall average of $167,535.00.

Big Seamore was the only reason why I came home anyway. He was blowing me up for two days (paging me) now. Ready to re-up on the sticky green, and a hustler had to get that cheese.

I jumped in the Barracuda and headed to the East Side to catch my boy Seamore. He was in the hood with the Prospect Posse. Seamore watched them handle business because he was completely out of work.

Seamore said, "I had a damn good week in Dallas. Plus I'm ready to spend some big cheese with you S.S. Boy."

"How much are you ready to spend Seamore?"

"About fifty thousand."

I said, "Damn homie. You want all of my weed."

Okay Seamore, "I will sell you pounds for six hundred dollars each, & will give you a good deal at eighty five pounds for the fifty. I'll also front you fifteen more pounds for seven hundred dollars each giving you a hundred pounds total. That will leave you a balance of about ten thousand dollars for fifteen pounds."

Seamore quickly said, "Shit, it's on. Let's do it."

"Okay then let's do it tomorrow morning Seamore. Call and wake me up about ten o'clock. Be at my house by ten forty five am alright?"

Big Seamore said, "That's cool. I'll be waking your hustling ass up at ten o'clock sharp."

I knew he would because he's an early morning person anyway. Big Seamore is always up early every morning. Soon after we finished talking business, the posse came over and handed me a bank roll of seventy five hundred dollars. They were ready to re-up also.

I asked the posse, "How much are you working with?"

"About six thousand dollars, but we still have ten pounds left. We don't want to run out."

Okay, "Well, I'll sell you pounds for the six, because that's how homies do it. I'll give you ten pounds for six thousand dollars."

Alright, "SS Boy, we'll take it."

They immediately counted out six thousand dollars & handed it to me.

Okay fellas, "I'll be here tomorrow before noon."

They all said, "That's cool. We know that you won't run off with our little six thousand."

We gave each other dap and I jumped back in the Barracuda. Headed over to OG's spot from California. Soon as I turned the corner on to his block, it was empty. There were no lights on in OG's house and the front door was knocked off the hinges. I knew what time it was then. OG had got cracked (busted). I hurried up and got away from there. I told that nigga, but he had to do it California style. Now he was doing it OKC style in the county jail.

I decided to go over to Mom's house and see how my family was doing. Mom cooked me a nice meal and made a few fried apple pies, which were the shit. We had a good time while Momma told me how much she was enjoying her new Lexus and her new diamond rings.

Momma, "I am going to pay off your car."

Then I dropped Momma thirty five hundred dollars to pay toward the forty thousand dollar balance. Now we only owed thirty six thousand, five hundred dollars.

I kissed mom goodbye after telling her, "Check on my house for me. I've been spending a lot of time in Dallas. I'm on my way back Monday. Be sure to check on the house even though I have security bars on all the windows and doors with a Brinks security system."

Sometimes that's not enough with my money in there all alone in the safe. I raced home to put up the ten thousand dollars I had left after peeling Mom off thirty five hundred dollars. Now I had a grand total of $177,535.00. That made a young hustler feel real good.

I understand what Pimping Beale was breaking down to me about he didn't need dope to get high, he got high off the money. I had a major buzz from getting this money in a fast way too. I ended my night relaxing in front of my Sony big screen, enjoying the evening alone to myself.

Needless to say, Seamore woke me up the next morning at ten o'clock am sharp. I was ready because I had dreams about that fifty thousand.

Seamore said, "I'll be there."

"Okay I'm up Bro."

I got dressed and headed to my stash spot in the country. Then picked up one hundred and ten pounds of sticky green. That left me one hundred and fifty five pounds. It would be a long time before I got some more. I wasn't in a hurry to get more either.

I decided to dedicate all of my energy and time toward pimping. Fuck catching a dope case. There was no telling how OG from California would act under pressure. He might decide to go platinum (sing a record, snitch) like Gator did, and tell everything he knows. It's not like he's from here anyway, but alot Cali brother's keep it 100(no snitching) but, not all of them.

Chapter 46

My best bet was to liquidate all of my inventory and have a going out of business sale. I could chill out for a while until shit cooled off. I needed to get back to Dallas and keep this steering wheel in my stables' backs.

I was home by ten fifty am. Big Seamore was sitting in my drive way in an old pickup truck with a lot of the neighborhood kids in the bed of the truck. That was a good camouflage. Big Seamore came into the garage and handed me a shoe box full of money. I gave him two large hefty trash bags with a hundred and ten pounds in it.

Also my brother, "Please give the posse the other ten pounds for me since you're going that way. I will holler at you later after I pick up Baby from the airport, okay."

"Handle your business SS Boy. We'll be rich in a minute and won't have to get our hands dirty at all. Imagine that."

Big Seamore threw the trash bags in the bed of the truck with the kids and threw me the peace sign. Seamore pulled out real slow, heading back toward the East Side. I went inside after letting the garage door down to re-count my money as I puffed on my first blunt of the day. That is the best high to me.

Now a hustler had major grip. I was sitting on $227,535.00. That was almost a quarter million cash. I didn't owe anyone but my big brother for giving me the game. I still had one hundred and fifty five pounds left, ten thousand dollars out on credit, and a stable of six dedicated hookers. I was feeling hella good.

At twelve thirty noon, I was out the garage door in the drop top SS Monte Carlo doing a hundred down the highway to pick up Baby from the airport. Banging on some Beenie Man. By the time I pulled up under the front door carport, Baby's plane had landed and she was standing outside waiting on her man. Baby had a tight grip on her purse too.

My dick got hard immediately just by the way she gripped that Gucci purse knowing it was full of money. Soon as she got in, I had a change of mood and changed disc from Beenie Man to Rome (I Belong to You). Baby was happy to see me and I was extremely happy to see her.

We headed straight to my crib. Baby emptied her Gucci purse on my king size bed. Then she poured out thirteen thousand dollars and some change. I put eight thousand in my safe. Now I had a total of $235,535.00 cash money, the most I ever had in my whole life. My stash was steady growing. We put the other five thousand dollars back in her purse.

I told her, "Let's go pay off the Honda Accord."

Baby was all teeth and gums. She was frisky as a little poodle puppy. We changed vehicles from the drop to the Escalade. I took her down to Norman to the mile of cars and we went inside and paid off her balance. That gave her a free title. Then we headed to the East Side so I could get my truck hand washed at T's detail shop off of Lottie and North East 23rd street.

T and everyone loved my truck and my bitch. They couldn't keep their eyes off neither one. Even though T had plenty of girls, he just didn't have any money making girls. Should I say he didn't know how to send them out the door with instructions like I did. After I got the Lac cleaned up, we went to Joe's Crab Shack for some good Cajun seafood and ordered drinks. We had a marvelous time. Just the two of us all weekend long.

I picked up a couple pieces of my monster jewelry; my iced out medallion and two of my monster rings. My shit was top flight. No one in the city had pieces like I did.

I told Rocky, "Add the ten extra karats to my bracelet. Never mind adding to the blue faced Rolex. I now have a Presidential Rolex full of ice."

Rocky said, "I'll have your other three pieces ready for you in two or three weeks."

"Okay cool."

I gave Rocky dap and left the store glittering like Liberace.

Baby was tripping saying, "Damn SS Boy. That is some pretty and very expensive jewelry."

"Yes it is, & I'm going to have to carry my pistol with me every time I wear it."

She replied, "You got that right."

We flexed around the city for a while before ending up at Pearls Oyster Bar off of NW 63rd street. Afterward Me & Baby went to my house to make a little romance together. Before long, it was time for Baby to catch her flight back to Nashville. A pimp sent her off with instructions on getting me more money.

Afterward racing home to pack my own clothes.

I called Mom to tell her, "I'm out. Hold down the fort for me."

A hustler punched out tearing the highway up getting back to Dallas. With plenty of pimping to do and plenty of dough to check. When I stepped in the mansion, I broke Little Momma for all my money for the past two days of work from my five dedicated hookers. That was seventy five hundred dollars. I really loved this pimp shit and pimping has never been dead. It's just these hoes been mislead. I took them to the spot Big Seamore turned me on to and dropped them off.

That Friday, Timer went to court and was again denied a bond.

The Commonwealth attorney said, "I am afraid that Timer is a flight risk. We might never see him again if granted bond. He is international and has plenty of money to travel anywhere in the world."

They were right about that. No way would Timer come back to jail if he made bond in Virginia. He would most definitely find the right connections to buy the case. I'm sure he has rabbit in his blood too, meaning he would run. Now he had to wait another five weeks before his next court date in preliminary court.

Maybe the Commonwealth would drop the charges after there is no evidence to present in court besides Gator. It would be Timer and his YG's word against lying ass Gator's. That is three against one, fuck a rat snitch.

Timer also said, "It's some big shit that came up. Call my lawyer because I can't talk to you about it over the horn. Use a pay phone when you call Ken Jackson."

I said, "Okay, I'm headed to the phone right now. Call me back in thirty minutes big brother."

I immediately jumped in the Cadillac and headed to the nearest pay phone to call Mr. Jackson. He was waiting on my call.

Mr. Jackson asked, "Can you talk?"

I answered "Sure, I'm at a pay phone."

Okay, "Good. Here is the deal. Gator has talked (snitched) in a major way. Now the feds are asking questions and trying to link Timer to several other crimes. They are trying to pin a few murders on him as well. Evidently, they don't have enough evidence to prosecute. The Commonwealth have looked at all of Timer's assets and real estate properties. Next week they are going to freeze all of his bank accounts and confiscate everything in his name."

I said, "Damn."

Mr. Jackson said, "SS Boy, it could be a lot worse if your big brother wasn't two steps ahead of them."

I asked, "What do you mean?"

He said, "Well, it would have been a lot worse if his mansion and Rolls Royce were in his name. The only thing in his name is his 600 V-12 Benz, a couple of savings accounts, a checking account, a Visa Gold/Platinum credit card, and the Suburban which was impounded."

Mr. Jackson said, "Timer wants you to take the Benz for a small fee of forty five thousand dollars. As is."

I thought about it and said, "Sure, I'll do it for my big brother. Tell him I'll just hold it for him until he gets out and he can pay me back my forty five thousand."

Ken said, "Timer isn't worried about the money. He just would rather get rid of the car instead of letting the Feds take it."

I said, "It's on. I'll buy it."

Mr. Jackson said, "Well, you need to look in his bedroom dresser drawer and find the title and send it to him immediately. Make it overnight delivery. Timer need to sign it and get it back to you with the quickness."

I said, "Okay, what else does he need?"

Timer also said, "Take the Rolls to his Mother. Or you can have her come get it and keep it at her house in South Padre Island."

"Okay Mr. Jackson, I'll handle all of that right away."

Ken said, "Get that car away from there and clean that house out good."

That meant remove everything illegal: guns, jewelry, weed, dope, and etc.

I told Jackson, "Tell Timer that I've got this end handled. Consider everything done. Thanks."

I hung up the phone, & headed straight back to the castle to clean up and give instructions to all the girls. We cleaned that house from top to bottom. I even washed all ashtrays. Putting the dope and weed I found right on the table to get rid of it.

Honey, "Find the title to the Benz. I need it right now. Also Honey, you are in charge. Put these ladies in check and give them assignments and rooms to detail. "Timer had twenty one rooms in his Mansion. It was already past five thirty in the evening. I might have to give the girls the night off because I had to make sure my big brother's house was clean. I would have to give it a white military glove test and go through that bitch with a fine tooth comb.

I fired up my new 600 V-12 and drove it to the store. I had to use the pay phone to call Timer's Mother. Luckily she was at home relaxing with her husband.

Mrs. Timer, "Timer wants you to pick up the Rolls."

Okay "I will be in Dallas tomorrow morning with my husband."

Mrs. Timer hung up in my face. I see now where Timer got that hanging up in a nigga's face from. Now I had to concentrate on getting this big body Benz out of here. Soon as I stepped in the house, Honey handed me the title. I left right back out the door and headed to the post office to mail it to Timer overnight. I had to handle my business to the fullest.

It was now almost eight o'clock pm and I figured that I would let everyone off work tonight. We just sat at the castle getting high and thinking about our game plan just in case the Feds popped up at the front door. I didn't have time to chill. I had to get the Benz out of there. The best place I thought of was in my garage in OKC.

And that's where I was headed with about ten different types of guns: 9mms, .45 automatics, M-14s, and several other kinds. I had to drive the speed limit. I'm pretty sure there were more guns in the house, but haven't been found yet.

Timer had a quarter pound of Indo in the house and no cocaine hopefully. It's hard finding everything in a mansion. Only Timer knows his house like the back of his hand. It had plenty of hiding places that no one else knew about. I had to travel down the highway with guns, about three ounces of Indo weed, and over twenty thousand dollars from what I clocked that week.

I was in a white on white 600 V-12 Benz sitting on chrome 20 inch rims, alpine down, clean as a mother fucker and it was now mine. I was really tripping. I couldn't believe that I owned a 600 V-12 Benz. Everything was going really fast and I loved it, but I hated that my big brother was in jail.

I was at home putting my twenty in the safe within three hours after leaving the mansion. Also putting the Indo up for whenever I got back in town. Took the guns to my stash spot. That gave me a grand total of $255,535.00, plus the one hundred and fifty five pounds. I was also taking an ounce of sticky green back with me on the airplane to Dallas in the morning.

I parked the Benz in the garage and chilled out at home. While blowing on the doddie (Indo) and relaxing. A hustler thought about the game real deep, and how far I planned on going with it.

The next morning, I called a cab to take me to Will Rogers Airport. My flight was scheduled to depart at ten forty five am through Southwest Airlines and would be arriving by eleven forty five am. A hustler had to be there so I could catch Timer's Mother and give her the scoop on the situation. Once I arrived at Love Field Airport in Dallas, I caught a cab to the mansion, & was there before twelve fifteen.

Mrs. Timer and her husband were already there. She gave all of us the low down.

She told us, "Don't even sweat the Feds coming here because this house isn't in Timer's name. This is my house and my lawyer is on standby. I wish they would come over here trying to search or take my house! I'm already angry at those white folks for holding my son with no evidence! He wasn't even at the scene of the crime. From what I understand, he was two miles away at a hotel minding his own business. I want to thank you for being so supportive and true friends to my son. It's hard to find true friendship. We are taking the Roll Royce with us. That's mine too and I wish those greedy peckerwoods would come and try to take my car! I'll hit them with a law suit the size of Texas!"

She took about a million dollars from Timer's safe along with his giant pieces of jewelry, which probably totaled over $500,000.00.

Chapter 47

Mrs. Timer said, "Everyone just sit back and relax unless you feel uncomfortable here. Ladies, this house is just as much yours as it is his. I could never put you out, no matter the outcome."

She and her husband gave us all a big hug. Momma Timer wrote down three different phone numbers to call if we needed to contact her or had any trouble. They got in the Rolls with all the cash and jewelry and punched out with their spirits and heads held high. I liked the fact that they were keeping everything in perspective and positive. She is a very strong woman and shot caller.

Momma T. also said, "As soon as I see Timer, I am going to slap him across his big head for fooling with some crash dummies."

Momma T. was mainly talking about weak ass Gator. She made us all feel much better and a little more relaxed.

I had to make a blunt run to the store for a box of green leaf Optimo's. When I returned to the castle, a player quickly rolled up five blunts and passed them around after firing them all up. The girls smoked four of them. I smoked one phat one all to myself. I couldn't smoke another one if I tried. I was coughing, fucked up, and so were the girls. I even mixed the ounce of Indo with an ounce of my sticky green and it was still the bomb.

"Everyone needs to get back in focus. Keep your eyes on the prize and let's get back on the grind in a major way."

I told Timer's stable, "Your man will be home before you know it. You should have a big surprise for him soon as he comes through the front door."

Honey said, "We most definitely will have that if everyone stays."

Timer's snows said, "Honey, what do you mean if we stay? Where are we going? We aren't going anywhere."

Honey said, "Good, neither am I. Timer never left us when times were bad. He always stayed down with all of us no matter what. Just look around at how we are living. If that is not enough, look outside at what each one of us is driving. So keep it real ladies. Let's show Daddy how much we really love and appreciate all he has done for us."

Her timing was perfect for me to intervene.

I told my stable, "Pay close attention because that was some real shit Timer's girls just got through discussing. You all might have to make the same decision one day on my behalf. I would like to separate the real from the fake right now. Who ever feel they can't make the same decision Timer's girls just made, you need to speak up now or forever hold your peace. You can step in other words. Let's separate the sheep from the wolves right now, or the real from the fake."

They said, "We are staying down."

Even the new turnouts were down. I also know when it gets hot in the kitchen, people get out. My hoes didn't have any pressure on them at the time. So automatically they will say that.

A month later, everything was still the same. My big brother was denied bond at court. Timer's lawyer filed a motion of discovery to receive the accusations that Gator made on him. That was enough for the

Commonwealth not to drop the charges and deny him bond. His punk ass was still in protective custody and lying to Timer.

Gator was stating, "I am staying down with you. I haven't said anything. There is no way I could turn state on you after all you did for me."

The Feds never did come to the mansion, but they did freeze his assets. They took the Suburban from him, which wasn't shit to Timer anyway.

Timer said, "I go to court again next month to see if I want to make a plea bargain or continue on to jury trial. I am not making any plea bargains. I'm taking my case all the way to the box, & file a motion for a fast and speedy trial. My YGs signed affidavits stating that I am innocent and had no knowledge of the crime what so ever."

I told Timer, "A young pimp had a major month. I knocked down fifty thousand. I'm getting stronger and stronger, & doing it how it should be done."

We gave each other much love and got off the phone.

I put thirty thousand dollars in my safe along with the ten thousand Big Seamore gave me. That gave me a record breaking high of $295,535.00.

Now I was on my way to Nashville in the Benz to pick up Baby. She had a bank roll for me.

My boys in OKC couldn't understand how a brother was wearing over seventy karats and rolling a top of the line V-12 Benz and a new Cadillac Escalade sitting on twenty inches, the drop top Monte Carlo SS, and an old school Barracuda. I was living lavish and dressing pimpish in top flight gear every day. Seamore's money was growing taller and taller too. That Friday, I left OKC headed to Nashville. Seamore paid cash for one hundred pounds. That was fifty five thousand dollars.

I said, "Damn. You got a helleva deal for almost five hundred dollars each."

I fronted him fifty pounds for six hundred dollars each, leaving him a balance of thirty thousand dollars. I just wanted to get rid of it. Fuck selling dope or weed. It was a full time job selling pussy. Can you blame me?

My safe at home contained $345,535.00 in cash. I was higher than a mother fucker with one helleva rush off of that money. Just like Beale told me. I could really feel where he was coming from now. I had thirty thousand out on credit and five pounds of weed which I kept for my personal stash. With six dedicated hookers & more state to state, coast to coast pimping to come.

I had my 600 Benz detailed and smelling good. Then got clean as a white dove in one of my Versace suits, Derby brim with the feather in it, all my jewelry, and my full length beaver coat. I had my shit on in the middle of the summer just like Ron Isley.

I made a stop at Bryon's Liquor Warehouse. Jumped on the highway headed east on I-40 toward Nashville to pick up Baby and my money. I was jamming to the Isley Brothers and feeling good. Thinking about my promise to Little Momma and Sunshine about buying them a car. When I get back to Dallas, Monday or Tuesday, it's on. A Man has to keep his word. That's all you got out here on these bricks (streets). A pimp had to come through for them and not let them down.

I made a nonstop drive to Nashville; only stopping to fill up and to take a leak. I drove for ten hours straight with my mind on my money and my money on my mind. Arriving in Nashville at six am Saturday morning.

I paged Baby from my mobile phone. She immediately returned a pimp's page.

She pleaded, "Come pick me up right now. I am ready."

"Baby I'm tired. I need some rest."

Baby said, "You can rest while I drive."

I agreed with her and headed on over to Meeko's to pick her up. Baby had over twenty thousand dollars for me. It was a good month for the both of us.

Baby asked, "What are you doing in Timer's Benz?"

I said, "It used to be Timer's before he gave it to me."

I went on to explain to Baby what had happened and where Timer was. Baby was so sad, but also loving the feel of that 600 V-12 Benz. That monster handled and rode down the highway with power. Baby drove for eight hours straight. I was good and rested up by then, & jumped back in the captain's seat and pushed the Benz the rest of the way to OKC.

We were at home by six o'clock that Saturday evening. I dropped another ten thousand dollars in my safe. That made it a total of $355,535.00. And mailed another nine thousand out to Baller Unlimited car lot; leaving a balance of $11,000.00. That made me feel really good.

I told Baby, "I can't afford to lay up with you for a whole week. Your man have to get back to Dallas and check his money. I have to be back by Monday."

Baby asked, "I thought you were going to spend some time with me?"

"Baby, you can come to Dallas with me if you like."

She said, "I need to visit my Mom and help her out a little bit. Mom is behind on her bills."

Me being the gentleman that I am, I had to help her out. I couldn't leave Baby's family out in the cold. I reached in my pocket and peeled off a thousand dollars to give to her Mom. Then I gave her five hundred dollars just to have.

Baby told me, "I will be in Dallas Friday morning. Pick me up from the airport. I'll stay until it's time for me to go back to work on Monday."

I said, "Okay, since you're calling all the shots and have everything figured out. We can do that."

Monday afternoon, I was back in the Escalade headed down I-35 south back to Dallas. I made it to the mansion before three o'clock that afternoon. Little Momma and the stable had another twelve thousand and five hundred dollars for me. That was for only three nights of work. Pimping was lovely and I could never see myself doing anything else besides managing.

I sent my stable out the door that Monday night with instructions. I was out there with them clocking and checking on my dough every hour or so. No slacking and pussy footing around. I broke those hoes for over six thousand dollars that Monday night. That just confirmed my theory; when a cat is away, the mice will play. From now on, I needed to stay on top of my pimping and quit putting my stable on automatic so much. But sometimes there was no way around it.

The next day, we went shopping for Little Momma and Sunshine some cars. I took Shelly to the mall for some clothes. They couldn't make up their mind on what kind of car they wanted. I would have to persuade and push them in the right direction on their selection of vehicles.

Shelly was happy to get her little wardrobe of whatever she wanted to wear and her hair and nail/toes done. Since Little Momma and Sunshine couldn't make up their minds, I decided to chill for the day on car shopping. We didn't know what we were looking for, so it didn't make any sense to keep riding all over Dallas.

That night, I worked the shit out of them again. I pimped over six thousand dollars out of them, giving me a new bankroll of twenty four thousand dollars. The next day, around noon, we were back out the door going car shopping. I took those girls straight to European Motors on Garland Boulevard, in Garland Texas.

One thing I did know for sure was that both of them loved drop top convertibles. This car lot had everything: BMW, Benz, Jaguar, Audi, and more. Little Momma immediately fell in love with an old school red 911 Porsche drop top sitting on chrome. Sunshine was digging the hell out of a black 1994 318 drop top BMW.

Both cars were in good shape and had good warranties. The ticket prices were in our price range too; not over fifteen thousand each. Both of the girls test drove the vehicles and fell in love with them. I believe the ladies had made up their minds.

The next job was for me to talk to the owner of the car lot. I had to get a super good deal since we were going to purchase two cars. Plus we might pay cash for them if the price was right.

The salesman said, "The price of the Porsche is $13,500.00 and the BMW is $11,500.00."

I asked, "What is the lowest you will take on them?"

He said, "This is it. I can't go any lower."

I cut the conversation real quick with him, & asked to speak to the General Manager.

I told him, "We will buy both cars cash right now for under $10,000.00 each."

The General Manager said, "Right now?"

I said, "Yes sir today."

He looked out the window to see what a pimp was driving, & seen my clean ass Escalade.

The General Manager looked back at me and said, "Okay, let's do it."

He was calling my bluff just to see if I would bite and I did. I reached in my pocket and peeled him off five thousand dollars.

And told him, "Write it up and put the cars in their names."

"I will be back in thirty to forty minutes. Make sure you have the cars cleaned up & also sign them up for full coverage insurance please & a warranty."

The G.M. said, "Have a seat in my office. Let's get this deal written up for you ladies."

Chapter 48

I headed to the mansion to pick up another fifteen thousand dollars. I was back in less than an hour. The girls and manager were waiting on me to show up with the rest of the money. We pulled off the car lot in the Porsche and BMW. All of us had big smiles on our faces and were headed back to the mansion.

That's why you have to be well connected. They let me pay cash without turning me in to the Feds. I bought two cars under $10,000 each.

We walked through the door and I told my crew, "It's on tonight. You all have broke me and a pimp can't walk around broke, you feel me?"

Little Momma and Sunshine said, "We'll get it back for you, Daddy. We are going to do real good tonight. Aren't we ladies?"

They all said, "Yes."

Then we all went outside to peep Little Momma and Sunshine's new cars. Special K, Shelly, and Kelly were just standing there staring at those cars with amazement. I'm sure they were wondering when they would be getting something like that.

I told them, "When you treat me right, I'll most definitely treat you right. What you put into the game is what you get out of the game. If you sell yourself short and play the game cheap, the game will play you cheap. It's just like having a bank account, if you only deposit ten dollars, that's all you can withdraw."

They all said, "We feel you. We are going to respect the game and play it to the fullest every day, all day."

I replied, "That's right."

Later that night, I sent Sunshine and Little Momma to Harry Hines, so they could drive their new cars and work at the same time. I gave Special K the keys to the Corsica.

I told her, "This is what you will be driving now. You are next in line to get taken care of baby. Now go work Harry Hines with Little Momma and Sunshine."

I personally took the two snow bunnies out to the other spot in south Dallas. I had plans on making these two snow bunnies feet look like deer hooves. It was time for me to really see what they were made of. I worked the shit out of them bunnies. Their little pussies were sore, stinking, and smelling like jack mack (lol).

I didn't give a fuck. We rode home with all the windows down in the Escalade. I pimped almost twenty five hundred dollars out of those two white hoes that night. I broke Little Momma and Sunshine for twenty five hundred dollars. Special K relieved herself of eleven hundred dollars. That gave me a total of sixty one hundred dollars that night. Plus I still had four thousand left after buying the cars, leaving me with ten thousand dollars.

Timer called home the next day to check on everything.

I told him, "Everything was just lovely. I believe it's time for me to invest in some Texas real estate. I need a ranch or something."

Timer said, "I got the hook up on it. I'll write you a letter and tell you which way to go and who to get with."

I handed the phone back to his bottom girl, Honey.

That Friday, Baby flew in from OKC to say her good byes for a month and to check us out. It fucked her up that I had two white hoes now and that Little Momma and Sunshine had new cars.

That put her on super high voltage and made her really fiend for that new Jaguar. She had envy in her eyes and wanted to stay in the mansion with us, but no way would that work. Baby would be sure to start some shit. I had to keep her separated from the rest of the stable.

Since she came to Dallas, I just couldn't let her sit up under me everywhere I went. I put her to work on the track where she was famous at. The bitch tried to talk her way out of it, but I still wasn't hearing it. I let her and the two white girls work together. They were walking up and down the track, flagging tricks down.

Baby wasn't that good on the track, I only pimped fifteen hundred dollars out of her for Friday, Saturday, and Sunday. Fifteen hundred was better than letting her sit up under me and bug the shit out of me, you dig? She should have stayed in OKC if she wanted a week vacation. Monday morning, I flew her black ass out of Dallas and back to Nashville with the quickness. She was already fucking up my program and I couldn't afford that. My motto is: what's not broken don't fix it.

A month later, I was house shopping and had my truck paid off. I was over $400,000.00 strong. Big Seamore paid me the little thirty thousand dollars he owed me, & was playing with six figures also. Big Seamore wasn't applying his pimping like I was. I figured out early in the game that hoeing was the best thing going.

My big brother was still in jail waiting on his trial. It wouldn't be for another four months. All the little YGs were out and on probation because that was their first time ever being convicted of a felony. Ken

Jackson managed to get all three of the YGs banned from the state of Virginia, community service, five year's probation & a fine.

Chapter 49

Timer had to pay another ten thousand dollars in order for that sweet deal to take place for the lil YGs. Gator could have gotten the same deal, but he talked. Timer fed him to the wolves by not giving him one red cent. Plus, the detectives didn't want him to get out anyway, because evidently, he made a deal to testify on Timer in jury trial. That's exactly what they wanted him to do.

Gator was anxious to get out since the little homies got off with their pride and names still good in OKC and everywhere else. They admitted doing the crime without Timer's knowledge and would testify in his behalf if necessary in open court. Now that's pimp shit. That's how real hustlers do it. Don't tell the folks (police) shit. The lil Y.G.'s didn't help the police build a case like Gator did.

"Gator was burning his candle at both ends," as Timer would say.

Gator was snitching to the authorities, & lying to Timer. He was acting like he was staying down.

Some kind of way, Timer tricked Gator into signing an affidavit and getting it notarized. Ken Jackson was feeling great knowing that. That affidavit will fuck up Gator's creditability in trial if he testified against Timer.

Mr. Jackson presented those affidavits to the Commonwealth attorney and they still didn't drop the charges on Timer. The Commonwealth is fucked up; it's only four Commonwealth states left. All the rest have been done away with. I don't know what is taking the United States so long to do away with the last four.

Two months later, thanks to Timer, I was living in my own mansion. It was sitting on two hundred acres on the outskirts of Valley Ranch where the Dallas Cowboys practiced. Now I had me a ranch. It costs over seven hundred thousand dollars. I got a deal out of this world. It had eight bedrooms, three family rooms, living area, game room, huge kitchen with the island stove, wine cellar, a formal dining room, two breakfast nook areas, a sunroom, weight room, two studies, ten foot deep swimming pool, two Jacuzzis, and a four car garage.

I called the cement company and had them to lay me a full length basketball court and a full size tennis court for a little of nothing. It cost twenty five hundred dollars, plus they measured a volleyball court and filled it with sand for me. My shit was top flight inside and out. My stable loved it and so did I. All my dreams had come true.

Timer's people hooked me up. They gave me a major deal. I dropped one hundred and fifty thousand dollars cash. I was in there within thirty days. My mortgage was sixty five hundred dollars a month. That wasn't shit to a hustler. I see that kind of money every day. My plans were to pay if off as quickly as possible. Just in case my stable decides to flip the script on me. After all this spending, along with paying off mom's Lexus for her, I was still over $300,000.00 strong.

My driveway was full of clean vehicles: Porsche, BMW, Cadillac truck, Drop top SS, and the 600 V-12 Benz. I had well over one hundred and thirty karats of top flight diamonds, & was living life to the fullest.

Back in OKC, my little Blood homie Redrum was balling out of control. He had the North Side sewed up and was coming down to Dallas to chop it up with a pimp on a regular basis.

Timer was still waiting for his trial date to come. The detectives had been sweating him about Pimping X. His body was found in the Red River off I-35 in between Dallas and OKC. Pimping X's punk ass boys mentioned Timer's name.

It took over a month for the authorities to identify his body. All of his teeth were pulled out, his finger tips were cut off, and he was left floating in the Red River sunny side up butt naked. They let the fish, snakes, and whatever else out there feed on him. Pimping X had a closed casket funeral. It was a photo of him on top of his casket. None of us went to his funeral. Fuck Pimping X. He played the game dirty and that's how the cards were dealt to him. The police were sweating the shit out of Timer.

Timer told the police, "I don't know what you are talking about. Pimping X and I were good friends. I hated for that to happen to my homie."

That left the homicide detectives mad as hell and furious like pit bulls.

"No matter what lies you tell us, we already know you did it. Your friend Gator told us."

Timer knew that was a lie.

Timer told them, "Well if Gator could tell you all of that, then he is your man. Charge him with it. I don't know anything about it. Now would you please excuse me & return me back to my cell?"

Timer went back to his cell to smoke a joint with some down ass brothers who he shared a cell with.

A week before trial, Gator's Mom and his only child were kidnapped in their home town of Chi-Town.

Gator immediately told the detectives, "Timer is the one who kidnapped my Mom and my twenty two year old daughter."

The detectives sweated my big brother again. They were threatening and accusing him of those brutal offenses.

Timer calmly asked the detectives, "How could I do any of those things and I've been right here? Since I've been here, I have been accused of robbery, murder, and kidnapping. All of this is a bunch of bull shit. You smart guys have the wrong man."

The detectives told Timer, "We are going to kidnap you and do the same thing to you that you did to Pimping X."

Timer really pissed them off when he asked the police, "Can you quit threatening and accusing me of those horrible things? How would you feel if you or one of your family members were abducted?"

Those peckerwoods almost jumped through the ceiling after Timer asked them that question. They immediately took him back to his cell with strong arm authority. They were dick suckers.

That Friday, Honey, & the rest of the stable, and I flew to Virginia. Timer's jury trial started at nine o'clock that Monday morning. He wanted the court room to be filled with his friends and family for support. If he was found guilty, we were going to turn that court room out with drama. I went just so I could stare Gator down while he was on the stand.

That would put more fear into his heart and mind. I just wanted to look at him and try to analyze him. How could he fall that weak? They were running in jewelry stores, laying people down, bashing the glass display cases with a ball pin hammer, and leaving with hundreds of thousands sometime millions worth of jewelry in a stolen car.

That Monday morning, the court room was filled. Timer was Armani down with Armani shoes on. He had a big smile on his face. Timer's Mom was able to talk to Ken Jackson for a brief second.

He told her, "Everything is looking good. Gator doesn't want to testify in open court against Timer for some strange reason. I filed a motion to withdraw all of Gator's statements against Timer. How could the courts use a statement if the snitch will not get on stand? Gator was the only one who could testify against Timer. He stated that Timer was the brains and play maker of the operation. None of the workers at the jewelry store could identify Timer because he wasn't one of the robbers nor was he the getaway driver of the stolen car. So Gator is the Commonwealth's only means of getting a conviction on Timer. Maybe Gator was afraid to testify because his Mom and daughter were missing. I don't know. Judge, I am making a request to vacate/dismiss my client of all charges and to release him immediately, due to lack of evidence."

The judge had no choice but to drop all charges against Timer and make him a free man. Everyone in the court room jumped for joy, except the Commonwealth attorney and the victims of the jewelry store.

The racist jury had intentions on convicting my big brother, but luckily they didn't get a chance to. None of the witnesses could say Timer robbed them nor did he help out in any kind of way. Timer did not assist in the robbery, bash the cases, nor drove the stolen getaway car.

We all gave Ken Jackson dap and a hug.

"I will pay for a cruise to where ever you and your wife want to go."

Jackson said, "That it is not necessary SS Boy."

I said, "Jackson, it will be a gift to show you my gratitude on doing such a great job on winning the trial."

We left the court room and I caught Mr. Jackson before he left the parking lot. I handed him five thousand dollars on the down low for him & his wife to take a cruise. Timer rode back to Dallas in the Rolls Royce with his Mom and stepdad. The girls and I caught a flight back to Dallas. Everything was cool and marvelous for a big hustler like Timer.

A month after Timer got back home and settled in; he bought himself a brand new Y2K drop top Bentley coupe. It was cleaner than a white dove.

I told him, "You deserve it Big Bro."

We played 21 on my basketball court at the ranch. I invested in a herd of one hundred cattle and five horses to walk and graze on my two hundred acres of land. We had a player's party on the ranch. We had all the pimps, hoes, and hustlers from the city. The Prospect Posse, Redrum, J Crack, Chub Roc, the rest of Redrum's crew, and hood rats who wanted to be down with some pimp shit. Timer's crew was there with plenty of women.

Everyone was ripped, out of control, and iced out. Redrum was cleaner than a mother fucker with a red suit and brim on. He was driving a black SS Monte Carlo drop top, sitting on 17in all chrome Daytons to the rubber, and chopping up gangster shit all night.

My party lasted all weekend. I had one of my cattle butchered and we ate beef ribs, hamburgers, T-bone steaks, briskets, filet minion, and roast beef. All hickory smoked on my huge bricked barbeque grill. Everyone had a great time swimming, playing ball, and volley ball the whole weekend. Timer's family also came and had a good time.

Needless to say, we had kegs of Texas's six point beer and all kinds of liquor. I pulled out a pound of sticky green. Timer had a quarter pound of Indo and a quarter key of bomb cocaine; which was only for the VIP players of the game. That shit ain't for everybody.

All the big pimps were there from several other states: Pimping Beale, Long Perm, Eyes, Cobra, Young Brian, Young City, K.C. Benzo, and the legendary Pimping Kanas city T. with the old school El-Dog drop top. Even the pimp of all pimps showed up for a minute or two, Mr. Don Juan out of Chi-Town. Even Snoop Dogg was there with a veteran pimp out of Oklahoma City, Okla. Named The One & Only, A true Vet with 40 years of pimping behind him & more to come.

I couldn't believe all the ghetto celebrities who were at my ranch. They all gave me hats off props and complimented me on my success and many more great years of pimping to come.

All of the pimps knew where Timer was the entire time.

Timer said, "I knew it. How can you keep something like that on the down low from some international, coast to coast players, and pimps?"

Later on, I caught Timer on a one on one basis.

I asked him, "Did Gator get probation?"

He said, "Well SS Boy, Mr. Gator kind of made the Commonwealth very upset when he decided not to testify right before the jury trial was about to begin."

I asked, "So what happened to him?"

Timer said, "Well, Gator ended up getting charged with six counts of first degree armed robbery. Each count carries 10 to 20 years each. He was looking at 140 years, but the Commonwealth ran all of his time concurrent into one violent 20 year sentence. 85% of his sentence had to be served before parole."

I said, "Damn, Gator snitched and still recieved 20 years?"

Timer said, "That's not all he got for burning his candle at both ends. The detectives and police still haven't found his Mother or his daughter. He lost his best friend that anyone could ask for."

I replied, "You got that right. Mr. Gator also lost his respect and his name in the streets. He can never come out and play again. Gator might as well hang his self because he is already dead. He just haven't laid down yet."

I asked Timer, "So you're telling me that:

1. Gator lost his mom and daughter.
2. Lost friendship, his name, and respect.
3. He snitched and still was handed 20 years in Virginia State Penitentiary with no help, or outside assistance.
4. He stayed in protective custody for years.
5. Gator will probably do all of his time in protective custody, that's if he doesn't have an accident like fall on a knife five times or something (lol), you dig?

Gator will most likely do the rest of his time in protective custody. Those down brothers you met in the county jail have homies in the penitentiary. They can reach him if he doesn't check into protective custody. He isn't safe no matter what penitentiary he is transferred to in the state of Virginia."

Timer ended the conversation by saying, "Now that's what I mean when I mention that phrase of burning your candle at both ends."

"I completely understand that phrase now, big bro. He had both ends of his candle burning, and the candle exploded right in the middle. That left him nowhere to run or turn. That caused him to lose everything. When a person decides to get in the game, you're making that whole decision for your family."

Like Timer said, "When you're in the game with him and other real ones, your whole family is in the game as well."

So don't make the wrong decisions like Gator did. It cost him a whole lot. He lost his family, friends, and twenty years in the state penitentiary. To make a long story short, never ever burn you candles on either end. Gator burned one end by snitching on Timer and the other end by also making the Commonwealth mad by not testifying on my big brother Timer. So therefore, he burned his candle on both ends. That costly move allowed Timer to fuck him on one end and the Commonwealth fucked him on the other end.

Conclusion

Burning the Candle at Both Ends is very true in all aspects of life. Never sell out or burn the only bridge to a friend, a love one, or even a person that you dislike or even hate. Never snitch or throw someone under the bus. This means even more than selling your soul to this old system of things. It's about morals, your name, and respect on and off the streets.

Me, myself and I would rather do my time and come on home with all my dignity, pride, and respect. I did that all three times of incarceration. Your name and word means everything; even more than freedom. Because guess what? After the authorities get all the information out of you, they throw you into the Lion's Den.

The last thing you want to see is a person like me, in the same cell or yard with you. You know what that means? It will be curtains for you. There will be a lot of sad singing and flower bringing, you dig?

Police even hate snitches. You weren't snitching when the money was flowing. Why snitch now and burn your candle at both ends?

I knew and know some of the coldest killers in the world with no remorse but guess what? Some of them folded up like cheap Wal-Mart lawn chairs when they went into the court room, stood in front of that white man, and started singing like the Temptations. People feared and respected them on the streets, but it's all gone now. You have no firearms while incarcerated. The only guns you have are between your elbows and shoulders and you have to know how to work them, believe me!

So my people, the moral of the story is not to sing. Always stand tall. We knew the consequences of the time before we committed the crime, true or false? You weren't crying and telling when the money was falling. Were you?

On one end of the candle you are burning:

    1. Your name, stars and stripes, and glory.

    2. Your respect and pride.

    3. Losing your friends, family, and future aspects of business ventures with real ones.

    4. Your livelihood.

On the other end of your candle, you are burning, dealing with authorities and etc......

1. Even a true police officer or marshal hates a snitch deep down inside. Too much paperwork and recordings are involved.

2. All while that person is making a statement to the authorities, that officer is wondering where and how will he or she survive after all this conversation. After they are finished with that person out to the wolves or Lion's Den they go. Hoping they get put to death or, on P.C. protective custody, away from danger and who wants to live like that?

3. Co-operating with the feds or detectives is like dealing with the mob, you're never out until they say you're out and that usually means death, or the next closest thing to it.

So never, ever, burn your candle on either end. Your name, dignity, self-respect, and pride mean everything out here on these bricks. My people, keep it zipped and sealed. Do your time and come on home. You will pick up where you left off, or even better. Plus you will have all your stars and stripes intact. People love a solid individual who won't crack under pressure. I'm not just speaking about underground activities. I'm also speaking from a positive and legitimate business perspective point of view as well.

To all of my real ones, don't trip. The rats will get what's coming to them. If you don't get to serve them someone else will. I'm not promoting violence or wishing bad on someone, but it is what it is. Sometimes you have to let the man upstairs fight your battles and protect you. I know that I have.

Who, me? I'm Bryce C. Turner and I hope that you all enjoyed my freshman project "Off the Front Line", as well as my sophomore project, "Burning the Candle at Both Ends." Look forward to my junior project, "Unexpendable."

Thank you for your support on my freshman project "Off the Front Line." I would also love to thank all of my supporters and sponsors again, B.T. 4 Restoration, Big Timer's Detail Shop, Worldwide Interior Restoration, Big Chief Publishing book store & more, and the sponsor of all sponsors, Jehovah God himself and his only begotten son Jesus Christ. My Mother, Bernice Turner, and my Pops, Obbie Turner for giving me life.

Thank you very much for your support, & hope that you can relate. Also I wish that you all enjoy my writing.

This book is dedicated in loving memory to some close personal friends and family.

REST IN PEACE and WE LOVE YOU. FROM YOUR BOY, B.T.

Billy{O.G. Patches}Newman JR., My brother from another mother, California Walter {heat cliff} Garland, Claude Bowie, Daryl {Peanut} Jackson, The beautiful Sara Hall, Inez Taylor, David Taylor, Mr. L.V. Goldsby, Mae Helen {punkin} Goldsby, Terry Eugene Goldsby, Nathaniel Goldsby, Vicky Goldsby. Mr. and Mrs. Mitchell, Mr.{Ardmore} Harvey, Mr. O.G. Greg Tucker, Mr. {Triple O.G. Killa} Darby, hustling ass Rod Von, Dwight Gist, Derrick Gist, Ms. Lena Mae Smith/Pope, Pimping Young Brian, Shit talking, Hoe busting Ms. Lisa Ford outta the N.O.{New Orleans}. Hustling Double O.G. Bobby Ray, My boy and college mate, Arnold {Terry} White, Mrs. Edith Ware, Ms. Carroll Summers, Ms. Lawerence, Mrs. Stevenson, Eric Jackson, my boy James (Guitar) Walker Jr., Mrs. Doris {Granny Watermelon} White, Mrs. Wilma Scott, Forrest (Dobby) Johnson JR., My Big Brother from another Mother Kevin (K.J.) Jones, Ray (Money Making) Stevens and last but not least, my first cousins Cowboy Craig (Butch) Dozier and outta Memphis Tn. Mr. Marcus {S.S. Boy} Turner, rest in peace cousins & to all of my loved ones. You might be temporarily gone but, never forgotten. We love and miss you very much.

From The Turner Family and Friends.

Sincerely Bryce C. Turner

(International Buck)

R.I.P.

Marcus Turner

"S.S. BOY"

R.I.P. Ray Stevens

R.I.P. Cowboy Craig (Butch) Dozier

www.ingramcontent.com/pod-product-compliance
Lightning Source LLC
Chambersburg PA
CBHW060235100426
42742CB00011B/1533